Strong Suit

"Deb Boelkes' new book, *Strong Suit*, is the single best guidance I've read on preparing women leaders to assume senior positions. Her voice is that of an insightful, strategic, and intuitive mentor, invested in *your* success. Her leadership lessons cut through the clutter that affects so much of business writing on leadership and gets to the heart of the matter—how to prepare yourself, be yourself, and succeed in the way that matters to you most. Sweep all the other business books off your shelf. This is the only one you need. And it is truly the one you've been looking for all along."

—MAJOR GENERAL MARI K. EDER
U.S. Army, Retired
Author of *American Cyberscape* and *The Girls Who Stepped Out of Line*

"*Strong Suit* is a collection of universal business truths, not only for aspiring women on their way up, but also for women who have reached the pinnacle and understand that they can always improve their game. Had I had this information at my fingertips decades ago, my own struggle would have been far less confusing and stressful. Deb clearly demonstrates that it is never too early to plan for success and never too late to consolidate success. This is an absolute must-read for women in or aspiring to leadership in any field."

"Deb is spot-on here on so many topics as I found myself nodding in agreement continuously throughout the read. Chapter 4: To Thine Own Brand Be True and Chapter 8: No Need to Be Lonely really hit home for me, as your personal brand speaks to your authenticity and is central to not only your beliefs and who you are at your core, but also to your future success. As you ascend the career ladder, it's normal to feel that you need to conform to your new business culture, but keep in mind that perhaps your non-conformity is maybe exactly what the business culture needed—a fresh perspective coupled with an against-the-grain mentality that challenges and elevates the organization to the next level. Staying true to yourself and surrounding yourself with like-minded and true, authentic support will carry you through the rough waters that you may encounter in challenging times, while also celebrating alongside you win after win."

"There is no question that becoming more aware of what captivates you, excites you, and engages you can help you be more successful in your career and life. Deb Boelkes' book is a must-read for women eager to learn, to improve, and to apply important lessons in life. She addresses many areas critical to a leader's success, including the value of an authentic personal brand, leveraging your strengths, and having a trusted mentor. Deb's wisdom and insights will aid your professional development, help you build your confidence, and guide you through challenges as you advance in your career. Her book, *Strong Suit: Leadership Success Secrets From Women on Top*, is full of engaging stories from successful female executives, and I couldn't recommend it more highly!"

—DR. SHERRY HARTNETT
Professor and Founding Director of the Executive Mentor Program,
University of West Florida
Coauthor, *High-Impact Mentoring: A Practical Guide to Creating Value in Other People's Lives*

"What refreshing encouragement from the pioneers who have gone before us! Too many times, women leaders conform to being and acting a certain way instead of being authentic—our personal brand is beyond important. I'm a mom of two young girls myself. In *Strong Suit*, Deb Boelkes uncovers the work-life balance myth because we truly have just *one* life. Pearls of wisdom are found throughout this fantastic book, and I look forward to passing the sage advice along to my daughters."

—LINDSAY HOYT
Founder and Board Chair, Cornerstone Classical Academy

"Reading this book was like getting an MBA for life. Deb Boelkes does it again with an eye-opening look into the thoughts and feelings of leaders at the top of their careers. No question is left unasked, and every answer given is heartfelt, actionable, and startling in the sincerity of experience. This powerful book took me into a deep introspection and made me reflect on my life and career. I learned some new questions to ask myself as I enter the next chapter of my career."

—LAURA STEWARD
Strategist, International Best-selling Author, and Podcaster

"*Strong Suit* is an inspirational must-read to catapult your career. Adopting the techniques that apply in the office as well as at home will be multi-beneficial and drive success. I found the thought-provoking introspections at the end of each chapter especially helpful and applicable to many aspects of leadership, from strategic planning to crafting simple emails—like adjusting tone to gain acceptance when delegating tasks. This book has caused me to rethink how I communicate to ensure that my message will be accepted when conveying complicated or shocking or simply unpleasant information."

—MARIA ZACK
Chief Executive Officer, Quantum Solutions Software, Inc.
Chair of the Board of Directors, Nations in Action

Strong Suit

Leadership Success Secrets From
Women on Top

Deb Boelkes

Author of **The WOW Factor Workplace**,
Heartfelt Leadership, and **Women on Top**

Published by:
Business World Rising, LLC
businessworldrising.com

Library of Congress Control Number: 2022921160
ISBN trade paper: 978-1-7340761-9-6
ISBN eBook: 979-8-9872846-0-5
ISBN audio book: 979-8-9872846-1-2

Business | Leadership | Management | Career

First Edition
Printed in the USA

To Vienna Kay
With your entire life ahead of you,
may you always play to your strong suits.

Contents

Introduction i

CHAPTER ONE: The Sky Is the Limit!
(The Power of Lessons Learned Young). 1

CHAPTER TWO: Be Open to Outcomes 41

CHAPTER THREE: Be Your Best at What Matters to You 85

CHAPTER FOUR: To Thine Own Brand Be True 105

CHAPTER FIVE: Every Day Is a Dress Rehearsal 133

CHAPTER SIX: Invest in Your Team
(and Activate the WOW Factor!) 161

CHAPTER SEVEN: Leverage Those Strong Suits 189

CHAPTER EIGHT: No Need to Be Lonely 217

CHAPTER NINE: WOW Culture Begins with You 237

CHAPTER TEN: Leading Through Challenging Times 267

CHAPTER ELEVEN: Learn from Your Mistakes 301

CHAPTER TWELVE: Hindsight Is 20/20 327

CHAPTER THIRTEEN: Special Section: Juggling
Career and Motherhood 359

CHAPTER FOURTEEN: Reflections on Success 425

CONCLUSION: Listen to Your Heart 451

About the Author 457

How to Work with Deb 459

Other Books in the Series 461

Introduction

Even if you're not currently facing a fork-in-the-road, life-altering decision, the knowledge you are about to soak in will enable you to become more aware of what captivates you, what excites you, and what engages you in life and at work. You'll be better able to identify and leverage all those strong suits you have, and you'll be better prepared to serve as a valuable mentor to others in the months and years ahead.

-DEB BOELKES

Have you ever wondered what really goes on in the C-suite or what it's really like to be a woman on top?

Have you ever wished you could be a fly on the wall, so to speak, so you could discover how other women in the executive suite got there while raising a family—without collateral damage?

Have you ever wished you had a role model mentor, someone who has "been there, done that" and is willing to share all their leadership success secrets and life lessons with you?

Do you wish you knew at least one female executive you could admire and easily relate to—someone who has your best interests at heart, and whose advice you can trust to help you become the best possible you—so you wouldn't have to blindly figure out everything on your own?

Heck, wouldn't it be nice just to have a mentor at all?

In June 2022, the mentoring software company MentorcliQ reported that 84 percent of U.S. Fortune 500 companies claimed to provide structured mentoring programs to engage, develop, and retain their top talent. Better still, 90 percent of Fortune 500s with female CEOs reported having mentoring programs for some or all employees.[1]

If you have been lucky enough to take advantage of such programs, you are fortunate. Not everyone has access to such opportunities. While running a peer mentoring program aimed at accelerating women's advancement to senior leadership, I remember coming across a 2013 study by Development Dimensions International, Inc. It reported that 63 percent of women in the workplace have never had a formal mentor. The study also found that "although nearly all women in senior roles (78 percent) have served as formal mentors at one time or another, very few of them had a formal mentor of their own."[2] As of this writing, I haven't found a more recent formal study to indicate the situation has improved. Does that surprise you?

During my 30-year career leading sales, business operations, and professional services organizations within Fortune 500 technology companies (the first half of that in Fortune 100s), I never participated in a formal mentoring program. While I was blessed to participate in a great deal of excellent leadership development training, I was completely on my own when it came to seeking mentorship, which I eagerly did.

> **While I was blessed to participate in a great deal of excellent leadership development training, I was completely on my own when it came to seeking mentorship.**

Identifying—and Addressing—the Challenges Women Face on Their Way to the Top

If you read my book *Women on Top: What's Keeping You From Executive Leadership?* (the predecessor to this book), you know that the longer I worked in global corporations, the more curious I became about why so few Fortune 500 CEOs were female. I finally decided to do something about it. I left my leadership position in the Fortune 500 technology space to establish a leadership development program aimed at accelerating women's advancement to C-level roles. At that time, only 3 percent of Fortune 500 CEOs were women.[3] Now, 13 years later, nearly 15 percent of Fortune 500s are led by female CEOs.[4] At least we're making some progress.

When I initially left the Fortune 500 world in 2009 to address the situation, I wanted to better understand the stumbling blocks female leaders faced so I could determine how best to remove them. That calling led to my journey as an entrepreneur.

As my first step on that journey, I assembled a start-up team of a dozen Fortune 500 executive women, each of whom had been a casualty of the 2008 financial crisis. Each woman possessed a wealth of knowledge and understood the issues to be addressed, based on her own firsthand experiences. Each was as passionate about the mission as me, and each agreed to join me in creating a business plan for what became Business Women Rising, Inc., a California-based corporation dedicated to the advancement of high-potential women to senior leadership roles in major corporations.

While building the business plan, we pored over surveys and studies addressing the most common barriers to women's advancement, as identified by Catalyst, McKinsey & Company, and other highly respected professional advisory firms. Our research concluded that the biggest obstacles women faced on the way to executive leadership included lack of self-promotion, lack of opportunities to network, lack of role models, and lack of mentoring—especially from other women who had already achieved senior leadership roles. Those issues clearly needed to be addressed, and we were determined to do just that.

Our research concluded that the biggest obstacles women faced on the way to executive leadership included lack of self-promotion, lack of opportunities to network, lack of role models, and lack of mentoring—especially from other women who had already achieved senior leadership roles.

Over the next six months, we designed a multi-tiered leadership development program for women at each step on the management career ladder—from high-potential individual contributors to C-suite executives. Our primary focus was fostering greater access to role models, mentors, networking, and leadership education. Our overarching goal was to create a stronger pipeline of women leaders and help them get promoted. To make that happen, we hired leadership trainers and executive coaches who had worked in the Fortune 100.

The aim of our programs designed for entry-level through mid-level managers was to help women at those early stages of management develop greater self-confidence and stronger strategic thinking skills. For our senior-level and executive-level members, we focused on improving their ability to inspire more innovative and engaged organizations. Overall, we fostered mentorship within and between each level of management. We measured our own success by the rate at which our non-C-suite members were promoted and the rate at which our executive members either became CEOs or moved on to lead bigger organizations.

The results were rewarding for one and all. If you asked them, I'm sure our members would likely tell you that they benefitted tremendously from the program, and most especially from the mentoring relationships they developed as a result. Most of our founding members still mentor each other to this very day, after more than a decade.

An Unexpected Diagnosis, an Unanticipated Path Forward, and an Infinite-Win Plan

By all measures, the program—and my life as an entrepreneur—went fabulously well for the first three years—until one mid-December afternoon. As I walked into my cozy kitchen at home to prepare dinner, I heard my husband come in the back door from work, a little earlier than normal. I instantly smiled to myself as this meant we'd have a little more time than usual to relax and debrief about our day.

As I met him in the living room, I could see something was amiss. Yet, I greeted him with a cheerful, "You're home early!"

He replied, "Yeah, I just got out of my appointment with the doctor."

Hmmm. I had forgotten about that. I looked at him in my inquiring-minds-want-to-know sort of way and noticed him swallow hard. After a few seconds of silence he said, "Looks like I have stage-three breast cancer."

What? Cancer? Breast cancer? I was floored. All I could say was, "YOU?"

It was the first time in our then 20-plus years of marriage that I ever saw him look frightened.

A dozen things immediately whirled around in my head, all at once. I thought to myself, *This can't be true. It must be wrong. Why would they think this?*

I managed to say, "Okay. What do we do now?" and hugged him as tight as I could.

After my husband shared the details of what he had just learned, I followed up with, "Okay. We have cancer. I'll be there with you every step of the way. I love you and I promise you this: You will not go through one single minute of this alone. What's our next step?"

Truly, the last thing I thought about at that moment was my business, even though Business Women Rising—by then rebranded as Business World Rising—had for the past three years been the foremost thing on my mind nearly every waking moment. To be candid with you, I later felt ashamed when I realized just how laser-focused I had been, perhaps to my husband's detriment, while getting the business off the ground. It's funny how none of those efforts seemed to matter in that moment.

Fortunately, I had received plenty of crisis management training over the years. I immediately put every bit of that knowledge to work. If ever I needed to be strong, calm, cool, collected, strategic, heartfelt, and optimistic, this was the time for role model action.

If ever I needed to be strong, calm, cool, collected, strategic, heartfelt, and optimistic, this was the time for role model action.

I normally *was* all those things—at work, at home, with the kids, leading our neighborhood's Community Emergency Response Team operations, you name it—and thankfully, that mental "muscle memory" kicked right in. I immediately decided to take a step back in many of these roles so I could focus on doing the most important job I had: to be there for my husband when he needed me more than ever.

I had always espoused the idea that no one should ever consider themselves indispensable at work. That included me, even though now I was the founder and CEO of the company. So, early the following week, I put the business squarely in the very capable hands of my team.

Between you and me, I never liked hearing people tell me, "Deb, you know, you are the company." Now was my time to prove those people wrong. It was time for me to step away and trust my team to do what I knew they could do so well. It was time to let them take the reins of the business.

I called an all-hands team meeting to explain the situation. I told them I would participate in business operations when I could, but my top priority would have to be my husband for the foreseeable future—however long that might be.

Most of the women in front of me looked a bit uneasy, but I assured them that I had complete confidence in their abilities. I had hand-selected each of them for a reason. All they had to do now was precisely what they had been mentoring all our high-potential clients to do: step up to the occasion and give it their best effort. They already knew everything they needed to know. Now was their time to rise and shine!

And that is exactly what they did.

To make a long story short, after being by my husband's side literally 24 hours a day for the next seven months—seeing him through a mastectomy, weeks of chemotherapy, and several more weeks of almost-daily radiation—he was released by his oncology team to start living a "normal" life again.

Those seven months were a time of accelerated growth and maturation—under fire—for all of us. My brave and amazing all-female leadership team mentored each other to step up their already-proven leadership game. No one buckled under the pressure. Everyone made it through, stronger and more determined than ever to succeed and live life to the fullest.

It's interesting how an unexpected late-stage cancer diagnosis can "magically" make you more appreciative of being and living in the moment. It helps you focus on making better use of the fleeting time you have. It helps you figure out and zero in on whatever your purpose in life really is. It helps you to live more passionately, every waking moment, to achieve with gusto whatever it is that you were uniquely put on this planet to do.

So, why is it that most of us never experience that kind of epiphany unless and until we have an earth-shattering wake-up call? Why do we wait to start living our lives with purpose and meaning? Why don't we focus on our callings, strengths, and passions all along, since we know our lives on earth don't go on forever?

Why do we wait to start living our lives with purpose and meaning? Why don't we focus on our callings, strengths, and passions all along, since we know our lives on earth don't go on forever?

Once my husband finally received the sign-off from his oncology team, he decided that after all he had now been through, he would give notice at work, help them find his replacement, and retire by the end of the year. He intended to live each day to the fullest, doing the kinds of things he would most enjoy, and he wanted me to retire, too. He absolutely did not want to spend his retirement alone.

Given the ordeal our family had endured, I completely understood. Yet, my husband's proposal came as quite a shock. While our boys were now out on their own, I was just in my mid-50s. Thoughts of my own retirement had never even entered my mind. My vision of living my life to the fullest, as of that moment, meant something else entirely. When I established my business, I felt that I had finally found my purpose in life. And after my seven-month time-out, I was ready to get back into the passionate pursuit of that calling.

I couldn't begin to imagine shutting down the business or walking away, especially given all our client commitments. Moreover, I intended to write several books that my company could use as the philosophical foundation for our peer-mentoring programs—and I had only just begun to conduct all the necessary research and executive interviews. I certainly didn't want to stop working on that project.

I had always believed that everything happens for a reason and that everything works out for the best. I had to believe that this situation was no different. So, as I had always done before whenever life presented seemingly overwhelming challenges, I reminded myself of the most important priorities in my life: 1) my faith and 2) my husband. Everything else came after that.

I prayed for guidance, and then doubled down on being the best partner I could possibly be to my husband—for every blessed day that God might grant us, however short or long of a period that might be.

Divine inspiration then told me to practice what I preached and put my deep-rooted leadership philosophies into action. So, I called my team together to brainstorm and explore if and how we might continue business operations. We mentored each other with all the caring and compassion we had in us.

After much deliberation, my team and I came up with what I call an infinite-win plan: I would hand over the reins of our peer-mentoring programs to the team. Meanwhile, my husband and I would do some traveling to decide where to live in retirement. Then, as time permitted—in my retirement—I would continue to conduct executive interviews and write the leadership books I had planned on creating for the business.

Over time, that plan for the books evolved. Rather than simply leveraging them as the philosophical foundation for our peer-mentoring programs, I now sell them to the public to help accelerate advancement for high-potential leaders everywhere.

You are a beneficiary of my team's mentoring sessions.

So here we are—and now you are a beneficiary of my team's mentoring sessions.

The Tremendous Power of Heartfelt Mentoring

Mentoring can be a wonderful two-way learning street. Both mentors and mentees question and learn from each other. Of course, mentoring relationships work best when mentors and mentees are friends, invested in each other.

My story is living proof that effective mentoring can provide tremendous benefits, not just to the mentor and mentee, but to the world beyond. When caring mentors and protégés are invested in each other, everyone can learn and grow personally and professionally. The positive impacts can be infinite.

I have always cherished mentoring moments with my team members and other mentees. We regularly discussed what was going on, what was working well, what could be improved, how objectives could be better accomplished, and what creative ideas might best help us move forward. Whether the conversation lasted one minute or one hour, the more we shared with each other, the closer we grew and the more confident we became as leaders.

I have always cherished mentoring moments... Whether the conversation lasted one minute or one hour, the more we shared with each other, the closer we grew and the more confident we became as leaders.

When asked for advice, a mentor's role is not to sit in judgment, but to share experiences and lessons learned from prior actions taken; to pose thoughtful, exploratory questions; and to offer helpful pointers.

During my early career in the Fortune 100 world, I learned on my own—without any formal human resources-sponsored programs—the importance of such mentoring. I certainly relied on mentoring as an entrepreneur and business owner.

Now, as an author, public speaker, business consultant, and community leader, I am delighted to serve as a mentor to virtually anyone who requests it—be they CEO or up-and-comer—provided we relate well, the mentee has a positive attitude, they come prepared to use our time effectively, and they are accountable for their goals and actions.

My Purpose in Writing This Book: to Fill the Mentoring Gap for All Female Leaders

Given the myriad of positive experiences I have had as a mentor and as a mentee, I wrote this book with the purpose of filling the mentoring gap for anyone who desires a glimpse of what really goes on in the C-suite, and what it's really like to be a woman on top.

I wrote this book with the purpose of filling the mentoring gap for anyone who desires a glimpse of what really goes on in the C-suite, and what it's really like to be a woman on top.

To revisit the questions I asked at the beginning of this Introduction: This book is for any woman who wants to know if it really is possible to have it all—a successful career *and* a successful family—without too much collateral damage. It's for anyone in search of a role model who has "been there, done that," and who is willing to candidly share her best leadership success secrets and life lessons learned, so you don't have to blindly figure it all out by yourself.

Whether you are just now completing your schooling and embarking on your career, or in the process of evaluating a different career path, or deliberating whether you can handle being both a mother *and* a career woman, or considering going back to school to retool, or just trying to up your leadership game—this book is for you. What you are about to learn in the next 14 chapters should help you make better, more informed decisions in any of those situations, and more.

As with the previous volume in this series, *Women on Top*, this book highlights the real-world experiences and insights of role model executive women who made it to the top of the corporate world, the not-for-profit world, the military, the government, and beyond—and remained true to themselves in the process. You'll quickly come to know these women, just as you would get to know and love a mentor.

Each of the women featured in this book and in *Women on Top* were specifically selected for meeting the very narrow qualifications I required of the executives featured in my first two books, *The WOW Factor Workplace: How to Create a Best Place to Work Culture* and *Heartfelt Leadership: How to Capture the Top Spot and Keep on Soaring*. Just like the "best-ever bosses" featured in my first two books, our women on top exemplify heartfelt leadership, and each has been recognized for the "Best Place to Work" cultures they created along the way.

In the ensuing pages, you'll find that each woman on top candidly shares the ups and downs of her career, along with how she went about achieving what turned out to be success beyond her wildest expectations. You'll hear each one lay out, in her own words, what worked and what didn't work over the course of her career. We'll cover important topics like capitalizing on one's strong suits, the importance of mastering soft skills, developing relationships at the top, learning from mistakes, and much, much more.

As in each of the prior books in this four-book series, I share some of my own leadership success secrets and life lessons learned during the years I led Fortune 500 organizations. I also share the eye-opening insights I gained as an entrepreneur and CEO of a business dedicated to mentoring scores of high-potential women leaders.

Within these pages, all of us have done our best to address the kinds of questions that we believe you might want to ask and discuss with a mentor. At the end of each chapter, you will find helpful pointers and the kinds of thoughtful, introspective questions a mentor might pose for you to consider as you proceed on your leadership journey.

Within these pages, all of us have done our best to address the kinds of questions that we believe you might want to ask and discuss with a mentor.

By the end of this book, I and each featured woman hope that you will have a better understanding of what it takes to position for and thrive in executive leadership. Our collective goal is for you to become the best leader you can be on your way to the top...while perhaps even becoming a better parent and life-partner at home.

Further Reading and Resources on Heartfelt Leadership

If you have not already read *Women on Top*, I encourage you to do so when you finish this book. It focuses on the many things that hold women back from being the best, most beloved leaders they can be. My goal in writing that book was for it, too, to help you become an even stronger leader at the next level, and the next, and the next—no matter where you are on the leadership ladder.

You might also want to read my first two books, *The WOW Factor Workplace* and *Heartfelt Leadership*, as they will further augment what you learn from the *Women on Top* series.

In my first two books, I collaborated with the world-famous psychiatrist and best-selling author Mark Goulston, MD. In it, Dr. Goulston and I each interview several exceptional "Best Place to Work" award-winning executives—both male and female. As with the *Women on Top* series, each executive highlighted in those books shares their own unique leadership success secrets and business philosophies, and they reveal how they evolved into the truly inspirational leaders they ultimately became. I also share my own Fortune 500 leadership experiences creating the kinds of workplaces where people loved to work each day and never wanted to leave.

In *The WOW Factor Workplace*, we explore the all-too-uncommon leadership principles required for building the kinds of organizations where the best and most talented people line up to get in. In *Heartfelt Leadership*, we tackle some of the most difficult leadership challenges managers at any level might face.

You will find both books, *The WOW Factor Workplace* and *Heartfelt Leadership*, chock-full of illuminating insights into situations and topics most people are afraid to discuss. You will find solutions to the kinds of workplace challenges you might be facing right now but may not think are possible to overcome. By the end, you'll be relieved to have discovered that it's true: Leading from your heart is not only doable, it's the best way to lead for enduring success.

Get Ready to Identify and Leverage Your Unique Strong Suits

Well, now it's time to buckle up and settle in as we begin a mentoring journey together that is sure to be an eye-opener for you.

Even if you're not currently facing a fork-in-the-road, life-altering decision, the knowledge you are about to soak in will enable you to become more aware of what captivates you, what excites you, and what engages you in life and at work. You'll be better able to identify and leverage all those strong suits you have, and you'll be better prepared to serve as a valuable mentor to others in the months and years ahead. Maybe you'll even become a highly respected and beloved woman on top yourself.

Best of all, you may finally grasp what it takes to forge ahead with confidence, starting immediately, on a more successful career trajectory.

So read on...and get ready to take full advantage of all the leadership success secrets and life-changing advice that's about to be imparted by seven amazing women on top.

-DEB BOELKES

1. Cook, S. (2022, June 17). *U.S. Fortune 500 Mentoring Taking Off: 2022 Mentoring Impact Report*. MentorcliQ. Retrieved November 3, 2022, from https://www.mentorcliq.com/blog/mentoring-impact-report
2. Neal, S., Boatman, J., & Miller, L. (2013). *Women as Mentors: Does She or Doesn't She?* DDI. Retrieved December 12, 2022, from https://media.ddiworld.com/research/women-as-mentors_research_ddi.pdf
3. Pew Research Center. (2018, September 13). *The Data on Women Leaders*. Pew Research Center's Social & Demographic Trends Project. Retrieved November 3, 2022, from https://www.pewresearch.org/social-trends/fact-sheet/the-data-on-women-leaders
4. Buchholz, K. (2022, March 8). *Only 15 Percent of CEOs at Fortune 500 Companies Are Female*. Statista. Retrieved November 3, 2022, from https://www.statista.com/chart/13995/female-ceos-in-fortune-500-companies/

ONE

The Sky Is the Limit! (The Power of Lessons Learned Young)

I believe you must show the world, every day,
that you deserve whatever it is you want
because you are willing to contribute.

-LINDA RUTHERFORD
Executive Vice President, Chief Communications Officer
Southwest Airlines

Why am I starting this book with a look back at my familial roots? Quite simply, I am fascinated by the role our parents, and their parents before them, play in formulating our beliefs, our value systems, and how we perceive ourselves. The values of those who raise us clearly shape how we evolve into the adults we ultimately become, even if we end up questioning some of those values as we mature.

Acknowledging that few, if any, parents demonstrate good judgment 100 percent of the time, some of us may decide to put more stock in the values of one parent over the other. We may decide NOT to follow the advice or practices of one of our parents.

Or we may ultimately elect to disassociate ourselves from one or both of them.

Due to various circumstances, some of us may be more heavily influenced by our grandparents than our parents. The value-based repercussions that emanated from events that took place and the social mores that were predominant back when our grandparents were young get handed down to us in some form or fashion.

> There seems to be little correlation between one's success in life and our parents' education level, wealth, career, or ancestral heritage. What does matter, however, are the values and lessons (both good and bad) that we learn from them.

The interesting thing I discovered over the course of interviewing dozens upon dozens of successful executives and award-winning Best Place to Work leaders is that there seems to be little correlation between one's success in life and our parents' education level, wealth, career, or ancestral heritage. What does matter, however, are the values and lessons (both good and bad) that we learn from them.

Humble Beginnings, Great Expectations, and Bold Ambitions

I was an only child. My father was born just before the Great Depression. He grew up poor by today's standards, but middle class for the Depression era. His father, who was riddled by kidney disease and unable to work, died before my father entered high school. Out of necessity, his mother became the primary breadwinner. She cared for both her invalid husband and her children during the day. She worked as a janitor, in downtown Los Angeles, cleaning office buildings at night.

My mother was an only child, born during the Great Depression. Her father owned a gas station on the lot next door to their home in South Los Angeles. When my mom was eight years old, her father died suddenly from a heart attack. Her mother, who until that day was a stay-at-home mom, then had to run the gas station herself to make ends meet.

The stories of my grandmothers' struggle to keep food on the table and pay the bills while raising children by themselves without any assistance, especially during

With determination, persistence, and a positive attitude, you can overcome any adversity.

the Great Depression and the Second World War, made a huge impression on me. I learned from them to never give up or simply settle for the status quo. With determination, persistence, and a positive attitude, you can overcome any adversity.

My mother went to work part-time as a filing clerk in a law office during high school. She used the money she earned to attend a small college within walking distance of the law office. She met my father while at college and continued to work at the law office as a secretary until I was born. After that, she became a stay-at-home mom.

My father never expected to go to college, so he joined the United States Navy at age 17 to become a fighter pilot during WWII. He ultimately did attend college, thanks to the U.S. Navy and the G.I. Bill, and became an accountant in the agricultural irrigation industry. When I was eight years old, he bought an agricultural pump business in Bakersfield, California, and moved us to California's Central Valley.

Both of my parents were strong believers that I could do anything I put my mind to. They also instilled in me the adage, "Anything worth doing is worth doing well." While they always told me that my grades didn't matter if I did my best, they made it clear to me, at a very early age, that I was probably not trying hard enough in the rare event I didn't get straight A's.

For example, in fifth grade, I did not turn in the required number of book reports for the semester. I don't know why not, especially since I loved to read. I guess I just found better things to do with my time. When report cards came out at the end of the semester and I had all A's except for a C in reading, my parents made me write all the missing book reports after the fact. From that experience, I learned it was much better to jump on assignments immediately and never procrastinate. As I grew older and assignments became more challenging, this habit served me well.

By the time I was in high school, if a term paper was assigned, I had it researched and completed within two weeks. Even in college and grad school, I had every research project done well before the deadline. I'm still like that to this very day; never let a moment go to waste.

> **Never let a moment go to waste.**

Lessons from My Parents on Business and Life

There was nothing I could not do in my father's eyes, and I learned a great deal about running a business from him. He coached Little League baseball when I was young, and he took me along to all the boys' tryouts and ball games. I observed how the boys learned to be part of the team. From that, I learned to be pragmatic and that crying got you nowhere.

My father also told me that math was fun and easy, and, guess what? I magically discovered he was right. He taught me algebra and geometry in junior high and trigonometry by the time I was a sophomore in high school. Math became a real strong suit for me.

After I completed elementary school, my father took me to work with him on Saturdays and school holidays, and every day during the summer. He taught me how to do timecard accounting and bookkeeping before I entered high school. He encouraged me to learn more about computers in college. It was one thing he knew very little about, but he believed they would be important in the future.

Of the many employees who worked in my father's business, the two office secretaries and I were the only females in the place. I loved being part of the office team, and I especially enjoyed talking to the clients who came in.

The best lessons I learned from my mother came early in my life. My mother made most of my clothes when I was little. She was a very talented seamstress, and she enjoyed making dresses for both of us. I was proud of the dresses and pinafores she made for me, especially the ones with detailed smocking or embroidery or floral appliques or beautiful buttons and little satin rosettes. Even as a young child, I thought the clothes my mother made were so much prettier than the store-bought variety my friends had. I loved going to the fabric store to help pick out the patterns and the materials for my school and party clothes.

My mother taught me to make my own clothes by the time I was eight years old. It took me a while to become adept at it, but a few years later, after my mother started to struggle with alcoholism, I always made my own clothes when I wanted a special outfit.

By the time I went to high school, I made my prom dresses and drill team uniforms and I wanted to learn to design my own clothes. I used the money I made working for my dad to buy the most complicated Vogue designer patterns I could find. I would switch the sleeves and necklines and skirts between the various patterns I purchased so my clothes would be entirely different from anyone else's. I loved the challenge, and I was proud of my results. I had a natural talent for it. Sewing and fashion design became strong suits for me.

My mother went downhill fast from excessive drinking by the time I entered junior high. After that, I hated being at home, and I never wanted my friends to come over to my house out of fear they would find out what my home life was really like. So, I got involved in all kinds of extracurricular activities to stay busy.

I volunteered at our local hospital as a candy striper; I joined Job's Daughters International, a Masonic-affiliated organization for girls and young women aged 10 to 20; I attended cotillion, where boys and girls together learned good manners, common courtesy, and ballroom dancing; I was on my high school drill team and pep squad; I worked in the school library in the mornings before school; and I was on the teen fashion guild for Bullock's department store.

During my senior year in high school, I was first runner-up in the Miss Newport Beach contest; I worked in a local specialty boutique and drug store; I worked at Disneyland as a dancer; and I essentially ran the household since my mother was completely incapable of doing so. Meanwhile I took Advanced Placement Math and English classes and maintained straight A's all throughout high school. I became quite an overachiever.

As I already mentioned, I feel that we are influenced by the people who raise us and the circumstances of our early lives. While my formative years were by no means free of challenges, I knew I was loved and had some advantages that helped me become the leader I am today. I attribute my now deeply ingrained overachiever trait to 1) the values imparted upon me by my parents, 2) the high expectations they had of me as a youngster—not wanting to disappoint them, and 3) desperately wanting to avoid losing control of my life as I felt my mother did. My experiences—good and bad—spurred me onward and upward to new heights.

My experiences—good and bad—spurred me onward and upward to new heights.

While conducting my research about amazing women who ultimately made it to the top of the career ladder, I had the mind-expanding opportunity to meet a few truly talented, smart, dedicated, yet down to earth and genuine role models of Heartfelt Leadership. It was encouraging, reassuring, and motivating to confirm that women—who underneath it all are just like you and me—really can make it to the top.

I found every one of the women highlighted in this book and my previous book in this series, *Women on Top: What's Keeping You From Executive Leadership?*, to be quite open and extremely interesting. Every one of them was willing to candidly share the ups and downs along with the "coulda, woulda, shouldas" of their careers. I hope you will find their extraordinary insights and the lessons learned of value as you proceed on your journey to achieve your own dreams of success.

Now buckle up and get ready to meet them.

Melissa Reiff
Former Chairwoman and CEO
The Container Store

When I wrote the first two books in this four-part series, *The WOW Factor Workplace: How to Create a Best Place to Work Culture* and *Heartfelt Leadership: How to Capture the Top Spot and Keep on Soaring*, I had very much wanted to interview the then-Chairman and CEO of The Container Store (TCS), Kip Tindell. Kip had a widely known reputation as a heartfelt leader, and he would have been a terrific example to highlight in those first two books. Unfortunately, we were unable to coordinate our busy travel schedules within the publishing deadline to be included in those books.

It was therefore quite a thrill for me to meet in person with Melissa Reiff, who, upon Kip's retirement, followed in Kip's footsteps to become Chairwoman and CEO of The Container Store, after having served 25+ years in numerous TCS leadership roles.

Melissa Reiff began her career with TCS in 1995 as vice president of sales and marketing. In 2003, she assumed the role of executive VP of stores and marketing. She became the company's president in 2006, joined the board of directors in 2007, and added chief operating officer to her title in 2013.

Melissa ultimately became CEO in 2016 and played a critical role in strengthening the company's employee-first culture. The company was recognized as one of *Fortune* magazine's "100 Best Companies to Work For" under her direction.

Now fully retired from TCS as of 2021, Melissa continues to serve on the board of directors of Etsy, Inc., where she is also chair of the compensation committee, and since April of 2021, also sits on the board of directors of Cricut, Inc., serving on the audit committee. Melissa continues to sit on the executive board of her alma mater, Southern Methodist University's Cox School of Business.

When I asked her, "When, where, and from whom did you learn the values that you live by today?" she answered this way:

I learned my values from my mom and dad.

> **[My parents] knew the importance of a strong work ethic while knowing that family must come first—if it had to come to a choice.**

I'm a baby boomer. Both of my parents worked. They were the result of the Great Depression, so they worked hard. They knew the importance of a strong work ethic while knowing that family must come first—if it had to come to a choice.

I had a very wonderful childhood. I have three older siblings, but there's quite a bit of space—about five years—between my next sibling and me. So, I was kind of an only child in many ways.

As I said, my mom and dad had a strong work ethic and strong values. From the very beginning, I was taught "no holds barred." I could do whatever I set my mind to, whatever I was passionate about, whatever I worked hard for, whatever I had the proper education to support.

I responded, "It sounds as though you lived the American Dream."

You know, it's true. I think that had a lot to do with my dad. In his eyes, I was always his "little doe." He taught me to *think* BIG—no mountain was too high to climb—and to *dream* BIG.

My dad always told me, "The best way is many times the hard way."

Things may seem hard, and they can be. It is always easier to just sit back and do nothing, say nothing, but sometimes you have to push through. The best way *can* be the hard way, in many situations.

I think the credit for my success goes back to the fact that I never thought there were any limits to what I could do. I was not raised to think there were any limits.

It is always easier to just sit back and do nothing, say nothing, but sometimes you have to push through.

It goes back to my upbringing and the people I surrounded myself with—even right out of school. All those mentors I had have had such an impact on me. I am so grateful to each of them.

So, I learned not just from my mom and dad, but from others as well. As I think back on that, what is interesting is that most of my mentors were men. They lifted me up, and they, too, told me there were no limits.

One person who instilled that in me, right out of college, was Lamar Hunt—he may not have even known how I looked up to him. Another mentor to me was Ronald Walker, President Nixon's special assistant and chief advance man.

Another one was a gentleman I worked with at Crabtree & Evelyn, William Everett. And, of course, Kip Tindell, who was one of the founders of The Container Store and was the long-time chairman and CEO. He certainly had a huge influence on my career and me.

Jodi Berg
Retired President and CEO
Vita-Mix Corporation

One of the most energizing women on top I had the pleasure to interview was Jodi Berg, PhD, who served as the fourth-generation president of her family's company (Vitamix). Vitamix blenders are loved by home cooks and professional chefs alike for their superior quality and innovative design. The company was originally founded by Jodi's great-grandfather, William "Papa" Barnard, when he started selling kitchen tools in Illinois in 1921.

Jodi grew up in Erie, Pennsylvania. Her family moved to Ohio when her dad joined Vitamix, and she was a junior in high school. Jodi began working for the company during high school—cleaning toilets, painting walls, working in customer service, and sorting mail.

After college, Jodi went into sales for Residence Inn by Marriott. After getting an MBA, she returned to Ohio to help set up a quality department at Vitamix, then became the director of quality for the Ritz-Carlton in Cleveland.

Jodi rejoined Vitamix in 1997 as head of its international division. At the time, Vitamix products were sold in only a handful of countries. Jodi served as president and chief executive officer for a decade, creating the iconic brand we know today, expanding into over 130 countries and creating an admired, purpose-driven culture.

I began our discussion by asking Jodi, "When, where, and from whom did you learn the values that got you where you are today?"

> I was very blessed when I was growing up. My parents told me that I could be or do whatever I wanted to be or do in life. They said it may not be easy, but it is possible.
>
> They never—through any of their actions or words—gave me any reason to think that they were saying that only because they were my parents. They truly and sincerely meant it. My mom had us listen to *Free to Be...You and Me* by Marlo Thomas and Friends, with the premise that anyone could achieve anything.
>
> During those formative years, multiple other people also instilled things in me such as the confidence to overcome any

obstacle. That was a very, very strong foundation. I always thought, *I can do anything I want. Like, why can't I?*

My dad was not associated with Vitamix when I was growing up. He started different businesses—an entrepreneur in his own right.

> **I always thought, *I can do anything I want. Like, why can't I?***

If you have ever been part of a startup business, you know that starting a business and raising two, then three, then four, then five kids is challenging and quite an investment. We grew up on a very, very, very tight family budget. We didn't have a lot, but we had each other. We got really creative, and we figured out how to make things work.

Nancy Howell Agee
President and CEO
Carilion Clinic

Another impressive woman on top who was taught early on to believe that she could do anything she wanted to do is Nancy Howell Agee.

Nancy grew up with an ambition to be a nurse. Not only did she accomplish that goal early on in her career, but she ultimately became the president and chief executive officer of Carilion Clinic, a $2+ billion not-for-profit integrated health system headquartered in Roanoke, Virginia.

The Carilion Clinic serves more than a million people in Virginia and West Virginia with more than 1,000 employed physicians. Carilion Clinic includes seven hospitals ranging from the third largest in Virginia to mid-sized community and small rural or critical access hospitals. Carilion Clinic also provides home health services, imaging services, pharmacies, and free-standing surgical clinics.

Nancy Howell Agee serves as an adjunct professor at the Virginia Tech Carilion School of Medicine, as well as Griffith University in Queensland, Australia. She serves on the boards of several publicly traded companies, including RGC Resources, Inc. (Roanoke Gas), American National Bank & Trust Company, and Healthcare Realty Trust. Nancy is a member of the boards of the Virginia Foundation for Independent Colleges and the Virginia Business Council. She chairs the state's economic development entity, GO Virginia, at the pleasure of the governor. Additionally, she is past chair of the American Hospital Association, representing the nation's 5,000 hospitals and healthcare systems.

The first question I asked Nancy was, "When, where, and from whom did you learn the values that got you where you are today?" Here's what she had to say:

I do not know. Maybe in the womb—at least it seems that way.

I am the oldest of three and the only girl in the family. In some ways, when I think back, it seems like I was always putting myself forward, one way or the other, for good or for bad.

I really learned a lot from my grandmother. I lived with her until I was about four, and I was always very close to her. I spent a lot of time with her growing up. She was kind of a woman before her time.

My grandmother was the manager of a large grocery store during World War II. Her husband was killed. She had four children to raise. Yet, she had such a joy, such a passion for life. She was a ton of fun. She liked to have fun, and she was never idle. If she had downtime, she was either playing cards or knitting or crocheting. She was always doing something.

She was incredibly encouraging to me. Neither of my parents graduated from college, and she would not hear of me *not* going to college. She would say, "You can be anything you want to be. You can do anything you want to do."

My grandmother believed it was okay to fail, but it was not okay to *not try*.

She gave me this huge foundation and I am grateful for that.

There was also a clear expectation in my family that you would work hard. So, there was a strong work ethic. My grandmother believed it was okay to fail, but it was not okay to *not try*.

I asked Nancy, "Do you have an example of your grandmother's encouraging you to do something by saying to you, 'Don't worry about failing. Just give it a try and see what happens'?"

Well, yes. Very early on, it was learning to play solitaire. Actually, I still play solitaire. It is very relaxing to me now. But we would play double solitaire. I'm sure I was horrible at it, but she was very patient. She was like, "It's okay. We'll just keep trying."

Later, particularly when I had some health issues in high school—I had a tumor in my leg and I had to have a lot of surgery—my grandmother was

[My grandmother] would say, "Get up and go! You can do this. Don't feel sorry for yourself."

very encouraging, but not mollycoddling. She would say, "Get up and go! You can do this. Don't feel sorry for yourself."

She didn't say it like that, but it was like, "Okay, let's go take a walk."

If I said, "I can't. My leg hurts," she would say, "Well, you'll feel better if you go do it."

She was a real cheerleader for me. She was adamant, right from the beginning, that I would go to college. From the time I was in eighth grade, she was always saying, "When you go to college..."

She laid that pathway for me.

Knowing from her bio that Nancy holds degrees with honors from the University of Virginia and Emory University, along with honorary degrees from Roanoke College and Jefferson College of Health Sciences, I asked about her undergrad and graduate degrees. She shared this:

I have a bachelor's degree in nursing, a master's degree in nursing, and post-baccalaureate work in leadership at the Northwestern University Kellogg School of Management. I studied oncology and ethics at both undergraduate and graduate levels.

A book I read years ago for an economics class is one I still recommend to colleagues and mentees: *Who Shall Live? Health, Economics and Social Choice* by Victor R. Fuchs.

"Do you think the medical issues that you had in high school stimulated your interest in nursing, or were you interested in nursing before that?"

I was interested in it from the time I was about five years old. For Christmas, I got a little nurse's outfit and a dog—that poor dog.

I have always had animals. That poor little puppy got a lot of Band-Aids. But, you know, becoming a nurse was a girlish fantasy back then.

Certainly, when I was hospitalized for a long time and had such wonderful care from such very caring people, my interest in nursing was stimulated. I knew I wanted to do something like they were doing.

Linda Rutherford
Executive Vice President, Chief Communications Officer
Southwest Airlines

If you have read any of my previous books, you know I have had long-standing relationships with several members of Southwest Airlines' executive team. Having celebrated their 50th anniversary in 2021, Southwest Airlines has long been one of the top-rated, most admired, and most awarded U.S. airlines. In addition to all their other accolades, Southwest was named one of *Forbes'* 2022 Best Employers for Diversity in America for a fifth consecutive year.

It was such a pleasure to get to know the vivacious Linda Rutherford, Southwest's executive vice president and chief communications officer, while working on my first two books featuring Southwest Airlines' President Emeritus Colleen Barrett, and the late Teresa Laraba, who until her passing was senior vice president of customers & culture.

Having joined Southwest Airlines in 1992, Linda celebrated her 30th anniversary with the company in June of 2022. She currently guides the efforts of Southwest's Culture Services, Media Relations, Employee Communications, Emergency Response and Business Continuity, Strategic Public Relations, and a host of additional employee- and customer-related service functions. Prior to joining Southwest, Linda had an extensive background in newspaper and magazine reporting.

Linda answered my standard opening question, "When, where, and from whom did you learn the values that have gotten you where you are?" this way:

> My parents were divorced when I was nine and my sister—I have one younger sister—was five. So, we were brought up by a single mom. My mother had never previously worked. My dad was the breadwinner. Before the divorce, my mom was a stay-at-home mom. When they got divorced, my mom had to figure out a way to make a living and create a safe space for my sister and me.
>
> I will never forget this: She went to work as a receptionist at a company that made acoustic ceiling tiles for commercial buildings. She made $4.63 an hour.

My mom was very real with my sister and me... We would always have what we needed, but we might not always have what we wanted.

> I always appreciated that my mom was very real with my sister and me. She admitted that there were going to be things that we might want to have, but we would have to do without. We would always have what we needed, but we might not always have what we wanted.
>
> So, she went from not working to having to create and build up skills to be successful in the workplace. She had to create that balance between needing to be at work and needing to take care of us.
>
> My mother always had the amazing ability to make an amazing dinner for four with whatever was in the pantry. She

never shied away from sharing our food if somebody needed to come over for a meal because they couldn't get one elsewhere. She always said she would give you the shirt off her back if she needed to.

I think that my work ethic, my fortitude, and my determined perseverance absolutely came from her. I learned from her that if you want something, you're going to have to work for it. No one's going to hand it to you. Things aren't always going to be easy. You must just figure out a way. I think I learned my resourcefulness from her.

I have met people who, when you ask them to do something, they will try to do it. But when they get stuck, they get stuck. They come back to you and say, "Well, I don't know what to do."

I really appreciate the people who say, "Hey, you told me to go do this, but that happened. So, I had these three options. I weighed them and then I did option B."

I'll be like, "Oh, I love it."

That is most definitely something that my mom taught me: Never just get stuck and mired down in whatever is happening to you at any given moment. You must figure out a way. If you bump into something, then turn, pivot, and find another way.

> **Never just get stuck and mired down in whatever is happening to you at any given moment. You must figure out a way.**

I asked Linda, "Is your self-confidence something that your mom instilled in you, or do you think that it's something you developed over time?"

> I would say some of my self-confidence probably came from my single-mom upbringing and her mantra of, "If you want something, you're going to have to work hard and just go get it."

> I believe you must show the world, every day, that you deserve whatever it is you want because you are willing to contribute. That was instilled early on. I also think it has built over time, as I have acquired more experience and more responsibility, and I have been able to see some success.

Kerry Healey
Inaugural President
Milken Center for Advancing the American Dream

Kerry Murphy Healey, PhD, is an internationally recognized leader in public policy and higher education. She currently serves as the inaugural president of the Center for Advancing the American Dream in Washington D.C., which is part of the Milken Institute.

The mission of the Milken Center for Advancing the American Dream is to advance economic and social mobility for all. They support and are supported by people who believe anyone with a dream and the drive to achieve it should have the opportunity to make it come true. While its online resources are already impressive, when the Center for Advancing the American Dream officially opens its physical doors in 2023, it will offer a broad array of programs, educational events, research initiatives, and physical exhibits.

Kerry Healey's impressive career has spanned both foreign and domestic policy. Prior to joining the Milken Institute, she became the first woman president of Babson College, a 100-year-old business school consistently ranked as the leader in entrepreneurship education.

Before her time in higher education, Kerry served as the 70th lieutenant governor of Massachusetts. As an elected official, she led bipartisan efforts to improve services for the homeless and those impacted by the opioid crisis. She increased protections for victims of child abuse, drunk driving accidents, and sexual and domestic violence. She was also integral in crafting the state's pioneering healthcare reform legislation.

These days, Kerry Healey is also a member of the Council on Foreign Relations and a trustee of the American University of Afghanistan and the American University of Bahrain.

I began my conversation with Kerry in the same way I begin all my executive interviews, by asking, "When, where, and from whom did you learn the values that got you where you are today?" Here is her reply:

Like most people, I received most of my values from my parents.

My parents were older than most of the parents of people from my generation. They were 34 and 41 when I was born. I am now 60 years old, so they grew up during the Great Depression and World War II. My father would be over 100 if he were alive today. My mother passed away at 94. In many ways, I have the values of that earlier generation.

For example, my father-in-law fought in Vietnam. My own father fought in World War II. So, the perspectives of these two generations were very different. Sometimes I feel like I am a little bit "out of time" and more closely identify with an earlier generation.

My parents grew up with the belief that the American Dream was real. The American Dream was something that was attainable to those who were willing to work hard, play by the rules, and prioritize education above almost everything else.

The greatest advantage my parents gave me was their love and support. All parents can do that for their children.

My parents were able to give me opportunities by simply being there for me as a loving family. They were not wealthy. They did not ever succeed by any financial measure. I always tell others that the greatest advantage my parents gave me was their love and support. All parents can do that for their children.

My mother had a wonderful American Dream story, a great success. She was an example to me because she was the first woman in our family to go to college. She went away to college at age 16 and studied on her own during World War II.

My mother's parents were immigrants. Her mother arrived at Ellis Island as a child with her mother and only a few dollars. As a child, my mother lived on a subsistence farm in Florida. Her family had to learn entirely new skills and become citrus farmers in order to survive the Depression. So, I look at her and I see the strength that she and my grandparents displayed and am inspired.

My mother eventually became an elementary school teacher. She taught third and fifth grades throughout most of her career. While many people might look at that as an ordinary life, for us, that was an extraordinary leap forward—a big accomplishment for a woman within my family.

Before the Great Depression, my mother's father was an architect and her mother was a hat maker. Neither of these professions had anything to do with growing oranges. But during the Depression, they needed to eat and so this was something that they had to learn to do to benefit their family and to survive.

I learned from my mother—and my grandparents on her side—that persistence, diligence, and hard work could take you very far.

My mother had great ambitions for me. She wanted me to go to the best college I could, even though she knew it would be difficult to afford. My father had a disabling heart attack when I was 15. So, my mother was supporting the family on a teacher's salary, which at that time was minimal, at best.

She firmly believed that if you got a good education and you worked hard, the sky was the limit. She told me that again and again. She believed it, and I believed it.

Of course, I cannot say that this opportunity existed for everyone. But simply the belief in that kind of opportunity carried me forward at times of great difficulty and kept me very focused on doing well in school.

I asked Kerry, "Did you have brothers or sisters?"

I did not. So, that made it a little bit easier for my mother to put all her eggs in one basket—my success. She needed me to succeed and be able to care for them in their retirement.

My parents were deeply religious people. My father was an extremely devout Roman Catholic. Over time, I've come to realize that many of the values that have been most important to me, personally, sprung from several of the Roman Catholic doctrines surrounding human dignity—the dignity of all people being intrinsic, something that you can't abrogate and something that cannot be taken from you.

These things that are very subtle in your teaching when you're growing up can, in time, really take root and grow.

It's interesting how these things that are very subtle in your teaching when you're growing up can, in time, really take root and grow. Now when I think about how I want to approach life—how I want to approach political life in particular—a focus on honoring human dignity in each person, and in each conversation, is extremely important. Those roots were founded in my parents' religious upbringings.

"Did you and your mom both work to pay for your college tuition in real time, and were you working while you were in school?"

Yes. I started working when I was 15, as soon as my father became ill. I started working to save money for college because I knew that I needed to. I continued to work during college, as well. I had a whole range of jobs, starting with working in a souvenir store.

I grew up in Florida. I worked in a souvenir store for three years at minimum wage when I was in high school, making t-shirts, selling puka shell necklaces, little shell creatures, and the like. At the same time, I used the money that I earned at that job to pay for community college, where I learned computer programming in order to get a better job.

At age 16, after a few computer programming courses, I was able to get a job at the local newspaper in research and development, where I got paid twice as much as working in the souvenir store. It was one of the first newspapers to have computer typesetting. I was excited to work there, not only because of the pay, but because they were doing very innovative things, using assembly language programming to do early word processing.

The experience of needing to work at an early age in order to help support my family and save money for college taught me the valuable lesson of respect for all kinds of work and made me appreciate the role of education in advancing my career.

Wendy Johnson
Former President and CEO
Dale Carnegie franchise, Atlanta, GA

For 18 years, until her retirement in 2020, Wendy Johnson served as president and CEO of Dale Carnegie of Georgia. For over a century, Dale Carnegie has been the worldwide benchmark for delivering professional training, consulting services, and leadership development solutions to sustain performance change. Their client base ranges from firms of just 25 employees to over 350,000 employees.

Wendy began her career as a flight attendant for Pan American World Airways, more commonly known back then as Pan Am. From there, she went on to work in the financial and medical industries where she served in a variety of management and consulting roles.

Prior to joining Dale Carnegie, Wendy represented Carreker Corporation (now Fiserv), a consulting firm specializing in the financial industry, where she served as global sales manager of the Risk Management Group. Her client base included 60 of the top 100 U.S. banks. She also opened markets in Australia, the United Kingdom, and South Africa.

Over the years, Wendy has served on a variety of advisory boards, including the Metro Atlanta Chamber, the Long Grove Bloodstock LLC, AIESEC, and the Women's Commerce Club. She currently serves as a board chair for the National Multiple Sclerosis Society Board of Trustees, Georgia Chapter.

Wendy shared this story about her childhood:

> I grew up in the San Francisco Bay Area of California. I lived in Sausalito as a child. Sausalito was a little offbeat, but it was a delightful little town. I remember playing in the park and trying to drink out of the fountain. By day, it was a family place. That's where I started. By night, Sausalito was known for coffee houses and beatniks who wrote poetry and socialized in coffee houses while smoking opium.

> San Francisco was such a sophisticated, lovely city when I was growing up. I remember when we took trips into the city to go shopping–because that was the only place we could shop—I always wore a dress and little Mary Jane shoes with socks. Unlike today, it was a very formal city.

> In the 1960s, it slowly became a very different place. People relocated there from all over for a chance to be free of societal rules. It all had a big impact on me—not all good. Looking back, I can now see that this "total freedom" culture obscures the recognition of right and wrong, which is essential to any culture.

I asked Wendy, "Who shaped your value system?"

> I would say it was my mother. She was the matriarch of the family and a tough cookie. She was a role model to me. She "walked the walk." She basically taught me the importance of hard work, being authentic, not whining, and respecting

authority. She also taught me that no work is beneath you. You do what you have to do.

No work is beneath you. You do what you have to do.

My mother survived the Depression and World War II. She worked at many jobs on the West Coast, hoping my dad's ship would come into port. There wasn't a job that my mother wouldn't do. After the war, she became a stay-at-home mom.

After we were grown, and prior to the death of my father, Mom decided to become a travel agent. She was in the first wave of real career businesswomen. Early on, she worked for free because she felt guilty that she did not know anything. She volunteered during her interview, "If you'll teach me the business, I'll work for nothing."

They let her work for nothing for three years.

"That reminds me of how Sandra Day O'Connor got started, working in a law firm after graduating law school," I interjected. "She ultimately became a U.S. Supreme Court Justice, but she worked for nothing when she first started out as an attorney because no one would hire a woman as a lawyer back then."

My mom didn't feel worthy. She didn't even value her skills. So, she did not get paid. But she did get what they called "fam trips"—familiarization trips and tours—where they bring in travel agents, at no cost to the agent, to see the destination city. Otherwise, she got no pay.

When my dad died, she had to muster the courage to go in and ask for monetary compensation. I observed that and thought it was tragic that she honestly thought she should work for nothing.

That was sort of a double-edged sword. I realize that she was trying to be fair to them because they were hiring her when she didn't know anything. But there came a point when she should have asked to be paid, and she should have asked for it much sooner. I observed all that.

She ended up making a career of it and ultimately became a well-known travel agent for seniors. She handled every single little detail for her clients, and I watched that, too. She worked in that role until she was 91 years old!

It was interesting. She would put on a slide show to introduce her clients to a destination city. They would sign up for a tour, and then she would give them all kinds of information about the documents they needed to get together to travel outside the country. Then she would have another meeting, a cocktail party, where she would check their documents.

On departure day, she would hire a bus to take them to the airport. The families of these seniors would bring their parents to the bus. She would again check all their paperwork before they got on the bus. She would even build in time for them to go home and get something they might have forgotten.

I observed that and thought it was tragic that she honestly thought she should work for nothing.

Then, when they returned from the trip, she would meet them at the airport. If anybody's bags were missing, she would fill out all the airline paperwork to find their bags.

It was amazing to me. I would say to her, "When you pass away, Mom, nobody will ever fill these shoes again. Nobody else goes to that extent with customer care."

She built this thriving business because she created *safety*. She wasn't just selling travel. She was selling *safety*. She was *dispelling fear*. She was the consummate provider of *high-quality service*. Whatever hurdle was presented, she would take care of it.

Although she was not a corporate executive, I learned all her business sales and service values. Behaviors that I emulated were hard work, authenticity, humility, trust, and fine service.

My mother's generation believed strongly in civic duty. She tirelessly devoted time to local political challenges in her community. Always using these outstanding values in her interactions within the community, she earned the reputation of someone who was fair and authentic. This even garnered the attention of California's then-Governor Ronald Reagan, who chose her to help select judges for the State of California.

"That's amazing, especially when you consider those were days when women did not necessarily have careers beyond being schoolteachers or secretaries or nurses. Even though she wasn't teaching you how to articulate your value in terms of asking for what she deserved moneywise, what a fine role model your mom was for you. She certainly understood what her value was to the customer and how to deliver on that. That's probably how you learned to be such a great salesperson."

Well, my dad probably taught me that, too. He was a salesman. My dad really believed in building bridges and relationships. That part was critical. But he died when I was 19 years old, so I didn't get a lot of time with him.

Lieutenant General Kathleen M. Gainey
U.S. Army, Retired

I felt especially honored to interview retired U.S. Army Lieutenant General Kathleen Gainey. With over 35 years of military service, this three-star general officer served over 20 years within the senior ranks, leading global supply chain management teams.

Throughout her career, General Gainey developed an impressive reputation as an effective communicator skilled in building consensus and synergistic relationships between government and industry partners to solve logistics issues with national security significance. Her military career culminated in her assignment as deputy commander of United States Transportation Command.

After her retirement from the military, General Gainey became senior vice president of logistics for Cypress International, and she also served as a senior fellow with the Institute for Defense & Business. Under Operation Gratitude, the largest 501(c)(3) nonprofit in the U.S. for hands-on volunteerism in support of military, veterans, and first responders, General Gainey served as co-lead for the National Coalition to Support COVID-19 Frontline Responders.

General Gainey had this to say to my question, "When, where, and from whom did you learn the values that have been important to you in your career?"

I think from my mom and dad. They were great mentors and coaches my whole life. They taught me how to treat people and how to handle myself in stressful situations. They both taught me that you must work hard. They helped me believe in myself.

My mom was an only child. My grandmother was 40 years old when my mom was born, which was late in life. My grandmother had health issues, so eventually my mother was the one taking care of her own mother. It was hard on my mom to do that when we were moving everywhere, especially overseas.

My dad had one brother, and being he was in the Air Force, they were not always around. So, my mom was caring for not only her own mother, but she also cared for my father's mother. She eventually moved both my dad's mom and her mom into the Army Distaff Hall to ensure they both received the right level of care. This taught me to never shirk one's responsibilities to family.

I interjected, "So your father was in the military. There must have been large chunks of time when he wasn't home."

Right. He had been an enlisted man. Then he used the G.I. Bill to go back to college. After that, he went back into the military.

My mom started out teaching. As a teacher, she would work whenever they needed money. She also had a cottage industry of making hats. She sold the hats at church bazaars to make money when she was not teaching.

Whenever we moved to a new community and my parents wanted us to attend Catholic school rather than public school, my mom knew they were going to need extra money. That's when she would start teaching again, either as a substitute teacher or as a full-time teacher.

When she was taking care of my father's mother and her own mother, while my dad was deployed, then there was no time for her to teach. She was strapped for time and energy, so she did work, but she didn't work all the time.

I was always reading-challenged because I am dyslexic. We didn't know back then that I was dyslexic. We just knew I was a slow reader. The schools always tried to hold me back, but my mom would say, "We can do this. We can work through this."

[My mom] always said, "You can do anything you want to do. You're just going to have to work harder at it."

So, she went to night courses to learn how to help me with reading. Then she got tutors for me—all the way through high school—to help me keep up with my classmates. She always said, "You can do anything you want to do. You're just going to have to work harder at it."

That was a great foundation with her values of "don't feel sorry for yourself," "pick yourself up by your bootstraps," "you can do this," "you just have to work harder," "you just get less time to play, less TV time," "okay, let's go—let's get back to what we need to focus on." She was a great role model for me. I got my organizational skills from my mom.

I was very much a girly girl. I didn't like bugs. I didn't like dirt. I was not a tomboy.

Do the best you can do in every job, not just the jobs you think are career-enhancing.

I was, by nature, a very shy person. Watching and listening to my dad, I honed my people skills. My dad would say, "Do the best you can do in every job, not just the jobs you think are career-enhancing. You are going to be known by your reputation, by how you approach things, and how you take care of people.

"If people see you are doing the best job you can do, that you are always trying to learn, and you are treating people with respect, they're going to help you along. If you are known by that, then people are going to give you opportunities.

"If you step on people while trying to get to the top, then that's what you're going to be known for and you are not going to advance. You'll just slide by. You'll get into little nooks and crannies and make things happen because people won't want to deal with you. But they won't be promoting you."

He would share stuff like that at the dining room table. He would also ask each one of us, "What did you do at school today?"

Then he would say, "Well, I did something stupid and here's what it was...I want you guys to learn from this."

> **[My dad] would say, "Well, I did something stupid and here's what it was...I want you guys to learn from this."**

As we wrap up each chapter in this book, I'll share some reflections about what we've just covered and present a few questions to get you thinking about your journey and to help you discover insights along with those valuable "aha moments" that often prompt growth. You can journal using these prompts or just spend some time thinking about them. They are a great way to start your workday or to recharge between projects, or anytime you need a reset.

REFLECTIONS:

For better or worse, the values and lessons we learn from our parents and grandparents—and the social mores of their time— shape the way we view the world and how we see ourselves.

It's common that many who eventually reach the top were raised hearing the encouraging and reassuring words, "You can be anything you want to be. The sky is the limit!"

Yet, if you didn't grow up hearing such sentiments of encouragement from the adults who raised or influenced you, never fear. Even if no one in your entire life ever told you, "You can do anything you set your mind to," you really *can* do anything you strive hard enough to achieve. You simply need to believe that you can do it and find a way. The famous quote by Henry Ford, founder of the Ford Motor Company, is true: "Whether you believe you can do a thing or not, you are right."

Achieving success is all about passion and persistence, especially when things get tough. As Thomas Edison, the inventor of the light bulb, said, "Many of life's failures are people who did not realize how close they were to success when they gave up." Therefore, if you find that doing something one way doesn't work for you, then pivot and try another way. Keep trying. Before Thomas Edison succeeded in inventing the light bulb, he said, "I have not failed. I've just found 10,000 ways that won't work."

Experience is what you get when you don't get what you want. Learn from every experience. Whether you achieve the outcome you had hoped for or not, take time to assess how you can improve on your performance and move on. There's no point in getting mired in regret or feeling sorry for yourself—that just wastes time and energy. And you'll need both to make your mark on the world.

> **The most successful people in their fields made plenty of mistakes, and you will too.**

Keep in mind, too, that no one is perfect. Not even the role model you think is so wonderful. The most successful people in their fields made plenty of mistakes, and you will too. Fearing imperfection is another pitfall that can keep you from your goals, your ambitions, and your dreams.

The bottom line: Never give up on something you really want to accomplish. If you want it badly enough, you will get there. All that stands in the way of achieving your dreams is your desire, your belief in yourself, and your willingness to put in the effort. It's completely up to you.

You *can* do anything you set your mind to. The sky is the limit!

INTROSPECTIONS:

1   What are some of the most important life lessons you learned from your parents/grandparents/the people who raised you? Did anyone else play a key role in imparting the values you live by today?

2   How have those values impacted your life?

3   What personality traits did you develop because of the values and lessons learned from the people who influenced you the most?

4   Are there any traits or practices that you observed in your influencers that you are consciously choosing not to follow? (Remember, no one is perfect—including your parents or guardians—and some of the valuable lessons you have learned may include what NOT to do.)

5   Of the values passed down to you, which ones would you pass on to others as key factors for success?

TWO

Be Open to Outcomes

*Once I began to travel, the world opened up to me.
I was fascinated with other cultures. What that
exposure did for the vision I had for myself was life
changing. I realized that there was so much more
for me out there than I had ever thought possible.*

*Over time, I realized one important thing. While I
loved the international travel and working with
people, I didn't want to be a stewardess all my life...
But I did want to sit in First Class—as a passenger!*

-WENDY JOHNSON
Former President and CEO
Dale Carnegie franchise, Atlanta, GA

Back in my grandparents' time, the career path anyone initially headed down tended to be the path they stayed on for life. Young (mostly male) trainees might start out as an apprentice to a shop owner who would teach them the trade and show them the ropes. Over time, the apprentice would become a journeyman—a skilled worker employed by someone else. A journeyman could spend their life working in that same trade for someone else, or they might eventually take over the business, while some might strike out on their own, typically in the same profession.

Around the same time, women had few choices. Before marriage, some might have become schoolteachers, nurses, housemaids or laundrymaids, cleaning ladies, secretaries, or shop clerks. But most women ended their professional careers upon marriage to run their households and raise any children they had. If the husband died, some might take over running their husband's business, as my maternal grandmother did, while continuing on in their other roles as well.

It has only been in the years since WWII that women have had more career options. As millions of men went to fight overseas, women stepped up and stepped into the roles they left behind. Although they faced challenges, including workplace harassment, low pay, and grueling work conditions, this was a period of empowerment that helped women redefine their roles and achieve financial independence and self-sufficiency.

Despite having more career options over the next few decades, very few women aspired to become a C-level officer of an organization before the 1970s. For the most part, that simply was not a viable option. But since then, within just a couple of generations, everything changed. Thanks to some very strong, brave, trailblazing women, like the amazing role model women on top who are highlighted in this book, future generations of women will never wonder if they have what it takes to lead the most important, successful, and influential organizations in the world.

The point is, career-building today looks completely different from how it once did—for men and women alike. Women have made impressive strides toward

> Within just a couple of generations, everything changed—thanks to some very strong, brave, trailblazing women.

breaking the glass ceiling, and now there's no limit to what we can do. But that doesn't mean our paths are always clear...

Wrong Turns, Detours, and Unplanned Adventures: Build a Road to Your Career Destination (But Expect the Unexpected)

I'm a firm believer in having well-defined career dreams, ambitions, and goals. But as you probably have experienced (and if you haven't yet, you will), our best-laid plans don't always work out the way we expect them to. Regardless, when we continue to work hard, build new skills, and hone our instincts, the journey often leads us to exciting places we couldn't have imagined.

My career path has led to plenty of unexpected places. I started out in fashion. At the age of 19, I went to work as a designer for a small women's ready-to-wear clothing manufacturer upon graduating with an associate of arts (AA) degree from the Fashion Institute of Design & Merchandising. The company where I began my design career had been established just a few years earlier by a husband-and-wife team who had no prior experience in the garment industry. At the time, the husband had been laid off from his job as a defense industry engineer.

The wife had designed one very simple Hawaiian muumuu-style dress that was admired by a local retail shop owner. The shop owner offered to sell the dress in her store if more could be made in other fabrics and colors. So, the two became entrepreneurs. They started a small clothing manufacturing business with only one design to sell. They quickly realized they needed to hire someone who could design complementary items. Fresh out of design school, I was cheap to hire and happy to land the job as head designer.

I had free rein to design whatever I pleased. I enjoyed the job, but working for bosses who rarely agreed on anything was not what I had expected. Sometimes they were in such disagreement they wouldn't speak to each other for days. I was caught in the middle. But I learned the business, mostly through trial and error, and through the mentoring of our fabric suppliers and my head seamstress.

About a year into this role, I married a young naval officer I had met at a fraternity party during college. His ship was going into dry-dock in Portland, Oregon, so I agreed to make the move, relieved to be out of the dysfunction of that husband-and-wife-run business.

In Portland, I became a designer for a long-established raincoat manufacturer that was expanding into fashions for young women and girls. I loved that job. I especially loved the mentoring I received from the VP of sales and from the buyers of our largest client, Nordstrom, a then-burgeoning department store chain for which we designed under their private label.

One year later, my husband's ship headed back to its homeport of San Diego. With this move, I leveraged the knowledge I had gained from Nordstrom and went to work designing junior girls' swimwear, albeit for another husband-and-wife-owned manufacturer. I should have learned the first time that this kind of arrangement wasn't a great fit for me.

Unfortunately, these owners did not work well together as business partners either. They yelled at each other much of the day, and door slamming was part of the routine. I learned to stay well out of their way—and how *not* to lead a company.

Yet, I found myself increasingly intrigued by what it took to run a business. I loved going on sales calls with our VP of sales. I loved speaking directly to the buyers in the stores that bought my designs. I loved walking the factory floor, learning what I could do, as the designer, to make the production process easier for the cutters, the seamstresses, and the quality control teams.

Soon I discovered I loved all the various aspects of managing the business even more than I enjoyed designing clothing. Because I had studied computer science during my freshman year at UCLA—before I transferred to fashion design school—I volunteered to get involved with the implementation of the very first computer system installed to run our financial accounting applications at my swimwear design job.

Changing Career Tracks: Going from Sketches to Systems

Before long, I realized I would rather run my own business than work for someone else. As I already emphasized, you never know where you will end up when you first start out. I wanted to be a CEO and make the important decisions. But with just an AA in fashion design, I believed I needed a business degree to be successful at the top.

> I realized I would rather run my own business than work for someone else. I wanted to be a CEO and make the important decisions.

About that time, my husband was reassigned to teach at the Surface Warfare Officers School at Naval Station Newport, Rhode Island. It seemed to be the perfect opportunity to go back to school full-time to finish up my bachelor's degree. While stationed in Newport for two years, I obtained both a bachelor's degree in business and an MBA in management information systems at the University of Rhode Island. By cramming three years of credits into 24 months, I set myself up to relaunch my career wherever my husband's next duty station happened to be.

But a funny thing happened on the way to completing my bachelor's degree: I was offered an unpaid internship as an applications programmer for Raytheon Missiles & Defense in Portsmouth, RI, in exchange for course credits based on the number of hours worked at Raytheon that semester.

I agreed to the internship for three simple reasons. One, Raytheon was much closer to my home than the university, so it would reduce my commute time and travel expense on the days I worked. Two, it required me to spend less time working than I would have spent in class and homework time for equivalent course credits. And three, I figured it would give me a glimpse into the operations of a major corporation.

What I never expected was the huge eye-opener the internship would turn out to be. I couldn't have possibly imagined the range of computer automation functions I would be exposed to, from human resource management to robotics, electronic weapon systems, and more…so much more than just basic accounting applications.

The following semester, Raytheon offered me a paid part-time position. I eagerly accepted and continued as an applications programmer, with somewhat more responsibility (and money to boot!), until I completed my MBA. This part-time position gave me even more visibility into how a major corporation operated while the breadth and sophistication of Raytheon's leading-edge automation projects awakened me to a whole new world of possibilities. Though I didn't know it at the time, this served as the catalyst that would take me in a completely different career direction after graduate school—more on that switcheroo in a subsequent chapter.

Someone once told me, "Be open to outcomes, not attached to outcomes." The outcome I was attached to was in the world of fashion design. Yet, the world of technology—with the opportunity to leverage leading-edge technologies to solve business challenges in entirely new, more productive ways and the opportunity to develop new, heretofore unimaginable goods and services—drew me in like a magnet. I became immediately hooked on the promise of a new tomorrow and never looked back.

Be open to outcomes, not attached to outcomes.

Because of the zig-zag experiences of my early career, I was eager to learn about the early career aspirations of our amazing women on top. I especially wanted to know if any of them had intended to become a C-level executive from the beginning or if they followed a more circuitous route, like I did.

As it turns out, the old adage rings true, "It's not the destination. It's the journey." Read on to learn about the twists and turns taken by these executives as they adventured along their career paths.

Melissa Reiff
Former Chairwoman and CEO
The Container Store

When I asked Melissa Reiff, "Did you always aspire to be the CEO of a company?" she quickly replied with an emphatic "no" and went on to explain:

I wanted to be a lawyer.

I graduated from Southern Methodist University (SMU) with a political science degree, and I was very interested in the law, so I thought that law school was my path. It was only when somebody came to me after graduation and said, "Hey, I've got an opportunity for you. I think you can do this," that I took it.

And like so many young people do, I never pursued my original path of law school and now here I am in retail! However, along the way, I had a lot of wonderful connections and relationships that got me to where I am today, and for that I am very grateful.

When I was a sophomore in college, I worked with Lamar Hunt's World Championship Tennis (WCT) as a courtmate, helping to run the tennis tournaments at SMU's Moody Coliseum. I worked for them in the summer, too, which was great fun and introduced me to many smart and caring people. It gave me the opportunity to learn and ask questions.

After graduating from SMU, I accepted a position with *Success Unlimited* magazine, based out of Chicago. For anyone not familiar with *Success Unlimited,* the company is not around anymore, but it was owned by W. Clement Stone, the founder of Combined Insurance Company of America. Mr. Stone coined the phrase "positive mental attitude." He was a great man in many ways.

At that time, I traveled with two gentlemen all over the country. We put on "positive mental attitude" seminars or rallies as we called them. We had speakers like Zig Ziglar,

Dr. Norman Vincent Peale, Paul Harvey, Dr. Robert H. Schuller, Denis Waitley, and, of course, Mr. Stone himself. We would sell tickets and fill 18,000-seat facilities.

For some reason, when I was 22, this gentleman, Ron Walker, a mentor of mine, saw something in me, I guess. I'm not sure, but I said to my dad and mom, "I can always go back to law school"—the typical thing—"but this is such a great opportunity!"

For some reason, when I was 22...a mentor of mine saw something in me.

So, for almost two years, I traveled virtually nonstop. I would stay in a city for two months at a time in a hotel. We would set up a boiler room in the basement of places like the American Airlines Center and hire a team to help us sell tickets, manage the money—just about anything related to coordinating and executing a successful rally.

I had a lot of responsibility. It was a scary time, but also amazing and very educational. Then I got married.

I asked Melissa, "Did you keep working after you got married?"

Oh, yes—my husband and I both did. He was self-employed, which gave us some flexibility, which was very important to us as we began our family.

My husband and I grew up together. We have been together since middle school. That was when we first started to "date," whatever THAT means. We have known each other for over 50 years now, and we have been married for more than 40 years.

Anyway, soon after we were married, I became pregnant w th our son, Jacob. Shortly after his birth, I began working, but this time, it was part-time.

I had met many great people while working during college—Lamar Hunt, for example, at WCT. Through those connecticns, I began working with a fabulous company, La Papillion, Inc., which was a manufacturer representative firm that represented around 55 or so beautiful lines of tabletops, toiletries, comestibles, stationery, housewares, storage and organization, and so much more. They were all beautiful and lovely product lines.

I had the pleasure of working with many retailers here in Dallas, including The Container Store. I fell in love with the product, with selling, and specifically with The Container Store. I was a principal with La Papillion for about 13 years before beginning the next chapter in my career.

After La Papillion, my family and I moved to Boston where I spent three glorious years with Crabtree & Evelyn as their national sales manager. That was from 1992 to 1995.

I fell in love with the product, with selling.

In August of 1995, I accepted a vice president role at The Container Store and moved back to Dallas. The rest is history. It's ironic, as I knew The Container Store back in 1978 while at SMU, when we opened our first store at Preston Road and Forest Lane in Dallas. So, I had visited the store. I always had a love for the concept of organization. At the time that I joined the company in 1995, we had 13 stores. We now have 94 stores.

"At what point did you have a glimmer that you might become the CEO?"

> As president and COO at The Container Store, I always thought that being the CEO would be really challenging and rewarding. It was kind of assumed, I think, that I would be Kip's successor at some point. However, for years and years, Kip and Sharon (Kip's wife and our chief merchandising officer) really ran the business together, with an incredible team, of course.

"So, it was well into your career before you really started looking at the possibility of becoming a CEO?"

> Yes.

Jodi Berg
Retired President and CEO
Vita-Mix Corporation

When I asked Jodi Berg, PhD, "Did you always aspire to be the CEO?" she replied emphatically:

> No. My parents told me I could be anything I wanted, but I did not see this as a job I would enjoy or be qualified for.
>
> I set out to follow my passions. When I graduated with my bachelor's degree, my passion was to serve, create moments, and help people aspire to greater things, so I was naturally

drawn to the hospitality industry. Within two years, I realized I could have a greater impact on the people around me if I was higher up in leadership, so I pursued my MBA.

While getting my MBA, I took just one class on quality. I graduated thinking, *This quality process, and the concept of, "If it is a problem, solve it at the root so that problem doesn't exist anymore" is amazing and powerful. I want to be in this space, but nobody's going to hire me with having just one class on the subject.*

I set out to follow my passions.

As it turned out, my uncle, the president of Vitamix at the time, was setting up a quality division. I went to him—which was so counter to anything I had ever thought about doing before—and said, "Uncle Grove, is there any chance that I can come back and help you do that, while I learn everything I can about this quality space?"

It was an incredible learning opportunity. I spent time in every single department of the company, learning everything they do, why they do it, how it fit into our ultimate goal of what we were trying to do, and how we could do it more efficiently and effectively.

I got paid peanuts, which was okay because I wanted to learn what quality was all about and why I had become so passionate about it. I really saw an opportunity, so I took it.

While I was working at Vitamix, the Ritz-Carlton won the Malcolm Baldrige National Quality Award. Two of my passions, serving others and quality, collided. Emily Yen—who was the director of quality for the Ritz-Carlton in Cleveland at that time—did a presentation for 500 people on the Malcolm Baldrige Award. It was the first time a hotel company, or even a service company, had won a quality award.

Two of my passions, serving others and quality, collided.

The Ritz-Carlton figured out how to quantify and systematically improve their processes and quality through the infusion of a strong culture. It was fascinating!

After Emily's presentation, I stood in this very long line to meet her. My brain was going a million miles a minute. I got up to the front of the line and I was so excited that I blurted out, "Emily, my name is Jodi Barnard, and I want your job."

I quickly clarified, "Oh, I mean, when you get promoted."

I felt like the biggest bumbling idiot at that very moment. But she laughed, thank goodness. Then I said, "I guess my passion for what you're doing comes through. If you don't mind, I'd like to shadow you. I'd like to meet with you. I'd like to learn from you so I can apply what you're doing back at Vitamix."

I then went on, "You are obviously incredibly talented. When you get promoted, I want to be the one who is the shoo-in for your job. I love hospitality and I now love quality. I can't imagine a more satisfying job than to be able to bring my two passions together."

So that's what I did.

One of my favorite aspects of this job was traveling across the U.S. and around the world teaching and speaking. I had discovered a third passion—I LOVED traveling, learning about different cultures, and embracing the diversity.

Within three years, I worked myself out of that job, because if you implement continuous improvement correctly, this happens. I said to my general manager at the time, "I've got six months. Here's my plan. You don't need a full-time person overseeing this anymore. But don't worry about me. I'll look for other options. I've got a six-month runway. You will have me 100 percent until I get to that point."

Within that six-month window, Vitamix created an international division and needed someone willing to develop it into something. All three of my passions were coming together. I developed an international division by creating a culture that empowered people to do their best.

We went from a handful of countries to over 130. But more important than that was that I found my purpose. I realized my passion for serving, continuous improvement, and embracing our differences fueled my life purpose of helping and empowering people to find and spread their wings, making our family company iconic and taking us around the world.

My passion for serving, continuous improvement, and embracing our differences fueled my life purpose.

Nancy Howell Agee
President and CEO
Carilion Clinic

Nancy Howell Agee began her career as a nurse. When I asked her—as I shared in the previous chapter— "When, where, and from whom did you learn the values that got you where you are today?" Nancy also expounded on how lucky she was to have had mentors who inspired her and helped her develop her leadership acumen along the way.

A couple of people stand out, especially a physician colleague, who became an unofficial mentor to me. Because we were both interested in oncology, in a community setting like we live in, we ended up writing a grant proposal together.

That was in the days before computers. I was in Charlottesville at the time, and he was in Roanoke. We had to physically mail manuscripts back and forth—if you can imagine that—and edit them. We created a real bond.

As I have thought about this, here is what I learned from him:

He was pretty powerful. He was the chief medical officer. He was a fellow in the American College of Physicians. He never *did not* have time for you—or for anyone. I mean, he spent so much time with his faculty and with the residents. If they were presenting somewhere, he was there in the front row, cheering them on. It was just remarkable how much time he spent and how supportive he was.

At the same time, he was very, very clear about expectations. When I say we shared manuscripts back and forth, usually it was him editing and me having to re-do it—as an example. But he was an amazing mentor for me.

Then, fast forward. Before I became the CEO, I was the chief operating officer. Becoming the COO was somewhat accidental, although if the position had been open, I probably would have applied. But it was offered to me without applying. My CEO, similarly, showed me a lot about (1) developing discipline around a challenge, (2) focusing so you could solve it, and (3) communicating. He shared everything. He was very open.

The position of CEO was something I didn't really expect to get. I hadn't prepared for it or planned for it. At the same time, I was very involved in a fairly major change in our organization. At the end of it, at some point, the CEO and the board became cross-wise a bit, and the board asked me to be the CEO. That's kind of the bottom line.

So, I had some great mentors. I think they made a big difference. A common denominator among all of them was that they had such passion and joy for what they did. They really believed in life and living and doing good for others.

> **The position of CEO was something I didn't really expect to get. I hadn't prepared for it or planned for it.**

I interjected, "I find when people love where they work, it's often because they've got somebody they report to who is a wonderful human being, who cares about others, who is passionate, and who has a joy for what they do."

> Yep. I hope that's a common denominator. That notion of joy certainly is a common denominator in the people I know, in the leaders I know, and especially in women—not just in women, but maybe women talk about it more.

"I would imagine, thinking nursing was your calling, that nursing was what you expected to do for your entire career. At what point did you aspire to be the CEO of an organization?"

> The truth is, never. It was kind of *right place, right time* I guess—or maybe *wrong place, wrong time*. [Laughs]

> Here's a different question: Have I enjoyed it? Is it the impostor syndrome? Or do I feel like I am in the right place at the right time?

> I think it's the latter. I have loved this role. I love what I do. I learn something new every day.

> The motivation goes back to my strong work ethic, doing the right thing for our patients, or in my case, for *a patient*. There were several instances where I did not feel that the organizational structure facilitated the kind of patient care that I wanted to give.

> It was not that anything was *wrong*, but here is a simple example: The kitchen closed at 10:00 p.m. I had a patient who had been throwing up all afternoon and didn't want to eat

until about midnight, but I couldn't get food for them because the kitchen was closed.

It was just things like that that bothered me. At some point I thought, *I can do better than this.*

So, I began to find my way into positions where I could have more influence and responsibility.

Things...bothered me. At some point I thought, *I can do better than this.* So, I began to find my way into positions where I could have more influence and responsibility.

"I have to think that in most health systems it would be highly unusual for somebody who started as a nurse to end up as the CEO."

Yeah, there are not many of us. There are some, but there aren't many.

Linda Rutherford
Executive Vice President, Chief Communications Officer
Southwest Airlines

Linda Rutherford shared this story about her early career aspirations:

My first job was with *Newsweek* magazine in their New York reporting bureau.

I remember packing up my U-Haul when I graduated from
Texas Tech, and my mom drove with me. We kind of made it a
little *Thelma & Louise* trip up to New York City. I sublet an
apartment, and she got me moved in.

As I remember, I did not have to be at work until a week or ten
days after we got there. So, our plan was to just go see a
Broadway show every single day. On the first night, we got
everything settled in the apartment and went to bed.

My mom and I woke up the next morning and had a cup of
coffee. Of course, we could hear all the horns honking and the
ambulance sirens. My mom said, "I think I'm going to need you
to take me to the airport."

I was like, "Why?"

"Because I'm scared here. If I stay another day, I am going to
take you with me. I know you want to be here, so you just
need to get me out of here."

I was like, "Okay," and literally drove her to the airport.

Linda's original dream for her life was to work as a beat reporter
for a major newspaper. Upon graduation, she secured the position
with *Newsweek* magazine in New York City, where she covered
celebrity news, major lawsuits, and the national political
conventions, all as part of the New York reporting bureau. But
after a while, she grew homesick for Texas and returned to Dallas.

After I came back to Texas from New York, I worked for a
number of different newspaper chains—Harte-Hanks

newspapers, DFW Suburban Newspapers, and then I worked for the *Dallas Times Herald* as a business features writer. I worked for the *Herald* until they closed on December 8, 1991, when they were purchased by the *Morning News*. Then I did a little bit of freelancing for six months.

I had been covering airlines for the *Dallas Times Herald*. Everyone was very kind when the newspaper closed. Of course, it had been around for 109 years. They said, "Hey, if you need to fly for an interview anywhere, let us know. We' l write you an industry pass for free."

I was like, "Awesome!"

Well, Southwest did one better. They said, "Hey, we have th s job for a public relations coordinator. Would you be interested?"

I was like, "I'm interested. What is that?"

They said, "Look. We'll explain it to you when you come in."

So, I came in. I knew the team really well, so we had a really good rapport. They said, "Look. We will teach you what you need know about the airline industry. We will teach you what you need to know about public relations. But the bottom line is, you know how to write. You know what makes a good story. You're sensitive to reporter deadlines. We want you."

So, my career at Southwest started as a public relations coordinator on June 1, 1992. It was truly a blessing. It has turned out to be a fantastic blessing, for sure.

I inquired, "Early in your career—either before you joined Southwest or when you started at Southwest—did you ever think, *One of these days, I could lead this organization?"*

Never. Sometimes I get asked to talk to university students, to kind of set them up for success and help them build confidence. I always have to admit that I'm the accidental executive.

> **I always have to admit that I'm the accidental executive.**

I had no hopes and dreams to do this. I didn't set out to do this. I just sort of started exploring. I thought I would be at Southwest for five or six years and then I would figure out something else to do. It just turned out to be too much fun. I was learning so much.

Journalism, back in the day, and what I would call public relations were probably very similar. Communications today is far more sophisticated. It has all been on-the-job learning for me, including the leadership aspects of the roles that I've had.

I had the same boss—a woman by the name of Ginger Hardage—for 23 years. That was a total blessing. I really got to learn leadership—those aspects of leadership—from her.

When I joined the company, Ginger was the director of public relations, so I went to work for her. For 23 of my 28 years at Southwest Airlines, she was my leader. She was my leader the whole time she was at Southwest Airlines, which was an extreme blessing. When Ginger was promoted into the senior vice president role, it was at that moment that I said to her, "Hey...so then I could do what you do and run the department day-to-day? Oh, I want to do that!"

It really was just one of those sparks. I hadn't been planning it or plotting it or anything. It wasn't until she literally said, "Hey, I'm going to move into this role," and there was an empty box on the org chart. I was like, "Can that be me?"

"Do you want it to be you?"

"Yeah, I do!"

I'd like to tell you there was a grand plan, but there really wasn't.

> **I hadn't been planning it or plotting it or anything…I'd like to tell you there was a grand plan, but there really wasn't.**

Kerry Healey
Inaugural President
Milken Center for Advancing the American Dream

As I was interviewing Kerry Healey, PhD, I said to her, "You've had such an amazingly varied career, from running a state government, to education, to television, and now running a new kind of cultural organization as part of the Milken Institute. You have been the woman on top of so many different types of entities. Can you tell me what your plan was when you went off to Harvard and what you were hoping to accomplish?"

I've always been very focused on problem-solving. I've always been very excited about being in a place where I can problem-solve.

I did imagine that I wanted to be in government when I was very young—when I was in high school or maybe even younger—because that is where you could solve problems. That's where things got done. But it wasn't very clear to me whether that was a place or career path that was available to women.

I think that while I imagined myself to be a leader in my early life—when I was in high school and going to college—once I got to college, I realized I needed to step back. I needed to spend some time building a foundation of skills, knowledge, and the finances that would allow me to come back, at some point, into public life and be valuable.

> **I needed to spend some time building a foundation of skills, knowledge, and the finances that would allow me to come back, at some point, into public life and be valuable.**

I asked Kerry, "Did you meet your husband at Harvard?"

Yes. But we re-met and, more importantly, started dating after college in Ireland. We both had scholarships that are given by Rotary International to allow people to study overseas. They are wonderful community-based scholarships that I always recommend to students.

The idea behind the scholarship is beautiful. It's a program to promote world peace through understanding. The guiding notion is that if you go to live in another country, you're going to be more empathetic to that culture. You're much less likely to engage in hostile behaviors, either toward that culture or that country. There's also the idea that people with those skills would be more likely to become leaders. I think that is true.

I spent a number of years in graduate education earning my PhD at Trinity College Dublin, putting my husband through law school, and working at a firm called Abt Associates, Inc., in Cambridge. Abt Associates was a public policy consulting firm that consulted for the U.S. Department of Justice's National Institute of Justice. I worked on criminal justice policy and research. We looked at recent findings in academia as well as what was happening in the field, such as what kinds of innovations were being created by prosecutors, police officers, and judges.

I didn't enter public life, or seek any leadership positions, until I was about 38 years old. By then I had two kids. They were, at that time, three and six years old. I ran for my first office when I was 38. I waited until the kids were old enough to go to school part-time so I could meet all my obligations.

I don't know if I was or was not a leader during that period of time. I don't feel like I was. But I feel like my desire to be a problem-solver was consistent throughout. I was coming up with solutions.

I would say, "This is what we ought to be doing about domestic violence," or, "This is how we protect people from being murdered by their domestic partners." I just didn't have a very big audience for those solutions. So, I would write an article or a white paper.

Writing white papers, articles, and giving papers at the American Society of Criminology is valuable work. But from a policy standpoint, I realized that all the research and work that I was doing was having very little impact. If I really wanted to be influential, I was going to need to take the next step. I was going to have to run for office and lead.

"So, it seems your focus was to get into government so you could be the decision-maker and create the policies that you had been working on. Did you have a long-term agenda at that point?"

> **I realized that all the research and work that I was doing was having very little impact. If I really wanted to be influential, I was going to need to take the next step.**

I did intend to implement the solutions that I had been working on for the prior ten years regarding criminal justice issues, especially around domestic violence and child abuse. But, once you are in office, there are so many things that need to be addressed, your agenda just grows. So, even though I was able to have a very positive impact on many of the things I cared about coming into office, my eyes were opened to a much broader series of needs in society that I couldn't possibly get near to impacting over the course of four years. Four years goes by quickly.

Wendy Johnson
Former President and CEO
Dale Carnegie franchise, Atlanta, GA

When I met with Wendy Johnson, I started out by asking, "What was the path you took to become the president and CEO of a training institute like Dale Carnegie?"

Well, it was a journey that had many different stops.

As with many women, our careers are sometimes formed by what's driving our personal lives. I started out as a Pan Am stewardess based out of New York and San Francisco.

As a language major in college, I was drawn to Pan Am, because they required flight attendants to be proficient in a foreign language. That was a requirement of the International Air Transport Association. International flights must have flight attendants on the airplane who can speak the destination language, in case of emergencies. As a result, you had to have a foreign language to get hired by Pan Am. I had been trained in Spanish and Italian, so they hired me...and there I was.

Every time I went to work, I left the country. When I started at Pan Am, I wanted to travel, but I never thought about it as a

Back in those days, women weren't encouraged to think about careers.

career. Back in those days, women weren't encouraged to think about careers. It was expected you would get married and have babies. Or you would be a nurse or a teacher. When I joined the airlines, on the first day of training, we were asked what being a Pan Am stewardess would do for our lives. I responded, "I'll be a better wife and mother."

I swear to you, I really did say that. I can still remember those words! I was so surprised at myself. I had no idea how this experience would impact my life.

Once I began to travel, the world opened up to me. I was fascinated with other cultures. What that exposure did for the vision I had for myself was life changing. I realized that there was so much more for me out there than I had ever thought possible.

Over time, I realized one important thing. While I loved the international travel and working with people, I didn't want to be a stewardess all my life (in those days, they called flight attendants "stewardesses"). But I did want to sit in First Class—as a passenger!

After six years, when the airline started to falter a bit—it was the beginning of Pan Am's decline—I decided that it would be a perfect time to make a career transition. Changing paths at that point wouldn't impact my income level. I wasn't making a large enough income as a flight attendant that it would cause me to take a pay cut to make a career change.

My background in the airlines really served me well, though. I was able to communicate. I could talk to anyone. I could build relationships. I was a risk-taker. I could solve problems. I used persuasion in my job, and I was unafraid of new environments and situations. So, I think all that allowed me to deliver in an interview very well.

I settled on going into sales because it fit perfectly with the skills I had built in the airlines—confidence, high energy, good communications, and risk-taking. Since I did not have a college degree, I thought I might have a better chance of getting a job in sales than in other professions. I applied for various sales jobs until I landed one. So, that is how I started my career beyond the airlines.

I have to say, making the switch from being a flight attendant into the corporate world was hard. Women weren't readily hired back then. Plus, I was already 27 years old. Most companies wanted to hire entry-level people right out of college so they could mold them into their own cultural image.

I settled on going into sales because it fit perfectly with the skills I had built in the airlines—confidence, high energy, good communications, and risk-taking.

I was a little more evolved and set in my ways than they wanted, and I was a woman. So, I had to find a company willing to take a risk on me. With no college degree, the very large companies like Procter & Gamble, IBM, and all those kinds of companies wouldn't even look at me because a college degree was an essential requirement.

But I did start a career in sales—a career that spanned many years. It was 1977 when I got my first sales job.

I asked Wendy, "When you got that first sales job, what were you selling?"

I have a funny story to share about how I got my first sales job. I worked through headhunters, and I made getting a sales job my life's work for that moment. I had so many interviews, but I always came in second or third.

I was living in Seattle. On this day, I was waiting in the lobby of a hotel for a call from my headhunter about an interview location in the hotel. I was called to the lobby telephone. It was my headhunter calling to tell me, "You'll be going to floor seven, room 710."

I said, "That's great. But you know what? I really need to mentally prepare for this. What is the company name and what is the product?"

He said, "Oh, I didn't tell you?"

"No."

Once he told me it was a major corporation, I said, "Well, that's a good company. I wish you had told me that sooner though. I would have studied the company. Which product would it be?"

Now there was just silence. I said again, "What product is it?"

"Douchebags."

"Are you serious?"

"Yes. Douchebags."

So, I went back to my seat and continued to wait in the lobby until that time when I was to go up to floor seven. But then I started laughing and I could not stop. All I could think about was that if I got the job, how would I tell people, "I was a Pan Am stewardess traveling the world, and now..."

Suddenly, a man comes up to me and says, "I've had a bad week, and you're sitting here laughing. Could you share with me why you're laughing because I need a good laugh, too."

I replied, "Why did you have a bad week?"

"I didn't accomplish what I needed to accomplish."

"Well, okay, sit down. Are you ready? I'm going to tell you."

So, I went through the whole story of how I had waited on kings and queens and businesspeople and vacationers, how I had traveled the whole world for over six years, and now I'm waiting for an interview for a job to sell douchebags.

Well, the guy couldn't stand it—he laughed so hard. He said, "You're kidding me!"

I said, "No. I'm not. But it's a fine company."

He said, "After hearing your story and recognizing your confidence and your courage and your flexibility, I've just decided I'm going to hire you!"

To that he said, "Okay. This is the deal. I have been looking all week for a salesperson to work for Transamerica Corporation in the Budget Rent a Car division. I'm looking for a salesperson for the northwest. I have interviewed so many people and I couldn't find anybody.

But after hearing your story and recognizing your confidence and your courage and your flexibility, I've just decided I'm going to hire you!"

"You're kidding me!"

"No, I'm not kidding you. I'm offering you the job. Here's my card. Call me on Monday."

I looked at him and said, "Well, that's great!"

Then he looks at me and says, "Are you still going to go on that interview?"

I replied, "You bet I am! I wouldn't miss this for the world. It's a great story!"

So, that was how I got my first corporate sales job. I went to work for Budget Rent a Car.

I sold corporate discount programs for rental cars through special credit cards. Their traveling sales teams would have our credit card, and this would give them special rates with Budget Rent a Car. I called on businesses door-to-door.

"Cold calling door-to-door has got to be one of the hardest sales jobs there is."

Yes, and it was not always pleasant. Have you seen the "No Soliciting" signs on buildings? Well, they can be serious. I got thrown out of these buildings—I mean, it was tough stuff. But I acquired a lot of skills.

On one of my cold calls, I called on Martin Marietta. I walked right in on a manager who was on the phone, as I was unaware of the physical structure of their executive office suites. When I walked right in on him, I immediately said, "Oh my, I'm so embarrassed. Please forgive me."

He waved me in and motioned to me to sit down. When he got off the phone, he started a conversation with me about my product and my background. After a while, he said, "I have a sales opening in this territory, and I would be interested in setting you up for an interview for this sales job. We are interested in bringing a woman on board."

Well, they flew me to Washington, D.C., where I was interviewed, and I got the job selling aluminum by the railroad car and the truckload. I sold products like ingot, billet, rod, bar, forgings, extrusions, sheet, and coil to companies like Boeing, Kenworth Trucks, and Peterbilt Motors Company.

So, within a year of going into sales, I moved right on to a Fortune 100 company. I guess every day and every interaction is a possible interview—and you never know when.

> **Every day and every interaction is a possible interview—and you never know when.**

Lieutenant General Kathleen M. Gainey
U.S. Army, Retired

Lt. Gen. Kathy Gainey shared this story about her early career aspirations when I asked her, "Going the military route, did you have a vision, in the beginning, that you wanted to become a general officer, or did you even think that was a possibility for you?"

> Never, never.
>
> 1) I never aspired.
>
> 2) I never thought that was possible.

"At what point did you realize, *I'm doing something I never thought I would do?*"

> Right after coming into the military.
>
> You start out as a platoon leader—that is regardless of branch. You're in charge of 20 to 30 people, depending on the size of that type of unit.

"That's assuming you don't go in as a nurse or something like that?"

> Sure.
>
> You are going to be a platoon leader and you are going to be responsible for getting those soldiers trained and completing

their job. You have non-commissioned officers (NCOs) below you who oversee the training and executing the mission.

Your job as the platoon leader is quite varied. You oversee getting them the resources, the training time, helping them execute the mission, doing the long-range planning, helping them in scheduling the firing range or scheduling the opportunity to go to the field, coordinating country clearances, coordinating convoy routes, securing the authority to be on the road, and so on.

Coming in as a platoon leader, suddenly you oversee people, their job, all the equipment, and their lives...*and* you are trying to motivate them, understand what their problems are, and how to help them.

When you are overseas, soldiers do not have their families around them. They do not have people to call or visit, so, therefore, you become their family. You become the one to help them solve their problems. It was very enlightening, and I enjoyed helping them.

> **Coming in as a platoon leader, suddenly you oversee people, their job, all the equipment, and their lives... *and* you are trying to motivate them, understand what their problems are, and how to help them.**

Maybe they have a spouse who does not speak English or maybe English is a second language for them. Or maybe they get into debt and suddenly you see them having problems and struggling. So you pull them aside and say, "Okay, what's going on? You're distracted."

So, you find out the family is cash-strapped. "I'm having to send money home because Mom's all by herself with six kids, my brothers and sisters," or, "I got myself into debt and I don't know how to get out of it."

So, you are teaching them key life skills to help them solve their problems.

Back in those days, most young people did not have checking accounts. The military paid everyone in *cash*. Literally, payday was *Payday*.

As the platoon leader, you went and withdrew the amount of cash needed to pay all your people. Then you sat at a table and they would come in to get paid. You had a listing of every soldier and what pay grade they were, and you paid them accordingly. "Okay, you're getting $450.00 today," or whatever amount it was. You paid everybody in cash.

Then came the time when, suddenly, we started paying them by check. I then had to explain, "We're going to go through a *check* process. You're going to be delivered a check and you're going to have to cash *that*. This means, your pay is going to go into a bank account that you must set up."

You had to teach these kids about a bank account and how to set up a budget and balance a checkbook. You had to teach them about credit cards and things like that, which were totally foreign to them.

"These are things people in the corporate world today would never think of doing. You are just there to do a business job, not teach people how to manage their personal life. It seems you had a very different role to play as a junior military officer."

Yes, because we did so much.

As a junior officer, instead of just teaching people or working in an office job, or maybe just coordinating the maintenance of the equipment, you also had responsibility for ensuring your soldiers could do their job. This responsibility went beyond just training them on military skills. It included life management skills, such as keeping a clean room, washing clothes, budget management, and often helping them go back to school to learn to read and write at the minimum level, etc.

So, you had to learn accountability. You had to learn maintenance. You had to learn people skills, management skills, and then the mission of truck driving—because we were a line haul trucking company. You had to learn how to run convoys and organize that, along with how to teach your non-commissioned officers to teach soldiers and get them proficient in their own jobs.

Sometimes you also had a staff to manage who were responsible for managing key functions and duties such as administrative, financial, supply ordering, inventory management, and the dining facility where everyone ate meals.

Just before I took company command, I was a documentation platoon leader in a mission where we took all the loose supplies and equipment and placed them into large 40-foot and small 20-foot shipping containers. We then scheduled those containers onto large commercial container ships to be delivered around the world.

That was my first opportunity to work with civilians. I had never worked with civilians before. The folks I had worked with prior to that had all been military soldiers. So, that required a whole new set of skills, which were more like the corporate world.

Then from there, you become a company commander where you oversee *three* platoons, sections that perform supply, financial management, and maintenance tasks. With a *company*, you can be leading anywhere from 100 to 200 people. Some types of companies, like a large maintenance company, can have up to 250 people. As a company commander for a heavy boat company, I led 187 people.

In all these jobs, I learned so much about myself and other people. I really enjoyed helping soldiers solve problems.

"At what age were you leading 200 people?"

Just before I turned 30. I turned 30 when I was in company command. I had to learn how to work with civilians as company commander, too.

Once I decided to go to graduate school, it became clear to me that I was going to have to stay in the military for 20 years. Well, I did not exactly *have to*, but my obligation for the Army-funded graduate school was a three-year payback for every one year they sent me to graduate school.

"At what point during your career did you decide to stay in for at least 20 years?"

When I was a senior captain and went to grad school.

"How many years had you been in the military at that point"?

I was ten years into it.

At 20 years in, you can retire and draw a retirement salary. So, then you have to think about it. Your obligation is going to be up at 16 years. Do you really want to *not* stay in for those four additional years and get a retirement package?"

My dad sat me down and said, "You ought to think about this. This means you're going to become a *lifer*."

"Oh no. No!"

"Let's do the math, Kathleen."

> **My dad sat me down and said, "You ought to think about this. This means you're going to become a *lifer*."**

"Okay. I guess you are right.
Yeah, so I guess I am going to be a lifer."

"Okay. Now that you're going to do that, what do you want to do by the time you've retired at 20 years?"

"Wow. I'd love to be a battalion commander."

"Okay. So start working toward that."

So that was the only goal I set. Then everything else just kept happening.

"Were you able to have such an insightful conversation with your dad because he was a military officer?"

Correct, but he had been an enlisted man for four years in WWII before becoming an officer.

"Did you then plan to just stay in until you hit 20 years?"

Right. I was just going to stay in to reach 20 years.

At that point, I still wasn't married—I still hadn't met Mr. Right. I just thought, *Well, women don't really advance much beyond that.* We had a handful, maybe one or two 1-star generals in the nursing field.

But the military is very good at dangling carrots in front of you. They did that by offering you the opportunity to command soldiers and perform more important functions.

REFLECTIONS:

If you are in any way career-minded, it's always good to have an end goal in mind and a plan to get there. That said, charting a specific course to a predefined outcome does not have to be a life sentence. Always stand ready and willing to take advantage of serendipitous opportunities that may come along when you least expect them.

Yet, while it's possible that someone might magically come along and open a wonderful door for you, you can't depend on that. You've got to be self-reliant and create your own opportunities. There is a great big world out there to explore and learn about, so remain flexible, yet be diligent.

If an intriguing new opportunity happens to come along when you least expect it, or if you become aware of a potential career opportunity that captures your attention and excites you, don't ignore it, and don't be afraid to step up to the plate. Go after it. State your intention and put a proposition right out there to a special someone who can help you get there. At the very least, do some homework and learn more about it. Ask for an informational interview. Even if a door doesn't open right away, you are making important connections, and you may cross paths later on or be the perfect choice at a later date.

Another important tip: Don't settle into your current position for the long haul—because opportunity can strike at any time. Even when things may seem to be going along quite well right where you are, remain flexible enough to make a shift if something else that you are passionate about and that captivates you comes along, especially if it clearly holds more promise to better leverage your strong suits.

> Even when things may seem to be going along quite well right where you are, remain flexible enough to make a shift if something else that you are passionate about and that captivates you comes along, especially if it clearly holds more promise to better leverage your strong suits.

And if you are well into your career, stay hungry for continued growth and learning. This starts with accepting the fact that you never know everything. Don't be afraid to try on a different hat now and then. Take chances. Just say *yes* and give new things a try. The upside potential of stepping in a new direction, if it leverages your strong suits, could be tremendous. Not to mention, it keeps things from getting stale. You'll enjoy much more fulfillment when you are engaged and chasing new goals.

Sometimes you must discard the cards you're holding for the chance to draw better ones from the deck.

Keep in mind, too, that while you may be happily moving along on your current trajectory, it's not always possible to anticipate what's behind every door. There could be dark clouds brewing ahead that aren't visible to you yet. The world that you are so comfortable with could radically change on a dime, without warning.

So, don't be so firmly entrenched that you can't gracefully change directions if the outcome that you've set your heart on doesn't happen the way you had planned, or doesn't turn out to be what you expected, or the job or the environment doesn't turn out to suit you. Sometimes you must discard the cards you're holding for the chance to draw better ones from the deck.

You'll never know what a blessing that next card might turn out to be until you go for it.

INTROSPECTIONS:

1. Do you currently have a career goal in mind?
   a. If so, what is it and what's your plan to get there?
   b. If not, take a time-out and think about what it could be. The sky is the limit.

2. Have you ever considered becoming a CEO? Why or why not?

3. Do you enjoy what you are doing, or do you feel like an imposter?
   a. If you are not happy with your current role, what would you rather be doing?
   b. Is there anyone who can help you get where you want to go? Can you commit to contacting that person for a chat?

4. Would you be open to exploring something totally different if something intriguing came your way? Why or why not?

THREE

Be Your Best at What Matters to You

I want to make every day matter. I want to make everything that I'm doing matter. Even if it doesn't make a difference on this particular day, I'm laying a foundation or I'm doing something that's going to ultimately matter.

-JODI BERG, PHD
Retired President and CEO
Vita-Mix Corporation

A s a child growing up, my parents and my grandparents were strong believers in the mantra, "You can do anything you put your mind to." They also continuously reminded me, "Anything worth doing is worth doing well," along with, "Don't even start if you aren't going to give what matters your best shot."

Thankfully, these messages sank in and helped me form a strong work ethic. From early childhood, all through college, and then throughout my corporate career, I always focused on doing the best job I could do at any given moment. I was usually my own worst critic if I failed to live up to my own high-set bar in terms of performance expectations. While I wasn't a perfectionist, I focused on exceeding expectations and made sure my team was inspired to do the same.

And as a side note, let's distinguish between doing our "best" and seeking perfection.

In the first two books of this four-book series, *The WOW Factor Workplace* and *Heartfelt Leadership*, one of the executives featured was Colonel Deb Lewis (U.S. Army, Retired). While working with her on that project, she advised me: *Done is better than perfect.* I've never forgotten that very important lesson, even though each of us, admittedly, must remind ourselves of it from time to time.

Perfection can be detrimental to your work and well-being—because "perfect" doesn't really exist in work, relationships, or life. Trying to make our work "perfect" slows us down and can trap us in a cycle of second-guessing and self-doubt. So, when I talk about doing our best, know that I am describing the zone where you are showing up fully, thinking carefully about the goals at hand, and working toward those goals with passion and purpose.

This dedication to doing my best is why my business focus as an entrepreneur has been on helping organizations become best places to work, where leaders at all levels inspire everyone to be at their best, day-in and day-out.

The Key Ingredients That Help You Be Your Best

Also in the first two books of this four-book series, I shared several stories about the leaders who inspired me throughout my career to serve as a role model in every endeavor. They taught me to be someone who could be counted on to deliver results that everyone would be proud of.

But for me to be that kind of employee, role model, and entrepreneur, I soon came to realize that there were some aspects to my work that could not be compromised. I found that to be at my best, day-in and day-out, it was important for me to:

- be proud of my company
- believe passionately in our products and services
- love what I was doing
- respect those I worked with, including my clients

If any of those key ingredients were missing, I found it difficult to thrive and be at my best. If I wasn't tapping into my personal passions, doing something meaningful that I enjoyed doing, it was difficult to deliver stellar results. I knew it was the same for my teams. I therefore kept a watchful eye open to ensure all the stars and moons remained in alignment and navigated my career accordingly.

> **If I wasn't tapping into my personal passions, doing something meaningful that I enjoyed doing, it was difficult to deliver stellar results.**

But as I'm sure you can imagine, it wasn't always smooth sailing. If any one of the factors fell out of balance, I asked myself what I could do to help regain equilibrium. Sometimes it meant bringing a new idea to my boss. Other times it was having a heart-to-heart discussion with team members. And sometimes it meant moving me or a team member to a different organization or finding a new position within my organization.

What I hope you will take from this is that we all need to discover the non-negotiable factors that must be present for us to truly give our best—and to take action if circumstances change in an unfavorable manner. Finding what matters to you makes a huge impact, not only in your performance but in your enjoyment of your work.

I'll bet my own personal must-haves above resonate with you. Maybe you have additional criteria on your list. If by chance you haven't spent time thinking about what really matters to you, it's high time to do so. Dig deep and write down what matters most. Refer to it often. If you happen to fall out of sync, you can return to your criteria and you'll be able to figure out how to get back in line with what is most important. That's what I do.

Working with Your Leaders to Arrive at What Matters

The amazing thing is, following my passions helped me grow and advance organically. I honestly don't recall ever asking for a promotion, but I certainly had plenty of promotions.

Now, that doesn't mean I didn't have sincere, heart-to-heart conversations with my boss about my career goals and objectives. We would definitely do *that* on a fairly regular basis. I knew my manager was focused on meeting his or her own career goals so I had to keep my own career objectives within their purview to ensure they knew where I wanted to head along with what I could achieve for the organization—if they helped me get there.

This is an important lesson. We tend to think mostly about our needs, our wants, our careers. But remember that your supervisors and leaders are also working toward what matters most to them. If you can help them achieve their objectives, you will set yourself apart as a highly valuable employee, and they will be inclined to help you reach your goals.

Because I thrived in leading-edge, bleeding-edge environments, doing things others had not done before, I made a habit of taking business proposals to my higher-ups for new processes, products, or service ideas. When I had a new idea, I would lay out how I would go about creating the team to pull it off. I would clearly define the benefits to be delivered to the company and our clients—if I was in charge of making it all happen.

When you're constantly working to add value to your organization, success tends to be steady. Once I learned how to sell my ideas, I would usually be awarded with a raise, a new title, and perhaps a new team or a new line of business to lead—all thanks to my reputation and past performance. Those above me knew I could be trusted to deliver and that my team and I would work together to bring the vision to fruition.

Those above me knew I could be trusted to deliver.

Fueling the Fires of Your Passion

If you're reading this book, you likely have ambitions for success as well. Where, you might wonder, does the stamina come from to continually perform at a high level? Moving into a new role every year or two has always renewed my energy. No matter how many hours I might put in, I rarely suffered from burnout because my jobs *gave* me energy and brought me joy. However, you don't necessarily need to change positions to get those bursts of inspiration. Volunteering for new responsibilities, taking the lead on projects that challenge and excite you, mentoring others, and setting and achieving goals are all effective ways to keep the fires of passion burning strong.

The key to my success was being happy in my role, delivering on every promise I made, and selling my vision for what I could do next for the organization. When I was happy doing all that, things went swimmingly. If I wasn't thriving, I knew it was up to me to figure out what was out of whack. I'd then figure out what it would take to get the roadblocks out of the way and go ask my boss—or whomever—to help make it so.

Sometimes I had to realign my role—or request other changes to better suit my personal ambitions—while remaining in alignment with the organization's overall mission. But I always did the best job I could do, wherever I was at any given time. I took pride in doing what really mattered to me—and that has made all the difference.

Now let's hear from the other bold and daring leaders about their pursuit of what matters to them.

Melissa Reiff
Former Chairwoman and CEO
The Container Store

Melissa Reiff had this to say about what matters most to her as a leader:

People really matter, and communication—thoughtful, clear, compassionate, and effective communication. I sincerely and genuinely *care* about people, particularly my family, of course, but also my TCS family and our vendors—our many partners. And when you sincerely *care,* you find ways to engage with them, and to do so, I believe it's important to try to always remember their name. It's not always easy and it may seem like such a small thing, but it can really show you believe they are important when you say their name. At least, it sure does for me when someone remembers my name.

You know, I never really thought about this until I came to The Container Store and my new colleagues would ask me, "How did you remember my name?"

> **When you sincerely *care*, you find ways to engage with [people]...it's important to try to always remember their name.**

They seemed surprised that I did. I remember being kind of puzzled. But regardless, establishing authentic relationships with people is so important in life. It really matters. It just does.

Jodi Berg
Retired President and CEO
Vita-Mix Corporation

Jodi Berg, PhD, shared this story about how she came to focus on being the best she could be—in the moment:

> When I was 30 years old, I got a chronic illness. Over a period of nine months, I just went downhill. They couldn't diagnose it. They didn't know what was happening. I went from working full-time and enjoying my life as a 30-year-old, to being bedridden in my mom's house, to being fed, to barely functioning.
>
> I went to one of my doctor's appointments and ended up having a seizure—a bad one—in his office. They couldn't get it to stop. My mom turned to the doctor and said, "What's happening?"
>
> He said, "I don't know. We need to get her into the hospital as soon as possible."
>
> Meanwhile, they're calling, "STAT!" All the alarms were going off. My mom said to the doctor, "How long do you think she should be in there?"

He turned his back to me, thinking that maybe I could not hear him because you never know—when someone is in a seizure—how aware they are of what is going on around them. I was aware of what was going on with my body and what was being said but I couldn't stop it. It was like watching a trainwreck and not being able to stop it. I heard him say to my mom, "Linda, right now I'm not even sure we're going to get her out."

I still remember lying there on that bed, hearing that, and thinking, *Oh no! No! No! You don't understand. I'm not done yet!*

I hadn't even gotten started living! I had spent 30 years learning, thinking that everyone else was so much smarter than me. There was so much I could learn from all these amazing people on this planet. I wasn't ready to be a contributor yet. It was at that very moment when I realized, *I've got to start contributing right away!*

You never, ever, ever know when you will no longer have more time. Spoiler alert: They did figure out what was going on. I was one of the lucky ones. *God had given me a second chance. Every day that I have, every moment is a gift that's been given to me.*

At first, it was an obligation—to use the time that I'd been given as a way to give to others.

You never, ever, ever know when you will no longer have more time.

That was a couple of decades ago. *Purpose Driven* was not a thing yet. I didn't even know that's what it would be called, but what clicked inside me was, *I want to make every day matter. I want to make everything that I'm doing matter. Even if it doesn't make a difference on this particular day, I'm laying a foundation or I'm doing something that's going to ultimately matter.*

At first, I was doing it because I felt like I had been given a gift. The right thing to do, when you get a gift, is to give back, right? For me, it was an easy switch. It was literally a turn. I realized how fragile life is, mine and everyone else's life. I was on a mission to make a difference.

Within a short period, I realized I was getting so much fulfillment and joy from it, it almost felt selfish. I certainly didn't expect that going into it. It's not just *because* you're doing something for others that you're going to get joy. It's because you're doing something that *matters. That's* what brings you the personal fulfillment and joy.

> **It's not just *because* you're doing something for others that you're going to get joy. It's because you're doing something that *matters.***

Now flash forward. I came back to Vitamix in 1997. I was heading up our international division. I fell in love with international business. I became fascinated with how people from different cultures saw the world so differently, yet in some cases saw the world in the same way.

One of the outputs of living through a *doing what matters* lens is that I no longer had aspirational goals of what position I wanted to hold, or what accomplishments I wanted to achieve.

Instead, I found myself striving to *make a difference* in whatever role I was in. Whatever position I was in—whether it was being a wife, a mother, a friend, or a daughter—I found incredible joy in helping people find their wings and fly in every role I held. The fulfillment came through my purpose, not my job.

Yet, promotions just kept coming. Opportunities just kept coming.

Wendy Johnson
Former President and CEO
Dale Carnegie franchise, Atlanta, GA

Ever the optimist, Wendy Johnson not only strives to be at her best at the things that matter most to her, she truly loves helping others be at their best at what matters to them.

At some point in my career, after I had moved to Atlanta, I elected to return to the banking industry. I joined a local software company in Atlanta where I managed sales, both nationally and globally, for one of their check fraud detection products.

This fulfilled a dream I had to work internationally. I had always wanted to either travel the world while working—so I could experience countries, more on the ground and less as a tourist—or I wanted to be an expatriate. I had thought it would be cool to be stationed in Hong Kong or somewhere overseas, but I never did get to do that. Yet, I fulfilled my dream to

travel internationally and do business in foreign countries—
which was all very challenging—and it fascinated me.

To be successful doing business outside your own culture, you
must study the culture of the country where you are doing
business. What works in America, in terms of business
processes and relationship development, does not necessarily
translate to another country. Cultures are often very different.
There can be a whole different dance you must do.

I learned to slow down and take time to build trusting relationships.

Working internationally
was a real growth
opportunity for me. I
learned that when doing
business with people in other cultures, you must spend a
great deal more time in relationship-building. I learned to slow
down and take time to build trusting relationships. An
example might be taking a long lunch over a beer or
presenting a client with a special American gift.

I commented, "Americans tend to be very bottom-line oriented.
We like to get straight to the bottom line of a deal."

That's exactly right. In America, we cut to the chase much
sooner in a given business transaction.

But you know, here in America, even in the worst of times,
Dale Carnegie was such a gratifying business for me. It fed all
of my love for helping others, and it fed my love for having
deep relationships with people. It fed my passion for having
employees who were always looking at the greater good,

rather than just making money. It was so very gratifying. It really was.

"I find your story so amazing, Wendy. Some people have the goal—from the time they begin their careers—to run a big company someday. It sounds like you never really aspired to be at the top. From what I've heard you say, it seems that you were just trying to make a living. But then you ended up at the top, almost out of self-defense!"

You know, Deb, you're so smart. That's exactly what happened. That's why I chuckled when I first saw your list of interview questions. I thought, *Gosh, should I really tell her the truth?*

"Oh, yes! I think your story is so inspiring, with all the challenges you had to overcome."

Well, thank you. Obviously, when you get inspired from the beginning and you end up where you are, sort of by mistake, and you haven't necessarily been paying attention to what you should act like and be like, you become a real work in progress. It's all been trial by fire.

Doing your best, at any given moment, is all you can do when you don't have a mentor or somebody else you can look up to; or have someone who taps you on the shoulder and puts you in a new position; or have a mentor who supports you by placing you in a training program so you can formally learn how to be a leader, and on and on. There was none of that for me. None of that.

Doing your best, at any given moment, is all you can do.

For me, it was all about being put right into the fray, sometimes making just terrible mistakes, and learning the hard way. But doing the best I could somehow got me through it all.

Lieutenant General Kathleen M. Gainey
U.S. Army, Retired

When I asked Lt. Gen. Kathy Gainey, "What would you say to those women who want to shine, stand out, and get promoted?" she had this to say:

My key advice is to do the best job you can do in every job. Ask a lot of questions. Learn as much as you can about all the different aspects of your work. Become competent in everything you do. Know the guidance of your organization. What does the instruction book say to do? Then, assess if you are doing it that way. If not, why not? Know why you are deviating from the guidance.

Help your people become the best they can be and empower them. Ensure they know what to do, how they fit into the bigger picture, and give them the authority to make changes for the better. Periodically give them feedback on what they are doing right and what they can improve upon. Then together chart a plan to address any areas you want them to improve on. I find this most effective when you do it in writing,

so they have something to
walk away with and reflect on.
They will thank you for it!
When they flourish, you
flourish.

**Help your people become
the best they can be and
empower them...When they
flourish, you flourish.**

The last piece of advice is to do what you love doing. If you
are not doing that, work on finding a different job. If you love
what you do, you will thrive. I loved the military and the
people I worked with. It was so much fun—it wasn't work.

I went into a civilian job after I retired from the military. It was
a great job with great people, great work hours, great money,
great boss, totally empowering. There was nothing wrong with
the job...except it wasn't a good fit for me because it didn't
involve people. I was doing analysis, and making PowerPoint
slides, and research, and sending it off. But I didn't work with
people, and I wasn't having fun.

I probably did a disservice to everyone, including myself, by
staying in the job. I promised my boss three years, so I gave
him three years. But somebody who loved that type of work
would have done so much better than me. The gal before me
was *very* successful. But for me, it was like drudgery. I hated
going to work because I didn't like what I did.

I asked, "Did you ever think that you might not love this job
before you accepted it?"

No! I thought I would love it. I thought I would be working
with companies and working with people, and maybe helping
to build teams. But I found that was not what the job was

about. I should have gone back to the boss and said, "This is not for me. Let's start looking for somebody who's more aligned with this."

I felt like I was a failure. I felt like I wasn't doing them justice, and it was my inability to make the job work with my skill set. I was like, *I am not a quitter. I will not give up on this job. I will figure this out!*

I realize now, that was a totally wrong approach.

"That's quite an admission. With a 35-year military career culminating in your being a three-star general, you were the best of the best of most everybody out there. You loved every day of your military life. You loved what you did. Then to have that happen. Wow."

That's why I now take volunteer jobs where I'm having fun. If I'm not having fun, then I can really stop doing that volunteer job.

You must love what you do to be great at it.

REFLECTIONS:

Anything worth doing is worth doing well. But I believe that to be truly great at something, you must have a passion for it, it must bring you joy, and it must matter to you in some way. These are the differentiators that ignite your work, to take it—and YOU—to the next level.

The things that give us the most joy are usually things that hold special meaning for us. Focusing on those things that we love to do and find joy in allows us to stand out from the crowd. In this way, *you* will matter, too. Your life will have more meaning.

Indeed, Jodi Berg drove home the importance of making the most of our time. None of us know how many days we have left on this earth. It could all come to a screeching halt tomorrow. So, start thinking of each day as a gift. Make the most of each day by contributing to your fullest. Find better ways to leverage the gifts you bring to the table—whatever you love and do best, and that will make a difference in your workplace. Stop waiting. Just do it.

Finding what matters most doesn't mean pursuing it all the way to the top of your field, or never stopping until you're the best in your company. Simply put, there will always be someone smarter than you, or more talented in certain ways, or who has better connections, or whatever. But here's the secret: You have your own special gifts, too. You have the qualities that make you *you*—and your unique characteristics are what make you valuable to your team and organization. Take stock of them, even if you must ask someone who knows you well to help you figure out what those special gifts are. Other people see your gifts, even if you can't.

Other people see your gifts, even if you can't.

Speaking of your gifts, don't discount the things that come easy to you. Instead, promote them. There's no prize for being shy about the things you do well. Stay humble, of course, but by all means, make the most of the knowledge, talents, and passions you have. Doing this, you can make more meaningful contributions to your organization and lay a stronger foundation for your own joyful future.

If you interface with people in different countries, keep in mind that other cultures have different norms, business standards, beliefs, and behavioral expectations. Practices considered de rigueur in some places may be taboo in others, so do your homework, build up your cultural intelligence, and do your best to be respectful. Don't expect others to kowtow to you. Learn to appreciate all these different perspectives and allow them to broaden your horizons. Building strong, trusting relationships with everyone you do business with will enrich your life. You might even find a new passion.

When you connect your work with the values that matter most, every single day counts. Every single task you undertake will count. Prioritize what matters most. Not only will others benefit from this, but it will bring you more personal fulfillment, just by knowing you are making a difference.

When you connect your work with the values that matter most...every single task you undertake will count...it will bring you more personal fulfillment, just by knowing you are making a difference.

Finally, if you find you are just not having fun in your role, volunteer to help your manager find someone else who would love to have that job. By helping find a great candidate to backfill your position, you can free yourself to move on—without regrets—to a role that will matter much more to you. Life is too short not to do what you love and that matters to you.

INTROSPECTIONS:

1 To be at your best, day-in and day-out, what environmental factors are important to you?

a. Make a list of those things.

b. Assess your current position. Is it a good fit for you, from an environmental perspective?

2 What kinds of things do you really enjoy doing, and what matters to you?

3 Do you currently have a role that allows you to focus on doing those kinds of things?

a. If not, how could you realign or redefine your role to better focus on what matters to you *and* help the organization better achieve its mission?

b. If it's time to move on, develop an exit strategy that will allow you to leave with grace and your head held high.

FOUR

To Thine Own Brand Be True

Your brand empowers you to build trusting relationships, gain the ear and attention of others, and influence outcomes. Those who learn to manage their brands are going to sail through life, at least those who learn that they have to put something into it—to prepare, be self-aware, and build human relations and communication skills.

-WENDY JOHNSON
Former President and CEO
Dale Carnegie franchise, Atlanta, GA

You can—and sometimes should—alter your career path as new goals and opportunities present themselves. It's also a good idea to develop yourself by learning and practicing new personal and professional skills. But there's one thing you should never compromise on: your personal brand.

"Personal brand" is somewhat of an umbrella term that might cover many different things. The values you live by, the traits and actions for which you want to be known, your areas of expertise, the things that motivate you, the way you treat other people, and your communication style can all be pillars of your brand.

Unlike your reputation, which is earned over time and made up of other people's opinions and perceptions, your personal brand is something you intentionally craft and allow to guide your actions. It represents how you want other people to see you.

At its core, your personal brand should be in alignment with your authentic self and with your objectives. You should not feel like you are wearing a mask or playing a part. Altering your personal brand to fit into a role or achieve a goal will almost certainly be detrimental to your well-being, fulfillment, and growth.

Here's a case in point. A friend of mine accepted a position with a big-name financial services firm in New York City. For years she had set her sights on working for this highly respected, high-powered company. When she finally landed the role, she became one of just a few women in senior leadership.

Shortly after joining the firm, she ran into one of the senior partners in the hallway. She immediately flashed her big, friendly, trademark smile at him; yet the partner's face remained stone cold as he confronted her with, "You're never going to be a success here if you continue to smile so much. You need to stop smiling."

She was a bit taken aback but assumed he was just joking. She laughed and lightheartedly responded, "Robert, you're so funny. How are you doing today?"

With steely eyes, he replied, "I'm serious. You need to change your demeanor or you're not going to make it here."

My friend was surprised and thrown off balance when she realized that the senior partner meant what he said. Unfortunately, because she had worked so hard to attain her position, she felt she had no alternative but to heed the senior partner's advice and modify her behavior. When she shared this story with me, my immediate thought was, *I wouldn't have spent another five minutes in a place like that.*

Yet, my friend stuck it out for almost a year despite longing to be her genuine, authentic, and pleasant self. Eventually she had to acknowledge that putting up a false facade every day made her deeply unhappy, and she left the firm. Its culture was completely at odds with who she was and how she wanted to be seen by others. If only she had realized this before joining the organization!

My Experience: Making Big Things Happen While Staying On-Brand

My friend's story reminded me of the time—very early in my own corporate career as a new hire at AT&T—when I met the one and only female director-level manager in our region. I never saw her crack a smile or participate in small talk. Her surliness seemed odd to me, especially since she was a director of sales. Because of this woman's demeanor, I had no desire to get to know her. Looking back, I wonder if she had been coached to behave that way.

I'm thankful that in all my years in Fortune 500 leadership, I was never coached that "professionalism" could be achieved only by being serious all the time. I was never encouraged to repress any of my core personality traits or to be anything other than who I am—not that I would have been likely to heed such advice.

I have always taken pride in being essentially the same person at work as I am at home, with my friends, with my children, and as a leader in my community. I am and always have been pretty much the same person everywhere I go. What you see is what you get. For better or worse, I am consistent. Even when the going gets tough or the unexpected crops up, you can count on the fact that I'll stay true to my personal brand.

> **I am and always have been pretty much the same person everywhere I go. What you see is what you get.**

What is that brand? Well, I have heard it articulated by others as: "Deb is fearless. She has infectious energy. She has tremendous passion for everything she does. She exudes enthusiasm. She is insightful about people. With Deb leading a project, whether small or on a global scale, it will be done on time and under budget, and everyone involved will have fun in the process."

I agree with that assessment, because those are all traits I embody and outcomes I consciously strive to deliver. But I've gradually distilled my personal brand down into something more succinct. When I originally established Business Women Rising years ago, my corporate branding and public relations consultant told me, "Deb, your personal tagline should be *Deb makes big things happen fast*. That's what everyone knows you for."

I liked it then, and I like it now: "Deb makes big things happen fast." After all these years, that personal tagline still fits all aspects of my life—at home, at work, and across my community endeavors. It is indeed what I do—and love to do—to this very day.

No Matter Where You Go or What You Do, You Have Only One Personal Brand

Personal brands and corporate brands have much in common. Although Fortune 500 organizations may spend hundreds of millions (or even billions) of dollars to carefully craft and maintain their brand image—using just the right colors, packaging, and advertising panache—at the end of the day, their real brand is whatever the public experiences. Their actions speak louder than their advertising displays. So be careful how you behave—as an individual or as an organization. As the old saying goes, "Perception is reality."

That being the case, it's interesting that over the years, I have heard so many senior leaders proudly exclaim, "I'm a totally different person at work than I am at home."

My internal response is always, *Really? If you're different at work and at home, who is missing out? Is your organization or your family being deprived of some of your strongest skills and traits? Is one or both of these groups not getting the full picture of who you are? Or do they see past the facade you've put up—which might negatively affect their perceptions of you?* To me, being a different person at home than you are at work or out in your community is akin to intentionally not taking advantage of your full power—your natural gifts—in all the most important aspects of your life. Why would you want to undermine yourself like that?

An executive friend once said to me, "We don't have a work life and a personal life. We have *one* life. I don't think being two different ways works in one's life. That's a big burden to carry. It usually means you have tamped down some aspect of yourself that could be really great to bring to work—or wherever."

> We don't have a work life and a personal life. We have *one* life.

Honor the Person You Really Are—Not Who Others Think You Should Be

Shortly after I left the corporate world, my team and I launched our leadership development program for high-potential women. We soon discovered that a significant portion of our senior members believed it was necessary to appear serious, calculating, and no-nonsense in the C-suite. When several of our members— at *every* level of leadership—admitted to behaving differently at work than elsewhere, we realized we needed to give the topic of *authenticity* a special emphasis.

One of the CEOs in our program actually burst into tears during one of our meetings when her peers finally convinced her to loosen up. "It's okay to just be who you really are with us," they encouraged her. "We are your friends. We know what you're going through. You can share your feelings with us."

Because this woman had always tried so hard to appear stoic, we were stunned when she broke down and cried. Having buried her authentic self for so long, she simply could not hold back her true feelings any longer once her peers gave her their heartfelt encouragement to let it go.

From that moment on, this CEO became a completely different person during our meetings. She was much more open and candid about the challenges she was struggling with, both in business and in her personal life. As she gradually rediscovered her authentic self, she shared that she didn't want to go back to the serious, stoic person she had been play-acting for so long. Over time, she became a kinder, gentler, more caring leader—and she found that others responded positively to the empathetic part of herself she had previously buried deep inside.

This CEO isn't alone in realizing that being herself could be an asset, not a liability. I once watched a video interview of Angela Ahrendts, then the SVP of Apple Retail and former CEO of Burberry. The interview was conducted at *Fortune's* Most Powerful Women Summit in 2016. The interviewer's final question for Angela was, "What would you tell your 16-year-old self, looking back?"

Angela responded this way:

> Be your best self. Know who you are. Know what you know and know what you don't know. Everybody has gifts that they have been given.

I think it is so easy along the way to become incredibly insecure about everything you don't know. I think along the way, people will tell you to—they will try to convince you to—become something that you're not.

Early in my days, a man from human resources told me I was doing a good job but I really wasn't CEO material—that I needed a coach.

I was young, so I said, "Oh, okay."

I was supposed to be in Minneapolis for a week so they could teach me how to present better, I guess. It was funny because the very first day they did these videos and then they played them back.

I liked it. I liked it! I felt the energy. I felt really positive. Then they spent the next five hours critiquing every single thing I did. "Don't move your hands. You talk too fast," you know.

At the end of the day, while I was supposed to be there all week long, I was so upset, I just looked at them and I said, "I like me. This is who I am. I don't care if I become a CEO."

I just looked at them and I said, "I like me. This is who I am. I don't care if I become a CEO."

Clearly, Angela's career trajectory proves that her instinct to like herself—and her refusal to tamp down everything that made her feel positively about her performance—was spot-on.

Be Intentional About Building and Sustaining Your Personal Brand (If You Aren't, You Might Not Like What Others Perceive)

In our leadership development program, it was typical for our junior leaders to say, "Nobody is watching me. The role model in our company is the CEO. That's who everyone observes and pays attention to."

I would always caution these women, "Well, the CEO may be the role model on top, but how often does the CEO interact directly with your own leaders, peers, and subordinates? You need to realize that every single day, all the people around you are watching *you*. Whether you know it or not, you are a role model in everything you do. You always represent your own personal brand. So, think about what that looks like. Consider how your actions, words, and attitude make others feel. Their perception—not your intention—is the reality."

I still advise young women that it's never too soon to take stock of who you are, identify what you do especially well, and understand what brings you joy in life. Based on those things, you can more clearly define, project, and develop your unique personal brand. This exercise might involve some difficult introspection, but it is worth the effort. Always honor who you are. Wherever you are on the career ladder, start laying a firm foundation for your personal brand *today*, if you haven't already done so.

Another senior executive friend once told me this about understanding one's personal brand:

Our personal brand is made up of the millions of encounters that we have with people every day of our lives. It is comprised of all the instances of how others see us and experience us. It's how we walk our talk (or not). It's how we help others (or not) along the way. It's how we make others feel. It's all those people out there who have observed and experienced you time after time who are the ones who really define our personal brand.

We should each set an intention for how we want to be known by the world and then honor that intention by living it every single day, wherever we go. When you think about it, brands are easy to aspire to, but they take a long time to get there. Brands are hard to stick to when the going gets tough. Most importantly, brands can be destroyed in an instant, just by one bad decision or one wrong move.

So, the more grounded we are in knowing who we are and what we want to be known for—and what our natural core strengths are—all the better. We can't be the best leaders for others until we are the best leaders of ourselves.

My experience is that it can be difficult for people to articulate who they are, what their values are, what their strengths are, who they need to partner with to shore up a blind spot, and what really brings them joy in life.

Knowing who you are, knowing that every single day you are honing and polishing your personal brand—and everybody is watching you—you'll be miles ahead.

Knowing who you are, knowing that every single day you are
honing and polishing your personal brand—and everybody is
watching you—you'll be miles ahead.

I can't emphasize enough: The key to honoring your personal
brand is to know who you are and who you are not. Start by asking
yourself, *What are my strong suits and what are my blind spots?*

The better you know yourself (including who you are not) and the
more intentionally you bring your whole authentic self to the
party—at work, at home, and in your community—the more
effective you will become, both as an individual contributor and as
a leader.

So, be diligent about honing your personal brand. Do so
introspection by introspection, encounter by encounter, day by
day, in all aspects of your life. Live the brand you intend to
project—the one that is authentically you—starting today. In the
words of Howard Behar, retired president of Starbucks: Our
success is directly related to our clarity and honesty about who we
are, who we're not, where we want to go, and how we're going to
get there.

Jodi Berg
Retired President and CEO
Vita-Mix Corporation

When I asked Jodi Berg, PhD, "Are you the same person at work as you are at home?" she said this:

I'm probably more emotional at home...I care just as much at work, but I don't have to personally live the pain as closely with people at work.

I'm probably more emotional at home, just because I have two young adult daughters who are very emotional. It is hard to watch people you really care about struggle. I care just as much at work, but I don't have to personally live the pain as closely with people at work.

I do not know if that makes sense, but I do think I am pretty much the same at home and at work. I think I just wear my emotions in my heart a little closer to the surface at home. I wear them, probably, closer at work than most. I care so deeply about the people I work alongside. I have been known to shed tears of joy and sorrow with and for them.

But, yes, I probably am very much the same person at work as I am at home.

Nancy Howell Agee
President and CEO
Carilion Clinic

I asked Nancy Agee, "Are you the same person at home that you are at work?"

Yeah, I think I'm the same person. I think I am. You would have to ask my husband. Perhaps I let my hair down a bit more, show frustration, disappointment, sadness. But generally, I don't change.

> **Perhaps I let my hair down a bit more [at home], show frustration, disappointment, sadness. But generally, I don't change.**

I remember my son being embarrassed about it. He once said, "Mom, you are the only person I know who arrives at a soccer game in a business suit."

I said, "Well, at least I show up."

As he got to be an adult, he came to appreciate it. And more recently he told me, on the night his daughter was born, he prayed she'd be just like his mom.

Linda Rutherford
Executive Vice President, Chief Communications Officer
Southwest Airlines

During my conversation with Linda Rutherford, we spoke a bit about her beloved manager of 23 years, Ginger Hardage. Before retiring, Ginger was senior vice president of culture and communications at Southwest. Linda shared this about her admiration for Ginger:

> She is an amazing human being. What you see is what you get with Ginger. She is 1000 percent genuine. She gets up in the morning wondering how she can make other people's lives better. She's been a blessing to know and to have in my corner, honestly.

I responded, "Speaking about being 1000 percent genuine, at what point did you start thinking about your personal brand?"

> I thought about it just a little, early on in my career as I was making the pivot from journalism to public relations: *What am I doing? Am I a poser here? What if somebody figures that out? I really don't know what public relations is.*

Knowing one of Linda's top-five Gallup strengths is "Self-Assurance," it's hard to imagine she ever questioned herself or her personal brand. Ginger Hardage quickly zeroed in on the pillars of Linda's personal brand: an unrelenting desire to learn, resourcefulness, and positioning for the future.

Ginger would tell you that the first thing she knew about me was my curiosity and my yearning to learn. Any time a conference or a webinar or a seminar came up, I would be the first one to raise my hand, saying, "I want to go. Could I do that? Can I sign up for that?"

She knew that about me. I had this constant desire and capacity to want to learn new things. That was sort of the spark that at least helped her understand how to advocate for me. She knew that if I ever felt like I was getting a little itchy, or if I had reached that ceiling of what I could do, she would throw a new challenge at me or give me a new opportunity to go learn about something that I had not done before.

That is the main reason why I have been in one place. If you had told me I would be here for 30 years, I would have never believed it. But her leadership style was to constantly raise that ceiling every time I felt like I was hitting it. That is probably one of the top-three reasons why I am still with this airline after all these years. I was always invited to find new ways to contribute.

She knew that about me and my brand. I wanted to find new ways to be of value to the organization. I was willing to and wanted to stay relevant.

I have this desire to stay relevant, particularly in a dynamic profession—communication—that is in a turbulent industry— the airline industry. I mean, the way we were communicating 20 years ago does not even exist anymore, at least not compared to how we are communicating and engaging with stakeholders today.

"Do you think you are the same person at work as you are at home?"

I think my family would tell you I am the same person at home and at work. Absolutely.

I have a son and a daughter. My son is 25, and my daughter is 22. My son graduated from college in 2020 and my daughter, who graduated in 2022, is going to grad school. I know I'm the same person everywhere because occasionally I get that criticism of, "Mom, I'm not one of your employees. You don't have to manage me."

> **I know I'm the same person everywhere because occasionally I get that criticism of, "Mom, I'm not one of your employees. You don't have to manage me."**

The way I stay organized at work is through some list-making, prioritizing, and tasking. Sometimes I do that at home, too, because there is a lot going on. That irritates my family. I'm the organizer. I make sure all the gifts are bought. I make sure the house is decorated. I make sure the house is cleaned. I make sure everybody gets where they're supposed to go. I'm the logistics queen. If we're going on vacation, it's because I've planned it.

I know they also appreciate me for that, but no, I feel fairly certain they would say I'm the same person.

I responded, "When you are just yourself wherever you are, you don't have to be somebody you're not and you don't have to put on some facade."

And that is exactly what I have been told in my environment here at Southwest. Southwest Airlines has been a great place for me to be. I can just be me. It is a good fit.

Kerry Healey
Inaugural President
Milken Center for Advancing the American Dream

With such a varied leadership career, I was especially interested to learn how Kerry Healey, PhD, would respond to the question about whether she was the same person at home as at work. She initially surprised me by saying:

No.

I cook a lot at home!

I replied, "Well, some people say they put on an entirely different demeanor when they go into the workplace."

I am finally now at a point in my life where I am very much the same person at home as I am at work. But this is probably the first job where I've been this way.

This is the first time, since politics, when I have been able to put together my own team from scratch, which is a delight and a joy. So I don't have to have that dichotomy anymore.

Certainly, earlier in your life, when you're dealing with kids and all kinds of demands on your life, yet you must appear professional and do professional things, I think it's more complicated. You might need to put on those kinds of facades at that point. But, at this point in my life, I'm not going to do anything where I can't be myself.

"Do you think it's easier to be yourself later in life, or do you think you could have done it differently earlier?"

I think that if you can embrace yourself earlier, you'll be more charismatic and more successful. Authenticity is at the core of charisma, and charisma is critically important for success.

If you can embrace yourself earlier, you'll be more charismatic and more successful.

What you'll notice is that there are very few female politicians who are charismatic. They are almost all constrained to put on a public persona that repels criticism. The way to repel criticism is to reveal less, but that doesn't attract loyalty, admiration, or empathy. I think the sooner you can be yourself, the better, but I absolutely understand why people don't.

Wendy Johnson
Former President and CEO
Dale Carnegie franchise, Atlanta, GA

Wendy Johnson had this to say about being true to your personal brand.

It is essential that you present yourself in a way that reveals who you are—your brand. Yes, you need to understand, you are a *brand*. People make decisions about you and are influenced based on their perception of your brand.

You have an internal and external image, as well as an interactive and an interpersonal image. You have a social media image, too. Your appearance, how you feel

> **You need to understand, you are a *brand*. People make decisions about you and are influenced based on their perception of your brand.**

about yourself, how you interact with others, and what kind of relationships you build all become the foundation of your brand.

Your brand empowers you to build trusting relationships, gain the ear and attention of others, and influence outcomes. Those who learn to manage their brands are going to sail through life, at least those who learn that they have to put something into it—to prepare, be self-aware, and build human relations and communication skills.

Lieutenant General Kathleen M. Gainey
U.S. Army, Retired

I asked Lt. Gen. Kathy Gainey, "What do you think it was about your personal brand that set you apart from the other women in the military?"

I think it was my focus on nurturing teams. And I was *assertive*, but not aggressive. Does that make sense? I think there is a fine line there.

I was making things happen, forward-thinking, trying to create solutions...being assertive in that way and not waiting to be told. I would see a situation developing and I would say, "Here's what I think needs to be done, boss, and here's how I am going to approach it," or if I had already started in that direction, I would say, "Boss, there's a situation developing. Here's what I'm doing about it."

I would keep my higher-ups informed while making things happen, but not in an antagonistic way. It was just being proactive.

On the other hand, *aggressive* is diving in without looking at the situation first. Maybe it is not good to go in right now. *Aggressive* is attacking without bringing in the team, *without* looking at the whole situation.

Aggressive is *not* sharing with anybody else so they think maybe you are making a power play. Or you are trying to take over territory or authority, instead of trying to respond to a situation that you see evolving.

Being *assertive* is keeping your peers and your people—on your left and your right—aware of what is going on, so they do not think you are jumping over them. You are just seeing a situation develop and you are apprising them of what you think needs to be done and the direction you are going in.

Being *assertive* is sharing with people, "Here's how I'm seeing the situation. Here is what we are doing about it. I want you to be aware so that when you see things going on, you'll know why we're doing this," so they don't feel threatened.

When I asked General Gainey, "Are you the same person at work as you are at home?" she answered this way:

Oh, no. But in some ways, you have to remember *not* to be the same person at home, at least when you are a military officer.

I will share this story: We had just gotten married. I came out of the office, drove by the motor pool, looked at a whole bunch of stuff. I was unhappy.

> **In some ways, you have to remember *not* to be the same person at home, at least when you are a military officer.**

I came home and walked in the house. Ed was at home cooking—he had gotten off of work first that day. I started barking orders at him. He was like, "Stop right there. Go back out that door. Come back in as Kathy Gainey, my wife—*not* the battalion commander."

I started to laugh, and he said, "I'm serious. Walk back out that door and come back in as my wife."

It was a good thing. We had just gotten married, maybe a month before, and I forgot to leave the aggravations of the office at the office.

So, ladies, be the woman he married, not that woman you are at work. Ed and I laugh because we talk about work and the military *all* the time together. I mean that never stops.

"Because Ed is…?"

A military officer. So it was very easy for us to share all the fears and concerns about work.

I would get great advice from him. He picked up different techniques from me with interpersonal skills, and about counseling, and about working with people. I picked up techniques on training and strategy from him.

He would say, "You know, I thought that idea was stupid, but, okay…show me how you do that because you are turning people around who were having behavioral issues. I'm not. I need to pick up that technique."

"How would you define yourself at home versus how you are at work?"

I was more of a friend at home than the leader. More like a teammate. It would be more like talking to a peer at work.

I'd say I was more of a friend at home than the leader. More like a teammate. It would be more like talking to a peer at work. The things that are similar were that I would ask Ed lots of questions. We created a great team.

We *shared* a lot of housekeeping duties. He did all the cooking. He did all the laundry. I did all the cleaning. I did all the bill paying. I did all the financial investing. But we would talk through every decision *together.* We approached life as a team.

We planned things because he likes to have a plan of attack. Even today, now that we are both retired, we still do a six-month calendar scrub every two weeks: What are we going to do? What are key events? What do we need to have as a factor, to block time for each other, to support each other?

I think at home the difference is that I can say to him, "You make the decision if you want, honey, because I'm emotionally spent."

Sometimes you don't have the time and energy to invest in each other. But we would work to try. We would at least tell each other, "I think today I'm emotionally spent. Let's do whatever," or, "I just need to vent. You don't have to solve the problem. Just listen to me vent."

> **I think at home the difference is that I can say to [my husband]..."You don't have to solve the problem. Just listen to me vent." At work, when you get up higher on the leadership ladder, there is nobody to vent to.**

At work, when you get up higher on the leadership ladder, there is nobody to vent to.

REFLECTIONS:

A corporate brand is an asset. Organizations large and small work hard to maintain strong cultures and brand images. In many corporations, governmental agencies, and elected positions, people identified as having high potential for leadership may be coached to modify their behavior to better reflect the organization's brand image, cultural values, and behavioral expectations.

Modifying one's behavior to fit organizational expectations may feel unnatural, but those who desire to be successful in such a place must either learn to fit the mold or move on. In general, modifying behavior to fit the cultural norm can be difficult to sustain unless the required behavioral shift is a natural developmental progression and allows the real you to fully blossom.

Many women face this choice in their careers, sometimes over and over. Having a strongly defined personal brand can help make your decision to stay or go a bit clearer. Ask yourself, *Do the changes I am being asked to make violate my values or goals? Will they cause others to perceive me in a way I am not comfortable with? Do they negate essential aspects of my personality? OR—are these changes compatible with my personal brand? Might they be good opportunities for skill-building and self-development? Could they positively impact my personal and/or professional life?*

Even if you are just starting out and haven't been coached to modify the way you present yourself, it's still a good idea to develop your personal brand because it can be a tremendous asset to you and to your organization. Those who aspire to leadership should strive to project the best, most authentic version of themselves from the get-go. Remember Kerry Healey's words: "Authenticity is at the core of charisma"...and charisma is one big key to success. The earlier you start being authentically you, the more charismatic and successful you will become.

Having a coach or a mentor can be helpful on this journey. Leveraging the insights of someone more experienced—someone who has been there, done that—can be a great way to learn and refine how you handle situations and present yourself to the world. And as Linda Rutherford noted in her conversation with me, sometimes mentors are able to identify and develop our strengths long before we are aware of them ourselves! So, take advantage whenever knowledge or sage advice is shared with you by someone wiser.

That said, don't assume that all advice is good advice. You should always reflect on what may or may not apply in your situation. Don't blindly let anyone convince you to become someone you are not, and don't try to force-fit yourself into someone else's image of perfection. Instead, do whatever will enable you to become the best version of your authentic self—the real you.

> **Don't blindly let anyone convince you to become someone you are not, and don't try to force-fit yourself into someone else's image of perfection. Instead, do whatever will enable you to become the best version of your authentic self—the real you.**

To do so, first take stock of yourself. Here are some important things to consider:

- Know who you are and who you are not—and who you intend to be.
- Be self-aware enough to identify what you know and what you don't know.
- Understand what brings you joy and what doesn't.
- Know your blind spots as well as your strong suits.
- Be honest with yourself about the kind of image you want to project as your personal brand.
- Be true to yourself.

You should also take time to understand how you are perceived by others. How do the words you use, the actions you take, and the attitude you project make others feel? The best way to know for sure is to ask other people to define your brand in their own words, because other people's perception of your brand is the reality. You may discover that you are not projecting the kind of brand you wish to be known for.

Based on this awareness, you can then more clearly define, refine, and further develop the unique personal brand that is right for you. Polish and hone your personal brand every single day, and remember that others are watching you. Over time, these things will put you miles ahead on a career path that is right for you.

> **Ask other people to define your brand in their own words, because other people's perception of your brand is the reality.**

INTROSPECTIONS:

1   Are you the same person at work as you are at home, or
     are you putting up a false facade in the workplace? Be
     honest.

2   If you are a different person at work than you are at home
     or in your community, why is that? Is it because you think
     you need to behave and present yourself a certain way? Or
     have you been coached to do so?
     a. If you've been coached to modify your behavior, how
        do you feel about the changes you have made? Are they
        stifling your authentic self or helping you to develop?

3   How would you define your personal brand?

4   How do people who know you well—at work, at home,
     and in your community—define your personal brand? If
     you don't know, ask them.

5   Is the culture and brand image of your workplace a good
     fit with who you are?
     a. If not, why do you stay there? What are you doing to
        identify other organizations or other roles that might
        be a better fit for your personal brand?

FIVE

Every Day Is a Dress Rehearsal

If you have any aspirations to be promoted beyond the position you have today, start acting that part now. Show people, starting today, that you are just the kind of person who should be in that position. You'll be amazed at what acting and dressing the part can do for your visibility, reputation, and others' expectations of you.

-DEB BOELKES

The phrase *fake it till you make it* sounded strange to me the first time I heard it. But in retrospect, it may be one of the most important catchphrases I ever decided to try on for size. Let me be clear up front: I'm not encouraging anyone to intentionally pull the wool over someone else's eyes, or to knowingly do anything fraudulent. But I am encouraging you to behave in the way you think your favorite role model executive might in a given situation. This way, you have an opportunity to prove to yourself that you have what it takes to act like an executive—and more importantly, one you would admire.

Before we go any further, I would like to explain how I interpret the saying *fake it till you make it*. It is absolutely NOT about being inauthentic. As we discussed in the previous chapter, trying to be someone you just aren't will only lead to unhappiness. Now, what we're talking about here is challenging yourself to perform in a manner that will help you achieve your desired career goal. "Faking it" in this context gives you permission to step outside your comfort zone, if need be, so you can model yourself after the leader you would most like to become.

Before Advancing to the Next Stage in Your Career, Have a "Dress Rehearsal"

Call to mind your most admired role model and ask yourself, *What would they do in this situation?* I'm not encouraging you to imitate your role model exactly, but to—in your own unique way—behave in a manner consistent with how they might coach you to behave. When in doubt, ask them! Then, absorb their advice and try it on for size, as if you were performing a role in a play. Think of *fake it till you make it* as a dress rehearsal for the next stage in your career or personal development. Give it your best acting shot so you can gain the confidence you need to believe in yourself.

> **Think of *fake it till you make it* as a dress rehearsal for the next stage in your career or personal development. Give it your best acting shot so you can gain the confidence you need to believe in yourself.**

Good acting is all about immersing yourself in the role. And in theatrical terms, a dress rehearsal is intended to perfect one's performance. Each cast member wears their costume and accessories so they look the part. They use the real stage props and backdrops. The orchestra and tech crew fully participate, just as they intend to when an audience is present. Similarly, *fake it till you make it* is most effective when you are all in. As far as possible, you should dress, communicate, behave, and lead the way you intend to when you reach the next level.

Your dress rehearsal for the executive suite should start early—as soon as you realize you may wish to pursue a role in management. Why not set yourself up early to get your name on the executive succession plan? In large organizations, executive succession planning is not just focused on the most senior levels—these organizations prefer to have a much deeper bench. Getting your name on the list is all about consciously setting yourself up for success.

Be Well-Prepared for "Opening Night" (i.e., Make a Strong First Impression!)

For this and many other reasons, keep in mind that first impressions are long-lasting—and your very first impression with a company is your interview. A sub-optimal first impression will make it more difficult for you to establish yourself as a future candidate for senior leadership. Therefore, consider your first interview, and every day thereafter, as a dress rehearsal for the C-suite.

Consider your first interview, and every day thereafter, as a dress rehearsal for the C-suite.

One of the first things I learned early in my Fortune 500 sales career—on the very first day of sales training, in fact—was that the best way to make a great first impression on a new client was to immediately present the best version of yourself. That may seem like common sense; after all, most people don't consciously try to make a bad, or even mediocre, first impression on others. The key word to focus on here is *immediately*. As in, you can't ease into establishing yourself as someone with authority and charisma. You have to project those things right off the bat.

It's long been said that it takes only seven seconds to make a lasting impression, for better or worse. Whether you are meeting a senior decision-maker, the CEO, key influencers, or a college intern, if you don't look and act the part within those first seven seconds, the person you are meeting might decide they don't want to hear what you have to say. Although it takes time to really get to know someone and prove your value, you should try to distinguish yourself as someone they would like to know better in just those first few seconds. The key is to help them feel positively intrigued by your presence.

It might feel uncomfortable to admit that first impressions carry so much weight. But all human beings—including you and me—can be that biased. Most people rely on their intuition to form instant perceptions of others. It's just the way human nature works. So, why would you want to make it a less-than-stellar first impression? Help others develop a bias that's in your favor.

Make Sure to Dress the Part for the Stage You're On (and for the Audience You Want to Impress!)

Like it or not, appearance matters. Always dress for success, no matter where you are in your career—or out there in the world. The first step in appearing likeable, knowledgeable, and believable is to dress appropriately. This is especially important if you want to have a successful journey up the career ladder.

> **Like it or not, appearance matters.**

In the earliest days of my Fortune 100 career, I religiously followed the guidance provided in *The Woman's Dress for Success Book* by John T. Molloy. It never failed me, but that was 40 years ago. Business was more buttoned-up back then, when almost all men and women in the management tiers of major corporations wore business suits.

Throughout my 25-plus-year technology career leading business-to-business sales and consulting organizations, I traveled extensively to meet with C-level executives in a variety of industries. Even back then, and certainly today, what was considered appropriate attire varied significantly between different industries, regions, and cultures. Even within the same company, senior leaders dress differently in various geographies. I certainly dressed differently in my Southern California office than I did in my New York headquarters office and when visiting other countries.

Over the years, dress codes have relaxed significantly, and in some organizations they have disappeared entirely. A one-size-fits-all approach to making a great first impression based on your attire— as so neatly laid out by the old *The Woman's Dress for Success Book*—simply doesn't cut it anymore. We no longer have tried-and-true formulas for dressing the part on every stage.

That said, there is one timeless rule that never goes out of style: Dress for the job you *want*, not for the job you have. Wherever you work—or want to work—pay attention to what the leaders are wearing at least two levels above your current position, and follow their lead.

Dress for the job you *want*, not for the job you have.

My personal rule of thumb, to this day, is to always dress up a bit more than everyone else. I try to look my professional-best and present myself as a CEO in business, in the community, and in the social realm. By doing so, I never feel out of place. I also know, regardless of whom I meet, that I will most likely succeed in making a good impression during those oh-so-important first seven seconds. If you choose to follow my lead, remember that you can always remove your jacket or accessories if you wind up in a new place that is more casual than you had expected.

If you feel you need more guidance on what to wear, seek out a successful female leader in your current or desired organization— someone you very much admire a few rungs up the ladder from you—and invite her to coffee or lunch. Compliment her sincerely on her style and ask for some pointers. You might even ask her where she shops. Most women are happy to share such things. More importantly, they will likely be impressed that you were courageous and interested enough to request the mentoring. As time goes on, you will probably find that you are able to extend style advice to others, too. The better you dress, the more likely it will be that others around you will start to elevate their own style.

Take the Stage with Courage and Speak with Confidence

Once you get past those first seven seconds, there are a host of things you might want to do to reinforce that great first impression and exude an approachable executive presence. Establishing and living your own version of executive presence was a regular topic of discussion in the leadership development program I founded.

Over the years of mentoring women at all levels of leadership in a variety of industries, I observed that women, in general, tend to minimize themselves in terms of their presence. They do this in many ways: from where and how they sit, to whether they speak or remain silent, and the tone and inflection they use when they finally *do* choose to speak.

> Women, in general, tend to minimize themselves in terms of their presence.

I can't begin to count the times I have heard women preface an idea with the statement, "This might be a dumb idea, but..." Or they'll say, "I'm sorry, but I have a question." Or when stating an opinion or a belief, they will pose the statement as a question through rising voice intonation at the end of the sentence (a statement should naturally fall in pitch at the end of the sentence).

In all my years in business, I cannot recall any man making a similar self-demeaning comment or turning a statement of fact into a question by modulating their voice—at least not in front of their peers or superiors.

There is nothing to be sorry about if you have a question. Chances are, if you have a question, other people in the room likely have the same question. Go ahead and forthrightly ask it without the self-demeaning preamble. You might discover that others are impressed that you were astute enough to ask for clarification. If the response to your question doesn't make sense, ask the speaker if they have considered an alternative approach. The breakdown in communication isn't necessarily your fault.

I have heard women admit in our mentoring sessions that once they reached the executive ranks and were finally at the decision-making table with the "big boys" (and yes, these leaders usually were men), they were reluctant to speak up in meetings. One example was offered by a senior leader named Samantha:

> Shortly after I got promoted to the executive ranks, my boss, who is quite supportive of me, called me into his office and said, "You know, Sam, you are frustrating the heck out of the other executive team members when you don't offer feedback during the weekly team meeting, but then at the next meeting you'll want to rehash an issue the entire committee agreed to last time."

I found it interesting that several of our senior-level members admitted to having this same challenge. The group came to the conclusion that the women in this situation felt a great need to know precisely what they were talking about before they jumped in and offered an opinion—or even participated in the discussion. Even though they knew the other executives at the table were willing to listen to them, these women were hesitant to present their own theories until after they had fully researched and analyzed each issue's various aspects.

As a result, we discussed ways for them to handle brainstorming in real time. The group concluded that they could simply say something like, "I reserve the right to come back to you next week with more on this, after I've dived into it more (or talked to my team), but off the top of my head, I think…blah, blah, blah."

Using this technique helped our members feel more comfortable with participating in real time. In fact, most wished they had learned this technique earlier, during the dress rehearsal. Better late than never!

Linda Rutherford
Executive Vice President, Chief Communications Officer
Southwest Airlines

I asked Linda Rutherford to share some insights about earning and leveraging one's seat at the executive table. She shared this:

Here is some of the advice I try to give new graduates who are entering this career space: What people want from me is to have a perspective, first of all, and secondly, the courage to share it.

> **What people want from me is to have a perspective, first of all, and secondly, the courage to share it.**

I think sometimes, for women, we defer. Sometimes we can be viewed as one thing or another, as women. We're either characterized as aggressive and bitchy, or we're too soft and quiet. I've always veered toward the more aggressive/bitchy side because I will share my perspective.

That was one of the things I worried about, coming into this role. I didn't want to come off as too strong. I remember a couple of years ago our CEO saying to me, "It really isn't fair for women to be characterized as that, when they have a perspective and they speak up. You need to know that I always want you to say what's on your mind. You have found a way to do it, where you're not commanding the room or you're not calling somebody out. Your style is fine. Just go for it."

I responded, "I have seen so many women struggle with expressing why they should be given a promotion. They are afraid to ask, even when they have clearly earned it. Have you ever struggled with articulating your value and sharing what you bring to the table?"

For whatever reason, I was having a mental block when I was in the VP role and my boss, Ginger Hardage, was in the senior vice president role.

We would often both be in the boardroom. Once a week we have what are called governance meetings. That is where the top executives go in and the subjects change. Different projects and initiatives come in.

Ginger was careful to explain the etiquette of the room to me. For example, even though there are no assigned seats, everybody sits in the same spot. We do not really have a dress code at Southwest—we are casual—but on those days you might want to dress up a little, that kind of thing—a lot of mechanical things.

For whatever reason, I could not grasp the dynamics of the room. I could not get into the vibe of the room. But every time I went in that room—and even though I am talkative and I have a strong voice—I turned into a mute person. I could not speak above a whisper. I would get completely drenched in sweat. It was just something about that room.

I remember telling Ginger, "I'm not comfortable. I am not comfortable in that room. I am not comfortable presenting. I do not feel like I am connecting with the people in the room. This is not going well."

She was like, "Well, why don't you talk to an executive coach?"

So, there is a woman here in Dallas named Karyl Innis. I went to visit with Karyl, and she was like, "Tell me what your role is. Tell me why you think you were put in the role. Tell me about the dynamics of the room."

After several sessions, she was like, "I think I get it."

"Okay. What's going on?"

"You think you have to impress these people whenever you get into the setting of this room. You have already impressed them, or you would not be in the role you are in. I want you, every single time you go into the room, to just close your eyes for a second and say to yourself, *I really like these people. Let's just have a conversation.* Just keep saying that to yourself, over and over, *I really like these people. Let's just have a conversation.*

"You don't need to go in and present to them and show them how smart you are. They are getting pre-reads. They are seeing the information. Now they just want to know your perspective on how we go solve this problem."

What an aha moment that was for me!

I had to train myself. It probably took about 18 months, but now I do not have that physical reaction when I walk in that room anymore. I truly know that these people are my friends, and we are just going to have a conversation.

I think that helped build my confidence. If I had a thought before, sometimes I would whisper it to the person next to me. But then the room did not benefit from that thought or that perspective. I have learned that my value is to share that thought or that perspective with everyone in the room. That is what I learned.

I have learned that my value is to share that thought or that perspective with everyone in the room.

That was really freeing, to be able to engage in those conversations in that way and not worry about offending anyone.

"What was different about that room? Was it that suddenly you were at an executive level, where before, you had not been part of that club?"

A long time ago, I read somewhere that in western anthropology there is this hierarchy we are driven to move up. But as we move up that hierarchy, we become more risk averse. When you reach a certain point, there can be that tendency to shut down. You do not want anybody to know or think that they have made a mistake, that they will see your weaknesses and then say, "This was not the right decision."

I think that might have been some of it. I did not want anybody to think they had made a bad decision by putting me in the role. So, I thought the easiest thing to do was to be quiet, because if I said something wrong, I would prove it.

I had to build up to all of that. But when I compare where I was eight years ago—in a room that made me sweat profusely, where I could not speak above a whisper—to where I am today, I am proud of myself for that.

I also hope that learning journey means that I can be more valuable to the organization, and to the people I work with, because I am going to speak up. I do care about what happens to the people I work with and the company I work for. I am going to defend and advocate. I will be all in.

I responded, "What you just said is so true. It's been my observation and my own personal experience that some women are a little afraid to put their opinions out there when they're at the table—especially when it's a table predominantly comprised of men who aren't afraid to share their thoughts and recommendations. Sometimes women don't want to share their opinions until they know it's absolutely the right answer, like, 'I have studied everything and I'm really convinced of this,' versus just throwing their opinion out there and seeing what people say about it.

"For women who are not in the C-suite—maybe they're either beginning their career or they're mid-career, feeling like they are plateaued at mid-level management—what are some of the surprises or things that you found to be different in the C-suite once you actually got there?"

I do not know if this will be unique to Southwest—because we're more casual, more collegial, and it does feel more like a family environment—but it's more casual than I ever thought it would be.

I think for a long time "the C-suite" generally, and the Southwest C-suite specifically, had a bit of a reputation for being really quiet, buttoned-up, and serious. But it's not! I mean, I hear laughter every single day. There are practical jokes that are happening among the officers. I think that's their little way of letting off some steam.

I think what people, particularly women, would never imagine is—again, you get into that space and your instinct is, "I'm going to show them what I've got, so they know I deserve to be here, but that isn't it at all. You got there because they already know that. Now they just want to know *you*. They want to connect with *you*.

They want to have fun with *you* because they don't have a lot of people they can let their hair down with.

> **You got there because they already know [you deserve to be there]. Now they just want to know *you*.**

I think that was the biggest surprise for me. I expected it to be a buttoned-up, über-professional environment. But instead, I found these people standing beside each other washing dishes in the executive office breakroom area, and people doing crazy practical jokes to one another and having fun. They feel—in that sort of safe, protected bubble—they can just have some fun with one another, and let off some steam when they need to.

Kerry Healey
Inaugural President
Milken Center for Advancing the American Dream

When I interviewed Kerry Healey, PhD, for the predecessor to this book, *Women on Top*, she shared that women tend to run for public office for different reasons than men do. Her observation was that men run because they are confident that they already possess the qualities necessary to lead. Most women generally run for office because they have a passion for a particular cause—a passion so strong that they are willing to accept the risks associated with being out there on the public stage.

Kerry surprisingly admitted she was no different from most women who dodge questions that require them to articulate their personal value. With that in mind, I asked Kerry what finally gave her the courage needed to get out there on that stage, speak with confidence, and run for public office. She replied this way:

> While you can certainly be useful as an advocate, if you want to be as efficiently impactful as possible, you need to have power. The best way to have power is to actually be the decision-maker. You need to be the person who's in a position to change policies and create new policies.

The best way to have power is to actually be the decision-maker.

> That's why I ran for office.

> That's why, at age 38, I said to myself, *Okay, I've spent ten years trying to make a living and trying to influence policy as part of a think tank, and that didn't work. There are no changes that I can see as a result of ten years of my labor. So I need to do something more impactful if I'm really going to get anything done.*

> That's when I started to prepare to run for office. That is probably what you could consider to be the beginning of my public career.

Kerry quickly learned that when running for office, especially the first time out, virtually every day is like a job interview. She was continually meeting new people. She had to stay focused on making the best first impression possible, over and over—in those oh-so-critical first seven seconds—every time she got out there on that public stage.

Kerry knew from the outset that her odds of winning her first election were low. So, she used that first attempt as a dress rehearsal for the next race and assessed what she needed to do differently the next time around to improve her performance. One thing she ultimately did was find a "big name" running mate—a "star" performer—while she ran in a supporting role.

> It took me about four years to be elected as lieutenant governor. It involved two unsuccessful runs for state rep, joining the state committee, successfully being elected chairman of the state committee in Massachusetts, and then actually recruiting Mitt Romney to come to run for governor in Massachusetts. Then he and I ran together.
>
> It was a fairly long process of making that transition from someone who was trying to influence policymakers to becoming a policymaker. But I can tell you that *being* a policymaker is the best way to get something done.

I commented, "That is a huge step to make. Until that point, you were more or less behind the scenes."

> Yes, totally behind the scenes. Totally.

"In Massachusetts, where you ran for office, did the lieutenant governor run separately from the gubernatorial candidate, or did you run with Mitt Romney as a team on the ticket?"

> You run separately in the primary, which is why my primary was so personal. Then you run as a team with whoever wins the primary for governor within your party. So, then I was on the same ticket with Mitt Romney for governor and I as lieutenant governor. There was also a governor and lieutenant governor candidate on the Democrat side.

"Other states may run those races a little differently," I observed.

> They do. They all run differently. Lieutenant governor means something different in each state, as well.
>
> I found it really surprising that some of our most important offices have election cycles that are only two years long. That would mean that you are perpetually running for office and have very little time to actually govern. We were fortunate that we had four years, so we could spend at least two and a half years governing before we had to turn our eyes to the next election cycle.

Wendy Johnson
Former President and CEO
Dale Carnegie franchise, Atlanta, GA

Wendy Johnson reflected on the Dale Carnegie program's focus on executive presence.

We recognize at Dale Carnegie that as leaders, we need to project a certain executive presence to create fellowship. So, one of our sessions was dedicated to exactly that—*Executive Presence: Being Perceived as a Leader.*

We believe that it's how others perceive you and it is how you conduct yourself at work that gets you the kind of attention you need to get results. It is about *demonstrating* that you have leadership skills, or that you have an interest in training to prepare to move into a leadership role.

At Dale Carnegie, we don't talk about how you dress. We talk about how you communicate, how you build trust, how you build relationships, how you handle controversy and disagreeable situations. It is also how you carry yourself— looking more like you *deserve* a leadership role.

> **[It's] about how you communicate, how you build trust, how you build relationships, how you handle controversy and disagreeable situations... how you carry yourself— looking more like you *deserve* a leadership role.**

The executive women we have interviewed agree that leadership presence is a big challenge for women. They need to close the gap between their perceived image and their actual image, communicate more effectively through active listening, and present themselves more effectively. As a result, we created another women's program called *Stand Up, Speak Up, and Be Counted.*

It is amazing how quickly women put our training concepts to use. They start to communicate and demonstrate their newfound confident leadership skills. Because of these new skills, for the first time, their management comes to realize that these women have great ideas and that they could be better utilized. Promotions often follow!

Lieutenant General Kathleen M. Gainey
U.S. Army, Retired

The term "command presence" can conjure up images of the military. I asked Lt. Gen. Gainey to talk about the more challenging aspects of demonstrating a command presence for women officers.

Frankly, in the military, we learn to cuss at a very young age. I had to break myself of that habit as a young captain, because I came back out of Europe cussing like a truck driver. I had to learn to stop doing that.

I asked, "With a father in the military, did you speak that way before you entered the military?"

Not at all. It's just something you pick up. My dad said, "If you want to be treated like a lady, you need to act like a lady."

He made me realize that was true.

I next asked General Gainey to address earning one's seat at the leadership table.

I see women who try to force themselves to have a seat at the table.

If you are coming into a meeting, especially where other organizations are present, you should *ask:* "Where does this organization sit? Are there designated spots? Who sits at the table? I'm from this organization," rather than demand, "I should be at that table."

If you or the organization you represent are expected to be at the table, great, but do not assume you are supposed to be at the table. People will say, "You should sit at the table. Make yourself a spot here. Pull your chair up to the table."

Sometimes it is better when the conversation is, "Oh. You are from X? Don't we already have somebody from so-and-so organization?"

Do not assume you are supposed to be at the table.

Try and find out in advance, if possible, so you do not have to *wait* to be told that you do have a place at the table. But if you suddenly find everybody is sitting down, do not assume you are automatically at the table. Just *ask*, "Where does this organization sit?"

Let somebody tell you, "Oh, you're at the table."

General Gainey also shared some of the challenges she had to overcome as she worked toward and then settled into her "seat at the table."

You must be a little bit humble.

Another thing to keep in mind is that in the C-suite, we must learn how to keep our emotions in check.

What I mean by that is, you'll get some bad news. You'll hear something and you might be so upset that you will walk out of that room and head down to your next meeting with a scowl on your face. You'll go to that meeting with anger and venom. You'll walk into that room, and you'll pass by people who will now think that you're mad at *them*. You'll take it out on the people who are briefing you, instead of saying to yourself, *That was* that *situation. Put it in a box.*

Develop a method to do just that—put that situation in a box and tamp that emotion down. Go into the next meeting, calmly smile, sit down, and pleasantly say to them, "Please go ahead with your presentation."

> **Develop a method to...put that situation in a box and tamp that emotion down.**

Now, it takes a toll when you do this, but you *must* do this. It helps tremendously to have somebody who helps you do that, someone close to you who can say to you, "Do you want to put that in a box before you go to that next meeting?"

Empower somebody to help you keep your emotions in check because people read body language. Then later, go back to your office and think about how you want to address the situation that upset you so.

That's another thing to know about the C-suite: You must learn how to read body language and realize that others are reading your body language. And remember, that applies especially in video teleconferences! You are not invisible, and others may have a full screen of all the players. They may not just see the person talking. I found this out the hard way.

People will know that when you put the pen down this way, t means X. Then, when you start tapping, they will pick up the signals you give off.

And you need to be able to read other people's signals.

"How important is public speaking?"

I think it is critical. It's something I did poorly, so I took several courses for public speaking, because I clutched the podium, terrified, and I would *read* my speech. So, I had to learn to get over that. I also took a couple classes in grad school for writing because I was a poor writer.

Later I also took a Toastmasters course—to better articulate my thoughts. So both Toastmasters and the public speaking course in grad school taught me how to break away from the podium, how to structure a presentation, how to engage with the audience, and how to focus in on people with my message.

When I do speeches now, I use 3x5 cards. I write out the whole speech and then I ask myself, *What are those key points?*

Then, I keep reading and reading it, and I highlight my key points. Then I put those key points on a 3x5 card, or a 5x8 card, so that they are the brain triggers.

"Did you ever become comfortable enough that you could confidently say, 'Sure, I'll get out there and talk'?"

Never. I am more confident as a speaker now, but I am never comfortable with it.

I just came back from Fort Lee where I gave five speeches. I used this technique that I slowly learned to develop. Still, my husband, Ed, will tell you that I totally agonized over presenting those speeches.

But you have a responsibility to give back and to share your knowledge with others, so I do it—not that I ever feel comfortable doing so, still to this day. I still struggle with it and prepare and rehearse. It goes with the job.

> **You have a responsibility to give back and to share your knowledge with others.**

REFLECTIONS:

If you have any aspirations to be promoted beyond the position you have today, start acting that part now. Show people, starting today, that you are just the kind of person who should be in that position. You'll be amazed at what acting and dressing the part can do for your visibility, reputation, and others' expectations of you.

One good rule of thumb is to dress for the job you want, not the one you have. If in doubt, emulate someone upline from you whom you believe has great executive presence. Assess whatever they do that makes such a great impression on you. Evaluate the way they dress and the way they behave.

If you are in doubt about how to playact the part you want, ask someone you admire—someone a step or two above you in rank—for advice. Invite them to coffee or lunch and ask for some pointers. Let them know how much you admire them and ask them how they learned to be the way they are. Ask them for pointers about the steps you might take to further develop the specific characteristics you would like to adopt. Then, absorb their advice and try it on for size.

Believe in yourself and appreciate the fact that every day is a new day. If at first you don't succeed, try, try again. This is exactly the point of dress rehearsals: to practice and perfect your

> **If you are in doubt about how to playact the part you want, ask someone you admire—someone a step or two above you in rank—for advice.**

technique before you "officially" begin to play a new role. When you make a mistake or are dissatisfied with an outcome, view it as a learning opportunity. Adjust the way you behave or respond next time. Finally, remember that every situation is new and different, so try a new approach now and then and see what happens.

Don't minimize your presence. Instead, play it up for all it's worth without being too domineering or becoming the clown of the show. Be aware of your body language and learn to read other people's non-verbal cues. Be deliberate about how you sit, stand, walk, speak, pay attention to others, ask questions, and offer ideas. Find techniques to become a more meaningful contributor in meetings, including during video conferences. People are watching you, even if you aren't watching them. It may help to think of every day as a great opportunity to make a fantastic first impression on someone new.

> Be aware of your body language and learn to read other people's non-verbal cues...People are watching you, even if you aren't watching them.

Regardless of what level you are at within your organization, keep in mind that everyone is on the same team. So, strive to be a most valuable team player. Remind yourself that your ideas are worthy and important, even when you don't have all the back-up information you might ideally want. You are paid for your ideas and opinions, so share them. Leverage what you do know.

As you settle into your seat at the leadership table, don't apologize for your perspectives or hold them back. You got to where you are because you are smart and capable. The people on your team want to know what you think. When you are the CEO, you have no choice but to share your ideas and opinions, so start acting that part now. Display your executive presence. Take advantage of the dress rehearsal—and enjoy the rest of the show.

INTROSPECTIONS:

1 How would you define the dress code for those in the leadership ranks a few steps above you? Do you dress as they do? If not, what adjustments could you make, starting now, to appear more professional and fit more seamlessly into that level?

2 What type of first impression do you make on others? If you aren't sure, ask trusted friends, colleagues, and mentors for their thoughts.

3 Are you afraid to share your ideas or opinions in group settings? If so, what techniques have you learned here that will enable you to start contributing in a more meaningful way?

4 Do you habitually use language that is self-deprecating or apologetic? If so, do you notice your male colleagues communicating in a similar way?

a. What words or phrases could you eliminate from your professional vocabulary to present yourself as more confident and authoritative?

5 Do you understand the unspoken rules of meeting etiquette in your workplace or in other environments where you are invited to participate? If not, consider asking a senior leader who is familiar with the meeting environment—and whom you admire—for some advice or mentoring to guide you. Some astute advice from

someone you trust just might give you the confidence you
need.

SIX

Invest in Your Team (and Activate the WOW Factor!)

If you invest in people, they will take care of you. When you make a mistake, they will correct it. When you need to know something, if you have created an environment where they can share information with you and not lose their head, not be yelled at, or screamed at, they will share things with you that you need to know—particularly when things are not going quite right and need to get fixed.

-LT. GEN. KATHLEEN M. GAINEY
U.S. Army, Retired

One of the most important responsibilities any leader has is to recruit, develop, and retain great teams. As the leader, you must ensure you have the right mix of complementary skills onboard to get the work of the organization done efficiently, effectively, and in a way that brings out the best in each team member. When that happens, you will WOW your customers as well as your organization.

Believe it or not, assembling and empowering a stellar team isn't that difficult to do, provided you accept the fact that this should be your top priority as a leader. The next order of priority should be to get any roadblocks out of the way so everyone on the team can deliver at peak performance—in unison.

When everyone on the team (including you as the leader) loves what they do, enthusiastically gives their best efforts, and helps those around them to do the same, the performance of the entire group will continue to rise to ever-higher levels. That's when you have what I call a "WOW factor workplace."

Do You *Really* Love Leading? (The Answer Is Crucial)

For WOW to become a daily reality, there is one fundamental prerequisite: You must love carrying out the responsibilities I have just laid out. If you as the leader don't love developing others or doing what it takes to remove impediments—if your heart just isn't in it—your reluctance will quickly become obvious to those reporting to you. Even if you are doing all the required tasks and checking all the right boxes, you will struggle to inspire the enthusiasm, innovation, and engagement that separate adequate teams from amazing teams. *You* will ultimately become the impediment that holds your people back.

> If you as the leader don't love developing others or doing what it takes to remove impediments...*You* will ultimately become the impediment that holds your people back.

If you want to build your best possible career, you must commit to not becoming that impediment, even if it means you must remove yourself from the leadership equation. If you don't relish doing what it takes to be a best-ever boss who thrives on developing highly engaged teams of exceptional performers, it will be far better for the entire organization if you instead focus your efforts on thriving as an outstanding individual contributor. Leadership is not an ideal fit for everyone.

Rest assured, there is nothing wrong with living out one's career as a top-notch individual contributor. Individual contributors are often the ones who become the most trusted experts—the go-to authorities who make things hum day-in and day-out. They know what it takes to right the ship when storm clouds appear. There can be tremendous fulfillment in such roles (along with commensurate compensation!). You simply need to assess which path is really best for you and then pursue the kinds of roles that bring you the most joy and satisfaction.

Believe me, everyone around you will be happier and more enthusiastic when you are happy and enthusiastic. Don't feel like a failure if you try a leadership role on for size, only to find it's not a great fit for you. If that happens, own up to the reality and proactively request to move on to a role that will make the most of your strong suits. Plenty of highly respected, noted experts have done precisely that at some point in their careers.

First, Get Over Your Reluctance to Delegate—and Then Start Developing

Before we talk about the positive things you can do to build and support your team, I would first like to address one common barrier to WOW-level leadership: a reluctance to delegate. Time and time again, I have observed that some managers, especially women, prefer to do certain tasks themselves rather than delegate those tasks and coach others to develop new skills. Curious, I dug in to figure out why this might be so.

I eventually identified several primary reasons why some leaders choose not to delegate:

- Some managers (new ones in particular) may be stuck in the mindset that their success depends on the technical skills they were judged on up until their promotion to management. They missed the memo that explained managers are judged by how well their subordinates do, not how well they do, at a particular task.
- Some managers believe it's too inefficient to delegate to someone who is half-hearted about doing the task. *If the employee isn't confident and enthusiastic from the beginning, they won't do a good-enough job*, the thinking goes.
- Some believe it's easier to do a certain task themselves than assign it to someone who wouldn't do it as well as they could. These leaders assume that if someone doesn't already possess the necessary skill set, delegating the task *and* developing the employee will take too much time and effort.
- Some managers don't want to sound like a "nag" by continually following up and offering constructive criticism.

I eventually came to realize that some of these tendencies are learned early in life. In addition to the conditioning girls receive from a young age to be nice and do caring things for others, girls—more so than boys—tend to engage in individualized athletic activities like gymnastics, dancing, track, or equestrian sports, where winning is all about individual perfection. Girls are coached to dot every "i" and cross every "t" rather than perform in coordination with teammates.

Men, on the other hand, grow up playing team sports like football and basketball. While boys, too, are coached to perform at their personal best, they are also taught that winning is all about being part of a high-performing team. Male or female, we take those early lessons with us into the workplace.

The thing is, being the best individual performer is not what leadership is about. There are better ways to get things done. Being a great leader is about encouraging, engaging, and developing every team member so they will be able to take on bigger and more important tasks in the future.

Whenever I had the luxury of starting a new organization, I sought out people who had a passion for doing the kinds of things that would enable the organization to meet its objectives. When starting from a clean slate, you can carefully select eager beavers who possess the strong suits needed for the team to function optimally.

But more often than not, as you work your way up the ladder, you will take over existing organizations with existing team members who may or may not

Exceptional leaders transform otherwise ho-hum organizations into cohesive, high-performing units by tapping into everyone's personal passions and coordinating everyone's unique efforts—like an orchestra conductor or the coach of a professional sports team.

be as passionate about the mission as you are. That's where the rubber meets the road in terms of your leadership skills. Exceptional leaders transform otherwise ho-hum organizations into cohesive, high-performing units by tapping into everyone's personal passions and coordinating everyone's unique efforts—like an orchestra conductor or the coach of a professional sports team.

Your Team's Performance Depends on Your Consistent Presence

I've certainly had my own share of managers who, instead of dedicating themselves to building high-performing teams, whiled away their days at their desks generating reports. When not in their offices, they could typically be found schmoozing with higher-ups. These "empty-suit" managers seemed totally oblivious to the importance of inspiring, coaching, or even simply getting to know their team members. What a missed opportunity.

Yet, I learned a great deal from these poor examples, because they quickly convinced me not to be like them. *Thanks* to them, I committed to becoming the kind of leader who always took the time to get to know and care about my direct reports, as well as the team members who reported to them, and on down the line.

I'll admit, getting to really know your direct reports (and their direct reports, and so on) doesn't happen at the drop of a hat. You can't just have one introductory get-to-know-you conversation and then assume you are off to the races. Really coming to know people—what's important to them, their strong suits, their blind spots, where they want to go in their careers, and how you can best motivate and develop them—takes time. It requires ongoing communication, because at any given moment, things can change. Needs and motivations can evolve over time. Sometimes unexpected blows happen on a dime. A great leader stays on top of what's going on with their people and pivots accordingly.

The good news is that really knowing your people—what they are good at, how you can motivate them to be even better, and how you can best get the roadblocks out of their way—is the most important aspect of your job. Nothing matters more than exciting, inspiring, developing, and empowering your people. Done right, it's a time investment that will pay huge dividends—for them and for you.

I know from experience that it's surprisingly energizing when senior leaders make the effort to do simple things like greeting people with a smile and calling them by name. (Contrast this with the feelings of resentment, worthlessness, or cynicism they may feel when their leaders hurriedly shuffle by and ignore them like they don't matter.) Wherever I went, and whatever role I had, I always kept this in mind. A team's success is born from the way the leaders treat, respect, and care about their people.

A team's success is born from the way the leaders treat, respect, and care about their people.

As I went up the ladder, I validated this theory. Virtually everyone who was one, two, or three steps below me seemed far more engaged and inspired when I went out of my way to not just say *hello* and call them by name, but also ask them about their family or a project they were working on. During these conversations, I made it a point to always ask if there was anything I could do to help them succeed. (Remember, one of a leader's top priorities is to remove impediments that are standing in the way of their employees' best performance.) This is all taken from the pages of Relationship Management 101: Treat others the way you would like to be treated.

Great Teams Are Built on Great Relationships

Everyone in the organization is on the same team. As a leader, you are the team coach. You play a vital role: helping everyone on the team perform at their personal best every day. So, treat everyone as a most valuable player—including those who are not within your direct chain of command.

Invite them to have coffee or lunch with you. Get to know each one as a human being who has a family and hobbies and passions. Let them know you appreciate all the various facets of who they are as a person. You just never know when something you hit on will spark a flame that could turn an average performer into a superstar. Simple acts of kindness can pay big dividends for everyone.

> You just never know when something you hit on will spark a flame that could turn an average performer into a superstar.

As a junior staff member, I loved it when my second-line manager (my boss's boss) would occasionally invite some of my peers and me to share a casual lunch in the conference room and simply shoot the breeze with us. This enabled us lower-level staff members to get comfortable conversing with the uplines, and it helped the higher-ups stay connected with the day-to-day realities happening on the front line.

As I worked my way up the ladder, I usually led remote and/or global organizations. So, I scheduled one-on-one calls or video conferences with my team members, at their convenience, so I could get to know them better. I also traveled a great deal because there is nothing like spending time together in the same place, face-to-face. The international team would get together somewhere at least once a year.

My direct reports knew they were welcome to meet one-on-one with me anytime. If they didn't take the opportunity to meet in-person or schedule a phone call or video chat with me at their convenience, then I initiated an invitation to join me for a conversation. My goal was to speak with each person at least once every couple of weeks. The agenda was theirs to define, but I always made sure to ask: "How are things going? What challenges are you running into? How can I help remove the roadblocks that are tripping you up? Are you still loving what you are doing? If not, what would you rather be doing? How can I use my magic wand to help you get where you'd like to go?"

I loved it when a team member would candidly share when something was tripping them up, or if they were growing dissatisfied with their efforts. Sometimes their challenge was as simple as not having the right tools or software for a project. Sometimes there was a personality conflict with a client or another team member. Sometimes they didn't enjoy their assigned duties. Sometimes the mission of another internal department was not in alignment with ours, so our teams were working at cross purposes and impeding each other's progress.

Once I became aware of whatever was hindering their success, I could take appropriate actions to resolve the situation. Sometimes resolution was as simple as my brainstorming alternative approaches with a peer department head. Sometimes I had to escalate an issue to the CEO and brief them on misalignments emanating from the top that only they could resolve. Sometimes supporting my team member meant realigning responsibilities within our department or moving the team member into a different position—sometimes out of the organization.

If I hadn't taken the time to engage in open, candid, and caring heart-to-heart dialogues with each of my staff on a regular basis, their issues would have only gotten worse and would probably have impacted others. But when I became aware of an issue a team member was struggling with, I could set about resolving it in fairly short order.

Bottom line: Getting roadblocks out of the way was a vital part of my job as a leader, and doing so was always worth the effort.

Likewise, I welcomed informational interview requests from anyone who asked, both from inside and outside the company. I found that people wanted to hear about my own journey and what I had learned along the way. When someone could relate to my career challenges and how I overcame them, they felt reassured and empowered to deal more effectively with their own struggles. It helped them to know that people at all levels have their own mountains to climb, and that it's possible to succeed despite the struggles. Sharing your own honest experiences will help your team members to know they are not in it alone, and that they are not the only ones who sometimes feel like an impostor. Everyone has been there.

Bottom line: Leadership is not about crossing the finish line first, by yourself. It's about coaching everyone on the team to be at their individual best, doing what they love. It's about everyone on the team crossing the finish line together.

> **Sharing your own honest experiences will help your team members to know they are not in it alone, and that they are not the only ones who sometimes feel like an impostor.**

If you dedicate yourself to helping everyone on the team discover whatever it is that they most love to do—of all the things they do well—everyone can experience the joy of meeting goals and working each day with an entire team of high achievers.

Legendary UCLA basketball coach John Wooden used to say, "Make each day your masterpiece." I have my own version of that saying: "Enable each team member to be a masterpiece, even if it's on another team."

When you do everything in your power to develop your team members and connect them to their strengths, your job as a leader—and in fact, every day of your life—will be more rewarding and worthwhile.

Melissa Reiff
Former Chairwoman and CEO
The Container Store

Prior to her retirement, I asked Melissa Reiff about the importance of developing great teams.

We have a great team, and we have great, *great* people.

Of course, we must always have an open mind, unite, and align to accomplish our goals. It is amazing what can happen when a team—a company—does that, with all of us on the same bus at the same time, with every employee in the company knowing as much as possible about the business.

> **It is amazing what can happen when a team—a company—does that, with all of us on the same bus at the same time, with every employee in the company knowing as much as possible about the business.**

Every quarter, after our earnings call, we conducted what we called "Melissa's Coffee Chat" with our company. Those of us joining in person would meet in our Gumby Café at our headquarters in Dallas, and each of our stores and distribution center employees would use Skype to participate. We talked candidly and transparently about our performance, our results for the quarter and year to date, our many initiatives and how we were executing against them, and so much more. There was time for questions and answers as well. I desperately wanted to hear what was on everyone's mind and answer any and every question possible. And our chats were fun! We celebrated our accomplishments as well as talked about improvements we must make. I felt this time together was critical in maintaining and growing our culture and assuring our path to continued success.

I mean, here we are—our company is 44 years old. Yet I still feel like we are just babies. In so many ways, it feels like we are just beginning. There is *so* much opportunity for our brand, our concept. And we have many differentiators in addition to a tight team, a respectful team, a team where everyone understands and has each other's back, that separates us from other retailers. We intend to continue to capitalize on all of them.

We are also very candid with each other, which I am grateful for. It helps so much with any red tape and bureaucracy, of which I am proud to say we have very little. I am very happy about that. We do not have time for any of that—we have too much to do!

During this discussion, Melissa mentioned the term *prime-time* team members. I asked, "What do you mean by *prime-time*?"

Prime-time is "part-time." We call our "part-time" employees *prime-time* because these employees are so valuable to our business—every bit, in many ways, as valuable as our full-time employees—75 percent of our employees are prime-time. Even though they may work fewer hours than our equally valuable full-time employees, we honor them more!

So, it's very important that we retain our great prime-time people, that we keep them happy and motivated, and that we invest in their future with us. We want them to understand everything, to be informed, to be an integral part of the team.

It's very important that we retain our great [part-time] people, that we keep them happy and motivated, and that we invest in their future with us.

We are all about excellence in service and providing complete solutions. We cannot help a customer in the true sense of the word—that is, help them accomplish their many projects—if our employees do not feel valued, knowledgeable, and confident in what they are talking about with each customer.

You know, one half of our business is custom closets. We have been selling closets and designing spaces for all areas of the home and office for over 44 years. When you are designing and selling, say, a $3,000 closet, or an $8,000 closet, or a $20,000 closet, you must be trained, knowledgeable, and be able to connect with the customer on many levels. If not, it is a lose-lose. The customer loses, and The Container Store loses.

I commented, "The customer has to trust you."

Yes! Everything is about trust! It's fundamental to business, and, frankly, it's fundamental in life. If you don't have trust, I don't know how you could build a business or any meaningful relationship whatsoever.

Jodi Berg
Retired President and CEO
Vita-Mix Corporation

Jodi Berg, PhD, had this to say about developing great team members:

> When I was overseeing the international division at Vitamix, I concluded, "If this brings so much joy to me, what if I ran a department in such a way that I helped everyone else realize what a difference they could make in the world because of *who they are*...not just because a difference must be made.

> Trust me, there are a lot of differences that must be made. The list is long. It's not a *pick what needs to be done from this list* kind of thing. The differences you can make are because of who you are, because of how you are wired, and because of *what matters to you.* Ask yourself, *What is it that I do so naturally that makes me so effective, and it is not a chore for me?* In other words, what are your superpowers, the things you are really good at and that give you tremendous fulfillment?

What are your superpowers, the things you are really good at and that give you tremendous fulfillment?

> When we're fulfilled and have joy, we willingly and eagerly do more of it. It's like the best intrinsic motivator. It is powerful when we connect our passion to making a difference that needs to be made in the world. Superheroes and villains both live with purpose—the superheroes are the ones making a positive difference.

So, I set out to release this personal and internal drive within my department as a result. We were incredibly successful setting up the international area. It was growing quickly because we not only did this together as a team, but we also sought out distributors who likewise had a mentality of *Why are we doing it? We're doing it because it matters, and we can make a difference in people's lives because of who we are, what we do, and how we do it.*

We made that one of the criteria we looked for as we selected our distributors. Soon, we found it was taking on this amazing life of its own. Success was coming, and we were enjoying the process.

After that I thought to myself, *What if we create an entire company with this kind of culture and we recruit people who share this passion for making the world a better place?*

We had already identified what our values were as an organization, so I asked myself:

> *What if we make those values integral into everything we do?*

> *What if people don't join the company simply because they like our values?*

> *What if they become part of the Vitamix team because those values pump through their soul and they're passionate about making a difference?*

> *What if I can help people determine what those personal passions and purposes are within them?*

What if I can help them make the connection
between their purpose and our company purpose?

What if I can help them live their purpose to make the
difference in the world that they want to make?

In the next chapter, Leverage Those Strong Suits, Jodi will explain in detail how she goes about helping team members determine their passions and strong suits, and how she helps them identify their personal purpose in life so they can make a real difference— not just to Vitamix, but in the world.

Soon we weren't living with passion simply to make the company purpose happen. We were living with passion for *our own individual* purposes that were synergistic with the company's purpose. We were personally motivated and fulfilled, and, in turn, the company mission and purpose came to life.

Some people understand their personal purpose. Of course, if they don't have a personal purpose, many adopted the Vitamix purpose. That's okay, too.

> **We weren't living with passion simply to make the company purpose happen. We were living with passion for *our own individual* purposes that were synergistic with the company's purpose.**

As I see it, there are three buckets of people:

- There are people who have their own personal purpose and are driven by it. The magic happens when there is a symbiotic nature between their purpose and the company's purpose.

- There is another group who never really articulated a personal purpose, but once we talk about it and they can identify it, then we can achieve the same thing—that symbiotic nature.
- The third bucket is people who have never been given the permission to live by or identify a purpose, or even have a purpose. Maybe they were like me before I had my near death experience. They never really got started living their purpose. But now they understand it and they get it. They grab on to the Vitamix purpose. They want to push that until they find their own. That is totally okay.

They are all purpose-driven people.

So, I surround myself with purpose-driven people.

We shared values, so I did not have to worry about people who are off in different places making decisions, causing us to have to fix things. We can all be laser-focused on the same purpose, knowing our own passions would contribute.

We shared values, so I did not have to worry about people who are off in different places making decisions, causing us to have to fix things.

That was how we navigated through unbelievable hyper-growth. The team was being led by somebody who had never been a CEO before.

I didn't know that I wasn't supposed to do it that way.

Nancy Howell Agee
President and CEO
Carilion Clinic

I asked Nancy Agee how she develops the members of her teams. She had this to say:

I have a saying—actually, two.

One is that I encourage folks to "take risks without being reckless"—to sort of take a calculated risk and understand the potential consequences. The other is, "Try it. What's the worst that can happen?" Said differently, don't be afraid to explore, be curious, innovate. It's okay to fail; it's not okay to not try.

> I encourage folks to "take risks without being reckless"...don't be afraid to explore, be curious, innovate.

Here's an example:

A young woman who worked here came to me with an idea. Her idea had to do with sustainability. She had great passion, great energy, and she came straight to the top with her proposal. She said to me, "I have this great idea. Let me go do it."

I replied, "You're not ready, and your proposal is half-baked."

I may have said it a little bit nicer than that, but almost that bluntly. I then said to her, "Here is what you need to do: You need to go back to school."

Then I pointed out to her how her proposal could be richer and better.

She went away disappointed, but fast forward two years: She got her master's degree, she put a full-fledged proposal together, and she is now the director of our sustainability efforts. She also tells the best stories.

It's very interesting. We hold these little TED Talks for employees, so I asked her to do one, where she talked about how the advice I gave her was not what she wanted to hear, but it was what she *needed* to hear. It was the same advice that her mother had given her—which was sort of cute. But she persevered and found a mentor, went back to school, and followed her passion.

Kerry Healey
Inaugural President
Milken Center for Advancing the American Dream

I asked Kerry Healey, PhD, "What can women do to foster their own advancement and build more cohesive teams?"

I think it's easy for people to take things personally or to think they have to do the work alone because they've experienced genuinely negative dynamics in many work environments.

With that being said, I do not believe it is ever helpful to view the people around you as competitors. You need to surround yourself with partners, colleagues, supporters, and promoters.

You must also maintain the perspective that you are not supposed to be in it alone. Your team is supposed to be helping you, and you are all in this together. It may be difficult at first, but it's a requirement for successful teams.

And finally, always behave in the most ethical and dignified manner possible. We have to respect each other's dignity in everything we do.

> **Maintain the perspective that you are not supposed to be in it alone. Your team is supposed to be helping you, and you are all in this together.**

Wendy Johnson
Former President and CEO
Dale Carnegie franchise, Atlanta, GA

Wendy Johnson ran one of the highest-rated franchises for the oldest and most widely recognized leadership development and communications training program in the world. It was no surprise that Wendy had a wealth of insights to offer about developing team members.

It was interesting for me to discover how some people thought of Dale Carnegie as a sales training company and other people thought of it as a presentation company, all because of that one basic self-help book, *How to Win Friends and Influence People*, written way back in the 1930s. It's one of the best-selling books of all time.

From day one, Dale Carnegie was a communications and human relations company that taught leadership skills. Dale

Carnegie himself believed that success was tied to one's ability to communicate and speak. The base medium used to change behaviors was public speaking. This helped build self-confidence.

Dale Carnegie began teaching public speaking at the YMCA in Harlem in 1918. What he discovered from his classes was that it is not just the ability to speak well that leads to success, but, rather, what you say and how you say it. From this finding, he created his famous human relations and communications leadership program, the Dale Carnegie Course.

In the Dale Carnegie program, which is conducted over twelve evenings or three consecutive full days, participants learn the 30 principles of great leadership and are held accountable to practice these new principles of communication and human relations on the job. In each session, the participant is required to give two-minute speeches reporting on their results. It is in these sessions that confidence and communication skills are developed.

Being able to speak up, make suggestions, and offer new ideas is essential to moving into a leadership role. We help people who are afraid to attend meetings and express their ideas to confidently attend and present themselves. At the same time, we help people who tend to dominate meetings recognize that tendency so they can dial it back and work on actively listening to others.

Building strong relationships of trust in the workplace is the key to success. Once people are given the gift of becoming confident communicators, people will seek them out. Their managers discover they are problem solvers and possess innovative ideas. Best of all, they start moving ahead in the organization. Good team leaders understand that not all people are born with these gifts.

The Dale Carnegie program is a great tool for executives to leverage if they want to develop more dynamic and effective teams.

Building strong relationships of trust in the workplace is the key to success.

Lieutenant General Kathleen M. Gainey
U.S. Army, Retired

I asked Lt. Gen. Kathy Gainey, "As you were promoted from one position to the next, what was usually your primary focus?"

The people. What I quickly learned is, people are your most important resource.

People are your most important resource.

If you invest in people, they will take care of you. When you make a mistake, they will correct it. When you need to know something, if you have created an environment where they can share information with you and not lose their head, not be yelled at, or screamed at, they will share things with you that you need to know—particularly when things are not going quite right and need to get fixed.

People who feel cared about will be the ones to volunteer when you need people to work the weekend shift. Instead of ordering them, you can simply start with, "Who would volunteer to work this weekend? If you are willing to take this on, I'll compensate you other days."

"Oh, okay. I'll do that!"

They will be there for you when you need them if you've invested in helping them.

I learned over time how to be a team builder, and I think I was an effective one. I found creating effective teams was the most critical thing.

If you take care of people *and you help advance them*—if you get them into the schools they need and you push them into the jobs that maybe they do not feel confident in, or you enable them to maximize their potential—then they will be there for you. I learned this because people pushed me into jobs that I was not quite sure I could do, but they said, "Try it!"

> **If you take care of people *and you help advance them*...[if you] enable them to maximize their potential, then they will be there for you.**

So, I would push my team members to try, and then I would give them the tools and the opportunity to show *themselves* that they could be successful. Because I knew that I gained confidence over time, I knew they could gain confidence over time, too.

But you've got to give them the tools to be successful when you push them into those jobs. You have got to mentor and coach them.

I responded with, "How important is that skill?"

It is huge. It is all about teams in the military—working together to create and achieve a common goal.

"Was there somebody in your chain of command who was watching out for you, assessing you, and helping you maximize your potential?"

I think there *were* many people watching out for me. Sometimes it was a peer who was maybe a little bit senior to me, and people who had been in a bit longer saying, "You need to branch out. Go for this job opportunity."

I also had bosses who helped me think through my career plans and what the next job should be for me. They always pushed me out of my comfort zone.

REFLECTIONS:

A leader's most important responsibilities are to build, develop, and retain great teams, and to bring out the best in each team member. Essentially, your most important investment—the one that will pay the biggest dividends—is in your team. Focus on enabling every member of your team to live with passion and purpose.

If you are in the game only to invest in yourself, if you don't thrive on developing others, or if you don't enjoy doing what it takes to remove any roadblocks that may be impeding your team's efforts— which may involve helping *other* teams do their jobs more effectively—you will become just another impediment to the organization's success. It's best that you get out of the way and invest your efforts in becoming the best individual contributor that you can be. Don't continue on the leadership track just because it's what you feel you "should" do, or because other people have told you that leadership ought to be the next step in your career. Do whatever gives *you* the most fulfillment.

If you do believe that leadership is your calling, remember that a team is composed of 360 degrees of relationships. It's amazing what can happen when you bring an entire team or company into alignment to accomplish the mission and goals in unison. To do this, you must invest in getting to know everyone on your team and coach them to develop their strong suits. You must make the investment in having the entire team get together every now and then, in whatever format makes sense for your organization, so they can all understand who's who, share challenges, brainstorm solutions, discuss results, celebrate successes, and ask questions—together. This keeps everyone aligned and moving in the same upward trajectory.

> It's amazing what can happen when you bring an entire team or company into alignment to accomplish the mission and goals in unison.

Make similar investments with your vendors and business partners. After all, they are part of your team, too. You are all in this game together, so make it an infinite-win—in other words, make it not just a win for you and your team, but also make it a win for the much broader constituency.

In all relationships, everything hinges on communication, trust, and ethics. Each of these are fundamental to business and life. Have honest and candid conversations about expectations and results. If things just aren't working out for a particular individual or business partner after you and they have given it your respective best efforts, then make the investment to help them find another avenue where they can be successful, somewhere else. In doing so, everyone—including your customers—will be better off, and the world will be a better place.

INTROSPECTIONS:

1   Think of your favorite manager or team leader (or even a friend or family member) who made an investment in you and helped you become a better version of yourself.

   a. What kinds of things did this person do and/or say that inspired you, made you feel cared about, and made you more confident that you could accomplish greater things in your position and/or in your life?

   b. Have you adopted any traits from this person that have enabled you to serve as a better leader to those on your team? If so, what are they? If not, what is one habit or behavior you could start integrating into your leadership style?

2   If you are currently a manager or leader of a team, but you don't enjoy the role, have you learned anything from this chapter that might help you look at your situation differently? If so, what specifically will you do differently in the days ahead?

a. Do you enjoy engaging with, coaching, supporting, and developing other people? Or might you gain more fulfillment from being an outstanding individual contributor?

3 How often do you see and speak with your team members? How well do you know them as employees and as individuals?

a. Can you identify each team member's strengths? What are you doing to develop and recognize those strengths?

b. What roadblocks are your team members facing? What can you do to remove those roadblocks and better support your people?

SEVEN

Leverage Those Strong Suits

Our superpowers are the things we just naturally do extremely well, that we enjoy doing—so it gives us energy. Believe it or not, we all have superpowers. We just don't think about it. But imagine what could happen if each of us focused on using our own superpowers more often!

Think about it. Ask those who know you well to tell you what you are really good at. From that list, identify the few items that you not only do well, but you love to do and it gives you energy. If it's something you do really well, you love to do it, and it gives you energy, then this is most likely a superpower!

-JODI BERG, PHD
Retired President and CEO
Vita-Mix Corporation

was once interviewed by a radio host who asked me, "If you could pick the primary thing that has made you successful, what would it be?"

That was a great question, and honestly, it caught me off guard. I thought about it for a brief instant and then answered candidly, "I have always done what I loved to do and did well. If at any point I found that I wasn't loving what I was doing, I would either redesign my role, or I would find another position."

Ever since then, I have asked that same question to other successful leaders. It's interesting to note that their answers are rarely the same. So far, I've heard no one mention their education or their specific work experience, although some may credit a beloved mentor. Most commonly, they will name a personal trait— their strong suit—something that is at the core of their personal brand.

On a similar note, one of my executive friends likes to challenge interviewees with these questions:
- What are your most deeply held values?
- What are your unique strengths?
- What brings you joy in life?

Great questions, all. Yet many people find it challenging to answer these questions, at least as they relate to a business setting. I have found that assessments can help you accurately identify many of your strong suits—that potent blend of strengths and passions that propels you forward—as well as give you insight into how to deploy them in the workplace.

CliftonStrengths Assessments Help You Zero in on Your Talents and Passions

When it comes to helping people identify and understand their strengths and passions, I'm a big advocate of CliftonStrengths, which was produced by Gallup and author Tom Rath. (You may be familiar with CliftonStrengths by the name under which it was originally published before rebranding: StrengthsFinder 2.0). One of Amazon's best-selling nonfiction books ever, its online assessment has been used by millions of people the world over to tap into their talents. Tom Rath claims that core personality traits and talents remain relatively stable throughout adulthood, so an investment in assessing yourself should pay dividends throughout your career.

I will be forever grateful to the Gallup consulting organization for serving as a primary sponsor of my leadership development company's semi-annual leadership symposiums. For a number of years, Gallup also hosted our peer-mentoring programs.

Because I believe a strong sense of self-awareness is vital for anyone who wants to be a WOW factor leader, everyone who enrolled in our peer-mentoring program participated in Gallup's CliftonStrengths assessment to identify their unique set of top talent themes.

If you have not yet had the opportunity to participate in a CliftonStrengths assessment, you might be wondering what a CliftonStrengths personalized

A strong sense of self-awareness is vital for anyone who wants to be a WOW factor leader.

insights report provides. Essentially, it helps you understand how each of your top five talent themes play out in your life. For example, even though most of our program members had

"Achiever" as a top theme, that one theme was manifested by each individual in a unique way because their other top talent themes differed dramatically. Therefore, each participant received a unique description of how their Achiever theme operated in their life.

One of the most interesting aspects of your personalized insights report will probably be its description of *what makes you stand out* when compared to the millions of people CliftonStrengths has studied. (Talk about a neon sign pointing to your probable strong suits and personal brand!) The report also provides ten "Ideas for Action" for each of your top five talent themes, so you will receive 50 recommendations that specifically enable you to make the most of your particular combination of strengths.

Case Study: "Achiever" Is a Common CliftonStrengths Talent Theme for Leaders

In reviewing each of our members' CliftonStrengths personalized insights report, I found it interesting, but not surprising, that regardless of their level on the management career ladder, over 80 percent of our members had Achiever as a top talent theme. Anyone with Achiever as one of their top five talent themes (a group that includes me) is described as someone who has a constant need for achievement.

According to my own CliftonStrengths personalized insights report, "Your Achiever theme helps explain your drive. You feel as if every day starts at zero. By the end of the day, you must achieve something tangible in order to feel good about yourself. And by every day, you mean every single day—workdays, weekends, vacations." Yep, that's me. No doubt about it.

If you are someone with a strong Achiever theme (and if you have chosen to read this book, you very well may be!), "You have an internal fire burning inside you. It pushes you to do more, to achieve more…Your relentless need for achievement…brings you the energy you need to work long hours without burning out…It is the power supply that causes you to set the pace and define the levels of productivity for your workgroup."

Know Your Team's Strengths—and Make Sure They Know Yours

While self-awareness is crucial for developing yourself as a leader, the CliftonStrengths assessment can also help you better relate to and develop your team. Gallup consultants told our program members that leaders who focus on each individual team member's unique strengths drive more engagement. For example, if you are leading anyone with a strong Achiever theme, you should keep in mind that for them, being rated as number one in their group, or being named the best in a certain category, will usually motivate them to do even more and better work. Of course, not everyone falls into the Achiever group.

> Leaders who focus on each individual team member's unique strengths drive more engagement.

Understanding the top strengths of everyone on your team can give you, the leader, a real leg up in understanding how best to uniquely motivate and inspire each employee to perform at their personal best. That's precisely what heartfelt leaders do, and it is how WOW factor workplaces become just that.

It's a good idea to share your own strengths with your team, too. This way, they'll have a better idea of what motivates you, what your priorities are, what your approach is likely to be, and even how to communicate with you. At Southwest Airlines, executives like Linda Rutherford include their CliftonStrengths top talent themes in their email signature block. Linda's CliftonStrengths are Futuristic, Arranger, Communication, Self-Assurance, and Includer.

As for me, in addition to Achiever, my CliftonStrengths are Futuristic, Learner, Maximizer, and Strategic.

Myers-Briggs Type Indicator: Another Helpful Assessment

Of course, there are a variety of other personality assessments on the market that can help people understand their personal traits, tendencies, and preferences. Another well-known example is the Myers-Briggs Type Indicator (MBTI), an introspective self-report questionnaire designed to indicate differing psychological preferences in how people perceive the world around them and make decisions.

According to Isabel Briggs Myers, who co-created the MBTI personality inventory many decades ago along with her mother, Katharine Cook Briggs, "The understanding of type can make your perceptions clearer, your judgments sounder, and your life closer to your heart's desire."

Myers-Briggs defines personality archetypes based on the following main factors: Introversion/Extraversion, Intuition/Sensing, Feeling/Thinking, and Judging/Perceiving. With this assessment, people are categorized into a "type" based on which of the four traits they practice.

For example, I am categorized as a Myers-Briggs archetype ENTJ, which indicates "Extraversion/Intuition/Thinking/Judging." In brief, ENTJs are talkative, high energy, and thrive around people. They seek action and tend to involve themselves in events. They prefer not to spend too much time alone. Yep, that's me in a nutshell, as well.

Discovering the Myers-Briggs Type Indicator for each person on your team can help you better understand why each person behaves and communicates in a certain way. It can also help you relate to and engage with each person more effectively and empathetically. When you understand how other people view the world and process information, you will have the tools to become a more inspiring leader to everyone on your team.

Of course, the assessments highlighted above are just two of the many options available. Every leadership assessment out there provides different insights into an individual's unique gifts, traits, and tendencies. Properly leveraged, such assessments can help each person become the best possible version of themselves, both in the professional world and in everyday life.

As I have alluded to before, WOW factor leaders are not just self-aware, they are also aware of the unique strengths, passions, and traits of every member of the team. Such understanding allows best-ever leaders to most effectively coach, develop, and guide each team member into the kind of roles that are not just well suited for them now, but will also best position them for where they want to go in the future.

In short, the better you know yourself, the better career decisions you will make. The better you understand each team member's strengths, passions, and character traits, the better you will be at helping everyone capitalize on the team's cumulative advantage.

Our Strong Suits Propel Each of Us Toward Our Own "American Dream."

In the United States, there is a long-held cultural belief in the American Dream, which—as we discussed in Chapter 1— essentially means you can be anything you want to be. I'm a huge believer in the American Dream. The women interviewed in this book are each a testimony to the American Dream. Yet, before you jump headlong into following any one career path, or someone else's vision for you, ask yourself if a particular job or career path would really make you happy and whether it would truly bring you joy.

I chose my first major in college—math/computer science—based on my father's dream for me (maybe it was really his dream for himself). It seemed to make sense at the time because I was always the top student in my high school math classes, from algebra and geometry to trigonometry and calculus.

> **Before you jump headlong into following any one career path, or someone else's vision for you, ask yourself if a particular job or career path would really make you happy.**

Yet after two semesters in college, not only did this field not fill me with joy, I found it boring and energy-draining. While I may have had the technical aptitude, I had no passion for it. I quickly realized I would never be great in the mathematical and computer science career fields—even if I graduated at the top of my class—because I didn't enjoy those disciplines. In other words, they were not really strong suits. If only I'd had a mentor to turn to for coaching and advice at the time! Perhaps I could have identified my strong suits earlier and streamlined my pursuit of my own American Dream, which awaited elsewhere.

If your American Dream lies in the ranks of leadership, understand that part of your role will be to help each member of your team achieve their own American Dream. If you suspect someone on your team is unhappy or unfulfilled, or if they simply aren't engaged, then have a heartfelt dialogue with them—as soon as practical—to identify what's going on. Encourage them to share their American Dream with you. Then together, brainstorm ways that you might help them achieve it—even if it means guiding them to greener pastures elsewhere—so they can better leverage their strong suits.

Speaking from experience, it can be incredibly fulfilling to be "the wind beneath their wings," regardless of where that path may take the other person.

Now let's hear what our amazing executives have to say about their own strong suits.

Melissa Reiff
Former Chairwoman and CEO
The Container Store

When I asked Melissa Reiff, "What would you say are your strong suits?" she responded this way:

My greatest strength, I believe, is communication—striving to always communicate clearly, with respect, passion, and confidence. Working hard to bring our team along so they are informed and always feel a genuine connection to their colleagues and our company goals.

I also feel my positive, can-do attitude is a strength—very different from an entitled kind of attitude. For someone to feel and act entitled is VERY unattractive and will really limit them in the long run, I believe. I always just felt that if you take initiative—the right way—if you look for opportunities, if you're creative and open-minded, and if you're positive and realistically optimistic, things will come your way.

Also, our leadership team would probably say that I have a lot of energy. I think that is a strength. I try to be somewhat sensitive to that, however; I don't think I'm hasty or careless, but rather always want to be decisive, strategic, and thoughtful—always wanting to move things forward and make great things happen for us all!

> **If you look for opportunities, if you're creative and open-minded, and if you're positive and realistically optimistic, things will come your way.**

Jodi Berg
Retired President and CEO
Vita-Mix Corporation

When I asked Jodi Berg, PhD, "What would you say are your greatest strengths?" she responded:

Okay. Now we might get into my *superpower* conversation.

One of the things I discovered when I was trying to articulate to people this concept of *personal purpose*, is that it can be rather difficult for people to understand what their personal purpose truly is.

Sometimes we don't necessarily know what our personal purpose is. It's not written out as a prescription. There's no plane flying across the sky, writing out for you, "Your personal purpose is..."

I found that helping people figure out their purpose in life can be quite challenging. So, I translated it differently: I help people figure out their *superpowers, which leads them to a purpose.*

To better understand this concept of superpowers, think about *superheroes.* Whether a superpower is instinctive to a superhero or not, or whether somebody told these superheroes that this is what they are supposed to do or not, each one of them is very purpose-driven. Each of them is out there to make a certain kind of amazing thing happen.

Superheroes achieve their purpose because they have certain superpowers. That's why they are the ones out there saving the world. They are good at what they do, and whatever it is that they do so well actually *gives* them energy, so they can keep going and going.

> **[Superheroes] are good at what they do, and whatever it is that they do so well actually *gives* them energy.**

Take Superman as an example. He's out there protecting the world from evil, and he's very purpose-driven in doing so. When Superman is out there saving the planet from evil, he can fly over buildings in a single bound and do all the superpower kind of things that Superman does. We are amazed and say, "Yes, Superman! Go save the world from evil! You've got these superpowers! Hooray!"

So, considering all of this made me think, *What if there were a way to help people realize their own superpowers?*

For normal humans like us, our superpowers are the things we just naturally do extremely well, that we enjoy doing—so it gives us energy. Believe it or not, we all have superpowers. We just don't think about it. But imagine what could happen if each of us focused on using our own superpowers more often!

Think about it. Ask those who know you well to tell you what you are really good at. From that list, identify the few items that you not only do well, but you *love to do and it gives you energy.* If it's something you do really well, you love to do it, *and* it gives you energy, then this is most likely a superpower!

On the other hand, there may be things that we're really good at, but they aren't necessarily a superpower because we don't enjoy doing it.

For example, I can read financial reports right up there with the best of them, yet doing so gives me no energy. I know I must do it, but it's not my favorite activity. In fact, I must force myself to dig into financial reports because it sucks the energy right out of me. It's like kryptonite to me. So, even though I'm good at it, reading financial reports is not a superpower for me.

There are certain parts of our job that we must do, even if it drains our energy. Balance every day by allocating some of your time to using your superpowers. By the end of the day when you go home, you might even have more energy than when you started the day! At the very least, you won't have used up all your energy at work, so you won't go home completely exhausted.

I interjected, "I get it. I really love interviewing people and sharing their stories—and I'm good at it."

There you have it: That's a superpower for you!

I really must thank you for what you're doing. You are making such a big difference in so many people's lives. You *are* using your superpowers!

The bridge to identifying a personal purpose is to have your personal advisory board—people who know you and who care about you—help you identify what big, audacious difference you can make in this world using your superpowers.

The next step is to identify your kryptonite. Then surround yourself with people who have superpowers that are your kryptonite—people who are really good at and love doing the very thing that pulls you down. But that is another level of the superhero journey—for another time.

Surround yourself with people who have superpowers that are your kryptonite.

Nancy Howell Agee
President and CEO
Carilion Clinic

I asked Nancy Agee, "What do you believe are the characteristics that set you apart from others and put you on the path to becoming a CEO?"

It can be very hard to know what differentiates you from others, I think, but I would say this:
- I am a clear thinker.
- I am a good communicator.
- I am a good writer.
- Thankfully, I am in a business that I love.
- I consider myself a servant leader.
- I am the quintessential glass half-full kind of person.
- I am empathetic.

Then I asked Nancy, "What do you think is the strong suit that has helped you get through the tough times?"

> I am the quintessential glass half-full kind of person.

First, I have a great team. Acknowledging that, I work on keeping a great team by doing the following things:
- I listen to them.
- I offer clear direction.
- I try to peer around the corner, so to speak, to see what is ahead, so we can create a pathway to get there.

Secondly, I'm willing to make hard decisions and stick with them, even if they are not popular.

Linda Rutherford
Executive Vice President, Chief Communications Officer
Southwest Airlines

When I asked Linda Rutherford, "What do you think was the key differentiator that set you apart on your way to the C-suite?" she responded,

Gosh, the *key* differentiator?

I'm endlessly curious. I'll be a student of things.

I think the key differentiator that sets me apart is my ability to learn quickly and immerse myself in whatever the immediate need is.

To that I responded, "What would other people say are your greatest strengths?"

I think they would say that I can very quickly grasp the root of a problem, or a challenge, and offer some potential solutions. I can move very quickly to the root cause of something and offer up ways to proceed. Like, "Now, here's the problem," and then, "Now, here are maybe five different ways we can try to solve it." I approach my thinking that way. That's resourcefulness, right?

One of my CliftonStrengths—high strengths—is Arranger. I can immediately look out there and see that everything has a place and be able to shift and pivot quickly.

I have also learned the importance of having a perspective and sharing it. I think that is one of my greatest strengths, particularly in the role I'm in now. People are looking at me for a perspective that they would not get on their own.

I can move very quickly to the root cause of something and offer up ways to proceed.

There is one other thing, which I will share with you. Several years ago, I read an article in the newspaper about a philanthropist here in Dallas. Her name is Ruth Altshuler. The mayor of Dallas, at the time, had assigned her the responsibility of Dallas's 50th anniversary of the JFK shooting—this would have been in 2013.

She said, "I really struggled when the mayor gave me this assignment. I thought, *Well, this isn't a party, but you also don't want it to be a somber moment. It needs to be recognized.*"

The reporter asked her, "Why do you think the mayor chose you for this role?"

She said, "I think the mayor knows that I'll do the right thing and I'll be bold. But something I know about myself is I'm often wrong but seldom in doubt."

I'm often wrong but seldom in doubt.

That was an *aha!* moment for me. I literally cut that article out of the newspaper because I was like, "Oh my gosh, that's me! I'm often wrong but seldom in doubt!"

In other words, I am decisive. I am loaded. And I'm going. I might not always be right, but I'm going! So, I would say a key strength is my confidence.

I am also comfortable in my own skin. I think that comes across in the work that I do. The people I work with know I'll have their back. They know I am not afraid to go and fight for something, to advocate for something, if it is going to be better for them and better for the company.

We might not always win, and I might be wrong—we'll find out on the other end—but I'm not afraid to try.

I certainly think you gain more confidence over time. Experience helps a lot, for sure. You learn what to do and you learn what not to do. I think that builds confidence.

Kerry Healey
Inaugural President
Milken Center for Advancing the American Dream

When I asked Kerry Healey, PhD, about the strengths that set her apart, given her broad-based career that spanned politics, running a university, and creating the new Center for Advancing the American Dream, she had this to say:

> First, I would say that I had very little self-awareness when I entered politics at age 42. I had no idea, really.
>
> But I think that one of the unique qualities of my leadership style, or that has allowed me to be an effective leader, is being resilient. I've lost a lot. I have lost way more than I have won, especially in politics.

Kerry went on to share how her resilience helped her in her role as president of Babson College.

> You are handed several challenges when leading a college or university, and I think it is extremely important to handle all those kinds of experiences with a sense of optimism, to not hold grudges, and just maintain an air of positivity. I think that's one strong suit of mine.
>
> I've also learned, over time, that self-confidence is another strength of mine—although I think that's probably reductionist, because I don't know what people consider to be self-confidence. Maybe it is more a lack of fear. I'm not afraid to lose. I'm not afraid to be criticized in public. I am not afraid of people disliking me.
>
> I have a certain level of disregard for physical danger—not an unreasonable one, but I realize that I am a little bit less concerned about these things than other people, sometimes. When I speak to friends and I talk to others, I do notice that I probably just have less fear.

I strategize, but I don't ruminate. And I don't get carried away with negative thoughts.

I commented, "Some people can be overly concerned about, 'What are others going to think of me?'"

> **I don't get carried away with negative thoughts.**

Right. I don't have those thoughts. I don't ever worry about what people are going to think of me. It's quite freeing.

"If you could just bottle that, you'd be a gazillionaire selling that to people! You're fortunate that you have that trait."

It's important if you're going to be in politics.

It comes from having conviction—the ability to stand by what you believe in. You are comfortable having people know what you believe in and you are comfortable with your life.

I have thought through why I do what I do and why I believe what I believe. Therefore, I am more comfortable if someone criticizes me because I can defend my beliefs. At the same time, I do genuinely try to stay open to learning from that person. I certainly don't ignore criticism. I want to learn from it. My first impulse is not to be defensive but rather to inquire more deeply.

> **I certainly don't ignore criticism. I want to learn from it.**

I think one of my strengths is that I do try to approach problems from others' perspectives. I actively attempt to put myself in other people's shoes at all times. I may fail, but at least I'm trying. That's better than not trying.

I also think that I'm willing to take on new challenges without the appropriate expertise. Traditionally, this is something that men are great at. They wake up every morning—virtually all of them, apparently—and when they look in the mirror to shave, they see a U.S. Senator staring back at them. Women generally don't have that level of self-confidence.

From a gender standpoint, I think it's important that I've been willing to take on new challenges, including running for lieutenant governor when I'd never held public office. That seemed way outside of my comfort zone.

While I have a PhD and I'd been a fellow at Harvard, I was not the typical candidate for being a college president or a university president. It was a big leap of faith for me to think that I could walk into that academic environment and understand the nuances of that culture.

The answer probably is that I did not understand the nuances of that culture. But I was able to figure it out over time and adapt so I could do the job.

I think that is a strength: the willingness to jump—to take the jump and try to do my best.

> **That is a strength: the willingness to jump—to take the jump and try to do [your] best.**

"Do you think your parents taught you that?"

I honestly wish I knew. I don't have a good answer for that, but I do think it's an important quality. I think fear can be a very limiting factor, especially among women.

I know that the unconditional love of parents definitely sustains you for many, many years and can give you a lot of self-confidence. To the extent that self-confidence is linked to lack of fear, there could be something there.

Wendy Johnson
Former President and CEO
Dale Carnegie franchise, Atlanta, GA

The longer I spoke to Wendy Johnson, the more some of her strengths became obvious. Yet, I asked her, "What do you believe are your greatest strengths?"

Gifts from my mother, I suppose, but I would say that two of my greatest strengths are hard work and a passion for whatever I'm doing. It's kind of infectious. People get around me and I am passionate, so they get passionate. I can create a sort of energy toward things.

It's kind of infectious. People get around me and I am passionate, so they get passionate.

Traveling the world and exposure to other cultures gave me a confidence and a communication ability that helps me create and sustain connections.

I am a servant leader and I care deeply about customer care.

I'm a risk taker and I'm an early adopter. If you tell me about something new, something I believe has value—because it's clear that it will help people or it will provide a better solution—then I can sell it in a minute. Being an early adopter of new ideas and solutions and being able to embrace new technologies has really helped me succeed.

I build bridges in relationships. I have the ability to create trustful relationships with people, internally and externally.

Those would be my strong suits.

Lieutenant General Kathleen M. Gainey
U.S. Army, Retired

While chatting with Lt. Gen. Kathy Gainey, I mentioned that some people have been raised to think, *I must work really hard to have this particular strength. If I am not working at it, then it's not a strength.* On the flip side, they may not even notice they have a particular intrinsic strength because it comes so naturally for them. Such things are their strong suits. For some people, it is easier to identify the strengths and weaknesses of others. They'll say, "I can tell you what *your* strengths and weaknesses are. It's obvious. Let me tell you."

I asked General Gainey, "Did you understand your strengths from an early stage?"

I don't think I even thought about strengths and weaknesses early on, but I knew I had a talent for teaching. I did leverage that. So, I guess I knew I was a good teacher.

Also, I liked working with people. So, I used my interpersonal skills and the ability to know task, condition, and standards to help my non-commissioned officers (NCOs) understand how to conduct training—about how to set the conditions and then think about how we would evaluate the soldiers after the training to assess whether the soldiers understood it.

So, I understood the *mechanics* of training. That's a big part of what you do in the Army. So that was a strength. I could help teach my NCOs how to train others. Some of it, they had just done by rote—following what other people did—but they really didn't think about how to evaluate the process, to ensure people were understanding the training and learning things correctly.

I think it was a strength that I was willing to ask, to learn, and I wanted to learn.

The two things that stayed with me throughout it all were the ability to work with people and understanding how to train people.

Another strength was the fact that I have good people skills. I didn't come in thinking I was king of the hill, knowing everything. It was an advantage that I didn't come in as a threat.

"From the vantage point of being a lieutenant general 35 years later, as you look back at yourself as a young officer, do you believe you had the same strengths and weaknesses throughout your career, or did you add to your strengths base over time?"

Well, I think the two things that stayed with me throughout it all were the ability to work with people and understanding how to train people. Those strengths, I think, carried throughout.

I think I developed additional strengths over time, too, such as:
- Learning to build teams—because I *did* have the interpersonal skills, I was able to get people to work together and focus on a common task, and
- Learning to ask others' opinions first, and not assume that I had the perfect solution going in. I listened and learned to ask people what they thought.

I would make much better decisions by coalescing what other people thought and giving them credit for their ideas. Then all of us could come to an agreement and execute.

REFLECTIONS:

Understanding your strong suits—or superpowers—as well as those of everyone on your team, can give you greater ability to uniquely motivate and inspire each team member. You'll be better able to drive overall team engagement. You will better enable everyone on the team to become the best versions of themselves and live a fulfilling life.

> Understanding your strong suits—or superpowers—as well as those of everyone on your team, can give you greater ability to uniquely motivate and inspire each team member.

To help the members of your team better understand their own strong suits, consider having them take the CliftonStrengths assessment and the Myers-Briggs Type Indicator (MBTI) assessment. Then take time to review their reports with them and ask for their feedback. Ask them if they find their results surprising or reaffirming. Discuss how you might better enable them to take greater advantage of their strong suits—their superpowers—within their current roles. Be sure to also cover what aspects of their jobs are like kryptonite to them. Determine if and how their jobs could be modified to bring them more joy at work and enable them to make a greater impact. If it means realigning roles within your organization or even helping someone find a role outside your company, consider doing so.

If you have not taken the CliftonStrengths assessment yourself, I highly recommend it. It will help you identify your own innate strengths and passions—your strong suits.

I also recommend taking the Myers-Briggs Type Indicator (MBTI) assessment if you haven't already. It will help you better understand your personality inventory. And as Isabel Briggs Myers put it, it will "…make your perceptions clearer, your judgments sounder, and your life closer to your heart's desire."

INTROSPECTIONS:

1   If you could pick just one thing that has made you successful up to this point, what would that be?

2 What are your most deeply held values?

3 What brings you joy in life?

4 What are your greatest strengths—your superpowers?

a. How might those superpowers contribute to your making a difference in the world (i.e., finding a personal purpose)?

5 What is your kryptonite?

a. How might you realign your role and/or delegate your responsibilities so that your kryptonite is shifted to someone who sees it as a superpower?

EIGHT

No Need to Be Lonely

If you're lonely at the top, you're going to fail. You must have colleagues and people who would walk through walls for you—or you are going to fail. Do not be alone at the top.

My team has sustained me through many difficult moments in leadership. Having an extraordinarily strong and loyal team around you is the best thing you can create for yourself.

-KERRY HEALEY, PHD
Inaugural President
Milken Center for Advancing the American Dream

You've probably heard the age-old cliché, *It's lonely at the top.* This well-known tenet, in and of itself, deters some women from aiming for a role in the C-suite. Who wants to be lonely day-in and day-out?

It's especially sad that women who have enjoyed strong bonds and intimate friendships with peers throughout their careers believe they must divorce themselves from these friendships as they make their way up the ladder. While it isn't wise to play favorites, you can still have amicable relationships and be equally friendly with everyone reporting to you as you rise to the top.

Jealousy Happens—and It's Not Your Fault. Don't Let It Impact Your Career Trajectory.

One of my C-level friends shared that as she promoted into the senior ranks, she became the target of backhanded office chatter more and more often. "I'd hear other women—my former peers— whisper to each other, 'Why her? I (or you) should have gotten that job!'" she said. "Men would flat-out accuse me of landing a certain job just because I was a woman.

"Now, I know I got the job because I had the breadth of experience needed, I put in the effort, I took care of my people, I stepped forward with great ideas, I took calculated risks, and I delivered on my commitments," she continued. "But the assumption that some of us get promoted to certain jobs just because we are women still exists. Men don't like it when they lose a big promotion to a woman."

I have had similar experiences promoting within major corporations. On a few occasions, former colleagues who had mentored me went on to denigrate me behind my back for being too young or inexperienced for the promotion I was awarded. They were clearly jealous, but there wasn't much I could do about it. I wasn't about to deliberately hold myself back from the running for the sake of their feelings. If someone else was determined to shut me off just because I was awarded a promotion that they believed they deserved, they were only hurting themselves. I had little choice but to move on and build collaborative relationships with others.

I nevertheless tried to maintain warm and supportive relationships with all my former peers, mentors, and superiors. I wanted to reinforce that I was still the same friendly and caring colleague I'd always been. I wanted to assure them that I was happy to mentor them in return and even sponsor them into new, career-broadening roles. In some cases, I made others aware of promotional opportunities I had learned of, or I referred them as candidates to hiring managers. Essentially, I tried to create win-wins whenever possible.

Yet, I had to accept that some individuals, no matter what I did, would tenaciously hold onto their jealous grudges. In those cases (happily, there weren't too many), I found it best to simply tune them out until they either changed their attitudes or moved on to greener pastures.

It's amazing how some people assume they should be promoted based on time-in-job, as though everyone should get extra credit for each year of service. While some governmental or educational institutions may operate that way, it's typically not how the merit-based corporate world works.

> **Some people assume they should be promoted based on time-in-job...[but] it's typically not how the merit-based corporate world works.**

Anyone who believes they have been unfairly passed over should look inward and evaluate their own performance. They should also consider the point of view of the higher-up decision-maker who is, at the end of the day, accountable for achieving business objectives.

A peer's promotion is not the time to play the victim or build walls in retribution.

It's also not the time for the person who received the promotion to build walls as a means of protection. Rather, it's more important than ever for the newly promoted leader to serve as the role model they are believed to be. True leaders encourage everyone around them to break down barriers and continuously grow their abilities and skills. In this way, the entire team develops and enhances their strong suits.

Climb the Career Ladder—But Don't Wall Yourself Off in an Ivory Tower

As the leader of a peer mentoring program for C-level women, I was in a position to observe just how many women build metaphorical walls around themselves by the time they reach the C-suite. Many of the CEOs who joined our program attended several meetings before they even began to let their hair down, so to speak. Of course, that's when they were truly able to begin building relationships with other smart women who could relate to their challenges.

It was no surprise to hear almost all of these CEOs confirm that they found it lonely at the top. Each had her own specific reasons, but most were consumed by the belief that they had to portray themselves—100 percent of the time—as unemotional and mentally tough. They felt that showing even a moment of empathy, indecision, anxiety, or even joy would cause their carefully built "executive" reputations to crumble. Because of this misconception, they deliberately shut themselves off from building friendships with other executives within their chains of command or on their boards.

> Most were consumed by the [misconception] that they had to portray themselves—100 percent of the time—as unemotional and mentally tough.

Thanks to the confidential nature of our peer mentoring program, and due to the fact that each of these women shared similar challenges leading their respective organizations, our C-suite members did eventually form strong and long-lasting bonds. In fact, they came to relish the relative safety our program provided in terms of candidly sharing their trials, tribulations, fears, and frustrations. They did not need to sugarcoat any of it. Each woman could simply be herself and even cry without embarrassment when her stress was so great that she couldn't hold back any longer.

Our C-suiters would likely tell you that one of the best aspects of belonging to a C-level peer mentoring program is the ability to solicit expert points of view for a wide variety of challenges. Most CEOs cherish having knowledgeable advice and peer confirmation when evaluating alternative approaches to complex business challenges—or personal quandaries. As you might imagine, it can be extremely helpful to discuss the potential pros, cons, and ramifications of each option in a nonjudgmental environment. Over a decade later, many of our former C-level members still mentor each other. I'm happy to see that.

For some, I served as their personal "shrink-in-chief." It didn't bother me in the least when they would call me late at night to seek my unbiased perspectives on handling some upcoming board action, or a child custody issue, or to share the despair of a cancer diagnosis or their grief over a parent sliding into the darkness of Alzheimer's. I cherished every one of these friendships. And when the occasion arose, I likewise appreciated their advice, counsel, and support in return.

I certainly understand how a CEO might come to feel lonely. But loneliness doesn't have to be an inevitable part of the territory. It is entirely possible for a CEO and other C-level executives to develop strong bonds with board members, industry peers, direct reports, and high-potentials downline. It is possible to mentor others and allow them to mentor you in return. Let's look at how you can accomplish that.

Surround Yourself with an Authentic, Supportive Inner Circle

As you are climbing the ladder, and especially as you near the C-suite, surround yourself—or at least form alliances—with smart, intuitive people you trust, respect, and enjoy being around, and who see things from a different perspective from you. Before you reach the top, make a practice of engaging in candid, thought-provoking dialogue with these people, because it will be essential that you do so as the CEO.

> As you near the C-suite, surround yourself...with smart, intuitive people you trust, respect, and enjoy being around, and who see things from a different perspective from you.

As smart and experienced as you might be by the time you become a CEO, no one knows everything. Having a close-knit inner circle can help you gain important perspectives on complex issues you might not otherwise know to consider. Sometimes the simple act of articulating a challenge, fear, or plan of attack to trusted advisors can give you a valuable opportunity to listen to yourself. Your inner circle can ask clarifying questions to help you assess alternative approaches, evaluate your reasoning, and develop strategies to overcome potential pushback. Especially as a CEO, it's essential to clarify these things *before* you run out onto the playing field, so to speak, and fumble the ball in front of the entire organization. Bottom line: Your team of trusted allies can help you make better decisions and improve your performance.

My best advice is to start forming this group early. As you network, collaborate, and form new business and personal relationships, always seek to identify people you could bring into your inner circle or onto your board at a moment's notice. Look for rising superstars who could readily fill your shoes. Start diagramming your succession plan well before you get to the C-suite. You may not need to enact it for a long while, but there are numerous other benefits to developing a deep bench—not the least of which is having a team of capable, engaged, and trustworthy colleagues supporting you!

Keep in mind that not all of these inner-circle relationships must stay entirely business-oriented. It is altogether possible to have fun with comrades inside and outside of your workplace. It may not always be easy to break free of your "work roles," and there may be valid reasons not to do so in some cases. But I typically advise senior-level leaders to maintain close, trusting *personal* relationships with other senior-level people within their organizations if their intent is to create and lead a WOW factor workplace.

Regardless of whether your inner circle is comprised of internal or external resources, go out of your way to engage in enjoyable relationship-building and knowledge-broadening activities together. Here are some ideas: If you live in the same community, occasionally go to breakfast, lunch, or dinner together, or have a potluck at one of your homes before or after a brainstorming session. Occasionally invite a speaker or subject matter expert to join you. This person could give a presentation or lead a group discussion on a topic unrelated to business. (Potential speakers might include the president of a local charity or other community project, a sports enthusiast or coach, the owner of a local boutique or home store, a restauranteur or chef, a wine enthusiast, a zoologist, a travel expert, a historian, your city manager or mayor, etc.) You never know what kinds of things you and your inner circle might learn that could later be leveraged for your organization's benefit.

Staving off loneliness at the top takes a concerted effort. And make no mistake: You'll have to do most of the initial work to form inner-circle relationships. If you haven't already, you'll find that others tend to be reluctant to make the first move in getting to know a higher-up or fellow leader. (Again, this stems from the misconception that leaders "should" be strong, serious, and unemotional at all times.) But almost everyone I know who has established such bonds tells me that the effort is well worth it. It simply requires you to step outside your old familiar ivory tower— which is probably more claustrophobic than you realize!

Look Outside Your Company for Connections

Yes, it's important to form close relationships with people from within your organization and industry. Their institutional knowledge, expertise, and shared trajectory will be invaluable in helping you identify objectives and set strategy—as will their unique ability to understand the specific trials and challenges you may be facing. But cultivating outside connections should also be a key priority for every leader—at every level on the leadership ladder. The earlier you cultivate relationships with leaders outside of your own industry, the more likely you will be to have established rich, meaningful friendships with other executives and CEOs by the time you reach the top.

In well-populated towns and cities, the opportunities to build meaningful and enriching peer relationships can be endless. Proactively participate in activities that may connect you with other executives beyond your own organization. Here are a few ideas:

- Join the board of a philanthropy that interests you.
- Participate in your alumni association or serve on a university-sponsored leadership advisory council.
- Get involved with a local theater group.
- Join a country club or sports club.
- Serve on a church board.

- Become a big sister in a program for girls and teens, or join a philanthropic organization dedicated to funding women's education, like P.E.O.
- Join the board of your local Rotary Club.

These are just a few ideas to help you start exploring your options. Take a look at the organizations, clubs, and groups available in your community, and get creative! If you've focused only on work and family all your life, you may be surprised by how many opportunities there are to build bonds with other smart people who have unique perspectives.

If you've focused only on work and family all your life, you may be surprised by how many opportunities there are to build bonds with other smart people who have unique perspectives.

Bottom line: There is no need to be lonely at the top. You merely need to put in some effort to step outside your self-imposed bubble. Start by making the investment to build more mutually supportive connections, both inside and outside your workplace. I guarantee, you'll be glad you did—and so were the female executives I interviewed.

Melissa Reiff
Former Chairwoman and CEO
The Container Store

Melissa Reiff shared the following with me about being lonely at the top while she was still in the CEO role:

> So many people gave me advice and counsel when I took this role. They would say to me, "You know, it's lonely at the top."
>
> I was like, "Yeah, okay, probably," shaking my head a bit. Well, there is certainly some truth to that.
>
> My prior role as president and COO for many years was certainly different from my role as CEO. I hear more things now, some things that I didn't hear before, as president and COO.

"Unkind things?" I asked.

> No, not necessarily, but input from other CEOs and comments—both complaints and compliments—from customers, etc.
>
> I had mentors and other CEOs tell me that it can be lonely at the top. In fact, a former board member, the wonderful Danny Meyer, asked me once, "You give nourishment to so many; who gives YOU nourishment?"

You give nourishment to so many; who gives YOU nourishment?

I had never been asked that question before and it really got me thinking. I told him that I truly get nourishment from our employees—all of them.

But it did help me to pause and ensure that I remained strong, focused, and physically and mentally healthy, in order to do my job to the best of my ability.

Nancy Howell Agee
President and CEO
Carilion Clinic

I asked Nancy Agee, "Did you find that it's lonely at the top, and if so, how do you deal with it?"

Well, it is funny. When I was offered the role of chief operating officer, by the then-CEO, he said, "Are you willing to lose friends over this?"

> When I was offered the role of chief operating officer, by the then-CEO, he said, "Are you willing to lose friends over this?"

I remember thinking, *What an odd thing to say*. But I said, "Yeah, sure."

The fact was that I did lose a friend. Sometimes I had to make decisions that my *friends* didn't care for. In fact, I lost a very good friend over some decisions we made. That was hurtful—and a good lesson on how important communication is and staying faithful to the mission.

Additionally, I've found you must be careful about talking something through. You must be careful not to just muse. So, I am grateful for people like our CAO, whom I can be clear with and say, "I'm just musing here."

People tend to assume idle thoughts are the gospel.

I will give you a funny example. I don't recall why, but I must have said at some point, somewhere, "I don't like that green tablecloth."

I have no idea if or when I said that, but I went into a luncheon one day where folks were honoring me for something, and there were all these white and green tablecloths. As I was walking in, the first thing one person said was, "I know you don't like green tablecloths. I'm really sorry. It's all they had."

I thought, *What is she talking about?* It's that sort of thing where people hold on to what you say.

But, in terms of it being lonely at the top, the good news is that I have a very supportive family, friends, and colleagues.

And as the CEO, you get involved in and invited to develop relationships with others who are in similar positions. So, I have a real network of friends, colleagues, and go-to people across the country whom I can pick up the phone and talk with anytime.

If you keep only to your own organization, I think it could be lonely and isolating. You can lose perspective. Often, the CEO can be protected from issues. Sometimes that is good because you want other people to solve things. Yet, at the same time, you need to know what the pulse of the organization is and what's going on. So, you have to work *not* to be isolated.

Kerry Healey
Inaugural President
Milken Center for Advancing the American Dream

I mentioned to Kerry Healey, PhD, "I've heard women say, 'People warned me about this. I didn't believe it, but I found out it is lonely at the top.' What do you have to say about that?"

It's not lonely if you have a good team around you. You can't be the only person responsible for success. You can't execute everything yourself. You can't succeed by yourself.

If you're lonely at the top, you're going to fail. You must have colleagues and people who would walk through walls for you—or you are going to fail. Do not be alone at the top.

My team has sustained me through many difficult moments in leadership. Having an extraordinarily strong and loyal team around you is the best thing you can create for yourself.

You are not there alone. You are either there with friends and supporters and brilliant people who can help you, or you are there with people who want your job and are waiting for you to fail.

It is well advised to take great efforts to build the best team you can. Support them. Give them growth and recognition. Make sure they have your flanks. The best defense you can have is a loyal, hardworking, intelligent team, and if you ever bump into someone you think is incredibly brilliant, you should hire them immediately.

> **The best defense you can have is a loyal, hardworking, intelligent team.**

"What do you do when you realize there is someone on your team who is just waiting for you to crash and burn so they can get your job?"

When you build a unified and talented management team, it is harder for anyone to attack a single member of that team. Everyone is protected by that model.

Wendy Johnson
Former President and CEO
Dale Carnegie franchise, Atlanta, GA

I asked Wendy Johnson, "When you finally made it to the top, running the Dale Carnegie franchise, what were some of the surprises you didn't expect to find when you got there?"

You do not get the feedback you were accustomed to in lower-level management jobs, where people gave you "attaboys" and they supported you.

If you have a need to be liked, or if you have the need to feel appreciated, you're not necessarily going to get it as the CEO. When you become the top dog, there will be people against you or against your decisions.

When you become the top dog, there will be people against you or against your decisions.

While in a perfect world, we get buy-in, collaboration, and agreement before we move forward, it doesn't always work out that way. Sometimes you must make decisions that affect people. While making these decisions, you weigh the financial/people impacts as best you can, but at the end of the day, your decisions affect people. You may not be popular.

I think it was lonelier than I thought it would be.

Before becoming CEO of my own franchise, I was just part of the team. But as the senior executive/owner, the buck stopped with me, and it was my money—you have a different perspective on how you must operate. It isn't always going to be the way your team thinks it should run—because it isn't *their* money. People tend to be more generous with other people's money.

To achieve successful implementations of new ideas or processes, I learned that I had to bring my team over to my point of view. I needed to gain their agreement or buy-in rather than just their compliance. Compliance is not sustainable, and command-and-control is not effective with our new generations.

Because positive feedback is in short supply, you must believe in yourself. I joined a CEO networking group. We shared our challenges and applauded our accomplishments. This helped to mitigate any loneliness I felt.

> **I learned that I had to bring my team over to my point of view…Compliance is not sustainable, and command-and-control is not effective with our new generations.**

Lieutenant General Kathleen M. Gainey
U.S. Army, Retired

I asked Lt. Gen. Gainey, "What are some of the surprises you discovered at the senior level?"

You must find someone you can talk to. That might be a friend, your spouse, a significant other, or a family member. You will need someone you can talk to, lay things out, and bounce ideas off. Just tell them, "I expect you to give me honest feedback," or, "Don't give me any feedback. Just listen to me so I can vent or think out loud."

I asked, "Is it true that it's lonely at the top?"

Yes. But other people are lonely, too. So, if you can, find other C-suite people who can keep your trust. It helps just to be able to talk, share common issues, and share how you are each solving things.

It helps just to be able to talk, share common issues, and share how you are each solving things.

"Were the other C-suite people—those you had confidence in and felt comfortable having confidential discussions with—military or civilian C-suiters?"

Yes, I had a little bit of both military and civilian friends who served that purpose. Sometimes it might have been a family member, mainly my dad. Sometimes it was another friend or peer who was in a similar stress-level organization. Sometimes those friends were Department of Defense civilians. Sometimes those people were just civilians from a totally different perspective within the community. Some were people with whom I had gone to college or high school.

REFLECTIONS:

There are multiple reasons why leaders choose to wall themselves off. Perhaps they believe they must present a stoic, unemotional, and capable front at all times. They may have been on the receiving end of jealousy-driven gossip and behaviors. They simply may not know where to turn for support and advice.

And as some of the women I interviewed shared, C-suite executives and boards of directors must sometimes make difficult decisions that impact close colleagues. Often, these decisions must be held close to the vest until they are made public. As a result, teammates and confidants may feel hurt, disappointed, or betrayed. Rather than deal with awkward emotional upheaval, some executives choose to distance themselves from internal relationships.

But living in isolation at the top is neither necessary nor the only option. Maintaining a supportive network of colleagues who can

Living in isolation at the top is neither necessary nor the only option.

provide unbiased feedback and alternative points of view is vital to your personal well-being and success as a C-level leader.

For this reason, every leader should set a personal developmental objective to cultivate connections with trusted peers. Within your executive team and outside your organization, look for individuals with whom you share common experiences, values, and goals, and who will have your back even through challenges and disagreements.

The good news is that you can start building strong, collaborative connections with other leaders even before you reach the top. In fact, the support of your inner circle might help you reach the C-suite sooner than you'd hoped.

INTROSPECTIONS:

1 Have you ever been the target of gossip or resentment after being promoted? If so, how did it affect you?

   a. On the other hand, have you ever felt jealous of a colleague's rise through the ranks? If so, did you blame others for overlooking you, or did you see it as an opportunity to re-evaluate your own performance?

2 What preconceptions do you have about how women in leadership roles "should" behave?

a. Do you believe that executives should be serious and stoic at all times? Or do you feel comfortable sharing your emotions and challenges with others?

3 Have you tried to develop supportive, nurturing professional relationships with peers or business colleagues—within your organization or industry—with whom you can candidly share business challenges?
a. If not, why not?

4 Is there an industry association, a university alumnae association, or a women's leadership organization within your community where you could potentially meet like-minded colleagues?

5 Do you have neighbors or family members with similar business experiences or leadership challenges who might offer you feedback on your business ideas?

6 Have you considered joining a confidential peer mentoring organization for CEOs/executives of similarly sized organizations?

7 Have you considered volunteering to serve on the board of a local not-for-profit or charity whose mission you are passionate about, where you could also get to know other local business leaders?

NINE

WOW Culture Begins with You

Whether your brand WOWs or disappoints depends on the actions and attitudes of every single one of your employees, from the CEO and the board of directors down. Your cultural reputation is based on how satisfied people are with the decisions and actions of anyone representing your organization. Any little slip-up by any one individual can undermine a WOW reputation that may have taken years to establish. Organizational culture matters.

Regardless of your role, the responsibility for establishing and enhancing your organization's WOW reputation and culture lies with you. So be sure to let your own personal WOW shine, wherever you are on the leadership ladder and wherever you may be in the community. You represent the brand. You represent the culture. YOU.

-DEB BOELKES

A podcast host once asked me, "What do you think it will take to create a movement that will change our work culture? When will leaders across the board start to realize that it's how you treat employees—how you care about them as people, how you inspire the members of the team—that makes the numbers happen?"

This was my response:

Instilling such a massive shift in organizational mindset might require a two-pronged approach. One piece of the puzzle will require a shift in how we prepare future leaders in business school. Responsibility for the second piece lies squarely with each of us as leaders in the workplace. We each need to let our own WOW shine wherever we are on the leadership ladder.

Business Schools Teach Important Skills...But Only Great Leaders Can Develop Future Great Leaders

Many who aspire to leadership assume that to be successful at it, they must attend business school, get an MBA, and master the mechanics of finance, accounting, and strategic planning. Certainly, it's important to understand these mechanics. As the old saying goes, *You can't manage it if you can't measure it*, which is why so many MBA programs emphasize course work in business analytics and quantitative finance.

> You don't create a WOW culture by focusing on metrics. It's the other way around. The numbers "magically" get made when you have a WOW culture.

Yet, what separates average managers from exceptional leaders is vision, charisma, and extraordinary people skills. Mastering the art of communication and relationship-building is vital for anyone who wants to become what I call a best-ever leader. Now, I have an MBA, but regardless of what I learned in school, the realities of business taught me that you don't create a WOW culture by focusing on metrics. It's the other way around. The numbers "magically" get made when you have a WOW culture.

Achieving WOW performance is highly dependent on how you treat your people. Great leaders are masters at aligning team members' personal goals with the organization's goals. Great leaders inspire passionate, enthusiastic people to do whatever it takes—in their own unique way—to delight customers. Top-line sales numbers and bottom-line profit numbers are organically achieved when leaders focus on building the kind of culture where people feel appreciated and are motivated to give their best efforts every single day.

Too often we hear human resources organizations and MBA programs calling these things "soft skills." Yet, they are very difficult to teach in a class or learn from a book. Perhaps one of the most difficult aspects of developing soft skills is the fact that everyone is unique. There's no hard-and-fast formula for connecting with another person. You can't assume that what motivates or encourages Employee A will have the same effect on Employee B. (Often, the results will be wildly different!)

The best—and in fact, the only—way to develop soft skills is by observing role models and adopting their behaviors, attitudes, and tactics. You may want to start by consciously treating people the way you would want to be treated and inspiring them to be at their best day-in and day-out. Then, *feel* the impacts that result from your actions. You know instinctively what feels good—what works and what doesn't work for you *and* for the other person. Sometimes you'll simply learn what *not* to do.

It's also helpful to engage in dialogue to uncover whatever it is that excites people and makes them feel great about coming to work every day. Everything you discover is valuable and will help you refine your own unique set of soft skills. Eventually, through trial and error, you'll learn what works best to inspire each of the individuals around you.

The Problem with the "Soft-Skill Gap" in Business Curriculums

As I alluded to earlier, most MBA programs focus on teaching management mechanics and leadership theories. Many of these programs offer courses that are taught by business professors with PhDs who have spent years conducting impressive organizational research. Yet few of these PhDs have relevant experience as inspirational business leaders, so few MBA programs focus on helping students understand and develop soft skills or empathetic leadership tactics.

While we see plenty of organizations full of MBAs, inspirational leaders remain a rare breed.

There is a big gap between understanding organizational theory and putting WOW into practice. Hence, while we see plenty of organizations full of MBAs, inspirational leaders remain a rare breed.

I believe the "soft-skill gap" in business education is also why so many mergers and acquisitions (M&As) fail. The financial synergies forecasted by the brightest MBAs seldom materialize because disparate cultures rarely mesh well. All too often, corporate culture is ignored during the financial due diligence and integration planning processes. Conflicting value systems and uncooperative employees end up derailing integration efforts.

Don't get me wrong: The traditional business school curriculum is crucial for preparing future leaders to thrive in the workplace. I would never recommend that courses like management mechanics or organizational theory be removed—nor am I discounting the expertise of individuals who have devoted their careers to researching and advancing these disciplines. Rather, I'm suggesting that an additional component be added to the basic business school curriculum. When students have access to courses on soft skills, taught by professors with a real-world business leadership background, they will be more fully prepared to fulfill their potentials.

Unless more leaders of Best Place to Work organizations step from the boardroom into the business school classroom, most MBA students won't ever really grasp what it takes to be an inspiring team leader. But I am hopeful that the soft-skill gap is gradually being filled, because more and more individuals like Garry Ridge, the now-retired chairman of the board of the WD-40 Company, are stepping into teaching roles. Garry, whom I featured in my books *The WOW Factor Workplace* and *Heartfelt Leadership*, now serves as an adjunct professor at the University of San Diego.

If you are enrolled in an MBA or other business program that does not yet offer coursework on soft-skill development, I would encourage you to participate in an internship with a major corporation. This will give you a taste of what real-world leadership looks like, and if you're lucky, you'll get to observe firsthand what soft skills are all about.

Lean Into Heartfelt Leadership, Whatever Your Level!
Changing the way we think about business education is important—but on its own, it won't help many workplaces transition from a numbers focus to a people focus. That's why I mentioned the second piece of the puzzle in my podcast interview: how you choose to shine in your own workplace. You can be the person who sparks a work culture revolution, right there on your own team, at whatever level you happen to be at now. There is no need to wait for a green light from on-high. You don't need a promotion or budget allocation, either. Just do it.

I know from experience that heartfelt leaders—those who excel at soft skills day-in and day-out—are the ones who inspire positive, lasting change and who turbocharge employee engagement. Best of all, heartfelt leaders can be highly effective at any level within any organization.

It may surprise you, but it's the entry-level leaders—the ones who interact most closely with frontline workers and focus on getting roadblocks out of their way—who really create the WOW. It's first-level managers who are best positioned to inspire customer-facing employees to make magic happen every single day. So if you are a first-level manager, get going. You don't have to ask permission. Just start that movement!

Of course, to have the broadest impact, cultural movements must start at the top and permeate all the way down. It's easiest for frontline managers to ensure that WOW happens with

It's the entry-level leaders— the ones who interact most closely with frontline workers and focus on getting roadblocks out of their way—who really create the WOW.

every interaction if upline managers are focused on the same thing. But all it really takes is someone, somewhere in the organization, who is passionate about helping their people become the best they can be at doing whatever they each love to do. Such leaders, wherever they are, will quickly stand out because their team's results will be undeniable. Why shouldn't you be that leader?

It's not an impossible task. In fact, creating an employee-focused work culture is easier than you might think. And if you do it right, your people will automatically perform at their peak because they'll be inspired. Daily inspiration will become part of your team culture because it makes everyone feel good to live that way. Heartfelt leadership creates a winning chain reaction.

I expect that once word gets out that there's a better way to run an organization, there won't be any going back to the old way of doing things. The old way simply won't be acceptable anymore. Everyone will want to jump on board the soft-skills train! Let's explore how some of our executives went about developing their soft skills and sparking heartfelt leadership revolutions in their organizations.

Melissa Reiff
Former Chairwoman and CEO
The Container Store

I asked Melissa Reiff, "What do you think has been the key differentiator that has enabled you to make magic happen here at The Container Store?"

Communication. I believe *communication is leadership*—they are the same thing in my opinion.

I think it is the ability to read people in a compassionate and constructive way—not in a manipulative way, but to really connect with people, to focus on them, and to always be in the moment.

Selfless communication is about putting yourself in the other person's shoes, taking the time to understand them, to learn about them, and then communicate with them as you believe they would want to be communicated with. It's customization versus just communicating the same old way to everyone because that is easier for you.

In my opinion, *selfish* communication is when you communicate to everybody the same way. You just kind of go, "Blah, blah, blah." You don't take the time to ask questions of someone else or try to understand how they might best receive the communication. Everybody hears and sees things differently. It's certainly not one-size-fits-all.

I would say that practicing effective, thoughtful, predictable, reliable, compassionate, and, yes, courteous communication—

> **Everybody hears and sees things differently. [Communication] is certainly not one-size-fits-all.**

every single day—is essential in sustaining a business.

One of the things we've worked hard on over the years—and this is so understandable, and I was certainly a part of it—is if someone is obviously in the wrong role, we were slow to sometimes move them on. Instead, we would sometimes create another role for them. Again, always trying to take care of our people—we love them all—however, sometimes it is better for them and the company to just move on. We were not always great at doing that.

In some situations, we moved people around to other positions. Sometimes it has worked and sometimes it hasn't. What I think we should have done, which is what we've been doing for some time, is to sit down with them and compassionately be firm, clear, kind, and confident about the decision—all at the same time.

While some people may view these kinds of conversations as "difficult"—out of fear that people will respond with emotion— it's not a difficult conversation, in my mind. It's just business when we talk about why this role isn't working and why it's best for the person—and for the company and the employees—to move onto something else, outside of The Container Store. Such conversations are sometimes necessary, and it's best for all concerned to have a candid conversation. If that conversation doesn't happen, it can be very demotivating for other employees.

I believe we owe it to this person. This is their life. This is their career. Lay out the expectations prior to this conversation and be very specific and very clear. Say, "Okay. Do you understand the expectations? Do you think you can reach these expectations, fulfill this role, and perform? Let's regroup in 30 days. If not, maybe the best thing for everyone is to part with the company."

To me, that is the right thing to do for any human being, versus moving them around and trying to make it work, and then 20 years later you look up and go, "Oh, by the way, you're not working out." That's just not right.

One of our foundational principles is *Communication is leadership.* But it's hard. It takes incredible discipline, effort, and a genuine caring and commitment. It takes a lot of brain power—at least it does for me—to be able to really focus and look somebody in the eye, to care enough to remember their name, to remember their face, to place them in the many compartments in my brain.

I feel like my brain is made up of these little, teeny squares, and I have only so many squares. So, if something is important, it stays in a compartment. If it's not important, then out it goes. Or if it's super-negative, painful, and serves no constructive purpose, it goes! I have no time for negative thoughts, particularly if I have no control over how to make it better. There's no point to it.

It's so interesting how the mind works. That's why I am so fascinated with brain health. I am in such admiration of the Center for BrainHealth, right here in Dallas, and of my friend Dr. Sandi Chapman, its founder and director. She is absolutely amazing. And I'm so proud that The Container Store has sponsored their lecture series every February for the past 12 years.

Jodi Berg
Retired President and CEO
Vita-Mix Corporation

If you've read my book *The WOW Factor Workplace*, you know that I believe creating a WOW culture is all about striving to be a best-ever boss in an environment where high expectations are envisioned and achieved day after day. A WOW factor workplace is somewhere employees so love what they do, and where customers are so delighted with the organization's products and services, that all parties are continuously uplifted and energized by their positive experiences.

One of the reasons I was so eager to interview Jodi Berg, PhD, was due to her reputation for making WOW happen at Vitamix. I couldn't wait to ask her what she did to create their WOW culture. But before I could even ask her that question, Jodi turned the tables and asked *me* this question:

So, Deb, your first book was *The WOW Factor Workplace.* *WOW* is a word we use all the time at Vitamix. It's a big word in our culture. In fact, customers are one of our corporate values, defined as *Customers: Listening, Learning, and Creating the WOW.*

How do *you* define the word *WOW*?

I responded, "Well, Jodi, it took a whole book for me to define the word *WOW*. But in terms of a workplace that is WOW—from a customer perspective *and* from the perspective of potential employees and current employees—it is a workplace that takes your breath away. It's products and services that take your breath away. It is a place you always want to be a part of, whether you're an employee or a leader or a customer or a vendor. It's one of your favorite places to be connected to."

To that, Jodi responded:

One of the things I discovered about the word *WOW* came from traveling around the world, asking people who speak different languages, "What's that one word, that when it happens, you just can't help but say that one word? Like we would say, 'WOW.' What's your word?"

They almost always said, "You mean WOW?"

I said, "Yes, but in your language."

"It's WOW."

"It's WOW?"

"It's WOW!"

Now, somebody should research this and do a much better
job than my talking to a few people around the world. But
what I found is that it is kind of like a sneeze.
You have to say the word *WOW* because you are so
overwhelmed in that moment of expression. It is hard to hold
it back. You cannot really keep yourself from saying WOW! It
just bubbles up and comes out.

So, for decades now, in my mind, it has been an incredibly
powerful word because it is tied specifically to, as you say,
"Take your breath away." It's an overwhelming feeling—just
that one universal word.

The opposite of WOW is all sorts of words—all sorts of grunts
and groans and noises of frustration. There isn't one reciprocal
word for when we are overwhelmed in a negative space. But I
think it is amazing that there might be almost a universal
word, across cultures and languages, when we feel *that*
overwhelmed with joy.

Now, do we use the word *WOW* in lots of other ways?
Absolutely. But that's kind of where it generates from.

I replied, "I had no idea about the global implications of the word
WOW. In fact, my response to that is WOW!"

See?

At Vitamix, we've incorporated it—not just into our value of *Customers: Listening, Learning, and Creating the WOW*—but on our production line, as well. We actually have a WOW station. It's the last station on the line where somebody will go through the box, and they'll just do one more look—checking to see if opening this box would make them go WOW.

Amongst ourselves internally, we jokingly say, "Now, don't forget to sprinkle in a little bit of the WOW dust right before you seal the box."

WOW is something that we use a lot in our culture.

"I love that concept: *WOW dust*. That's another concept I've not heard before. It reminds me of one of my very favorite managers, back when I was in the corporate world. When I took the position to run a division within her organization, she gave me a magic wand. It had thousands of shiny, multi-colored, glittery little stars floating around inside a clear plastic handle. You could shake it, and it would look so magical—like the way you would shake a snow globe. It looked so WOW.

"When she gave it to me, she said, 'You might need this from time to time, so here you go. This should work like magic for you. It certainly worked for me!'"

It was a WOW wand. I think that might even be better than WOW dust!

Another thing that we discovered about WOW is that the WOW builds up.

If you have a WOW moment, and then you have another WOW moment, and then you have another WOW moment—because of the same cause, or the same reason—those WOWs just build up, and build up, and build up, until you get to a point where you can't help but just explode—not just with WOW, but with telling everybody you possibly can about where that WOW came from and that you were WOWed by it.

Another fascinating thing that we discovered about WOW—and we use this in our talk to every new employee during orientation—is that every single one of us, throughout the entire company, is responsible for creating the WOW.

> **Every single one of us, throughout the entire company, is responsible for creating the WOW.**

But we also run the risk of deflating the WOW.

It's important to understand that no matter how much WOW has built up, the moment you add just a drop of the opposite of WOW—it is like putting in a microscopic drop of black paint into an entire container of white—it will never be sparkly white paint again. It will forever be some version of off-white. If you put enough black in, it now becomes gray and cannot ever again be categorized as white.

Any negative experience with our brand—one that is the opposite of a WOW—is going to quickly deflate any benefit that we had. So, we must be incredibly diligent in everything we do, at every touchpoint—how we build the products, how we deliver on them, how we communicate with people—to make sure that we are always creating that WOW.

Here is another thing. How we create the WOW is not just through the customer's first encounter, but by creating the WOW throughout the customer life cycle. Everyone has a customer life cycle, right? We call them *Moments of Truth*— where we need to create the WOW.

How we create the WOW is not just through the customer's first encounter, but by creating the WOW throughout the customer life cycle.

With our strategy, internally and at all moments, we must minimally be as good as our brand promise. Yet at critical customer Moments of Truth, we must really create that WOW and take it over the top. Our goal is to help our customers not only be successful in their Vitamix journey but LOVE the process.

The ultimate outcome is to create so much WOW that our customers become salespeople, naturally and authentically spreading the WOW to that many more people. It's really a part of our entire business model, from beginning to end.

I commented, "If you don't understand what makes a great workplace, what makes a great product, what makes a great customer experience, what makes people just gravitate to you, what makes you the magnet of happy people, if you don't understand what all that is, then you can't possibly make it happen."

Right! That's right.

I must share a little story with you about that: When my dad asked me to take over the household division back in

2002 - 2003, I fell in love with it. I just fell in love with our household division, our products, AND our customers.

Now, Vitamix is a family business, so I probably have a little bit of Vitamix geeky stuff in my blood, running through my veins, but I would often steer a conversation with a customer toward food choices and eventually ask them, "Why are you making that choice?"

Until the end of 2003 or the beginning of 2004, the answer from people choosing a vegetable-centric diet was most often, "Because it's the best thing to do for the animals and this planet. I'm sacrificing something personally to help the animals."

Then, during 2004, things started to change. People started to answer my question with, "Because I feel amazing when I eat that way. If I feel amazing, then I get to be more of what I want to be," whether that is for personal reasons or altruistic reasons. Suddenly, people were recognizing, *Food choice matters to me, and it makes me feel better.*

They were using words like *organic* and *local,* words that we had been using for decades within Vitamix. These were messages that, literally for decades, we'd been trying to help people recognize. Suddenly, these ideas were naturally starting to come out and people were sharing them.

I realized this food choice trend might very well be *the* opportunity for Vitamix—the company that my great-grandfather had started. It took decades and decades of joy, sweat, tears, and hard work to help people think differently about food, especially when a lot of the world was going to fast food, processed food, and convenience foods. Yet, we never gave up the torch of, *Food is the fuel that you put in your body. If you put the right fuel in, you'll get the performance that you want as a result.*

I was starting to hear people relaying the very message my great-grandfather was sharing decades ago and we have shared ever since. I asked our marketing firms about it, but they said, "No. We're not seeing any of that. It hasn't hit the radar yet."

> **I was starting to hear people relaying the very message my great-grandfather was sharing decades ago and we have shared ever since...That was the beginning of our creating the WOW!**

Yet, *I knew* it was out there. *I knew* it was happening. *I knew* this was our time. This is our time as a company to transform and become the company that we had always wanted to be—with *transform* being the operative word.

We started putting all the different things in place to ride this wave, increase its momentum, and drive a permanent shift in how people think about food. That was the beginning of our creating the WOW!

Nancy Howell Agee
President and CEO
Carilion Clinic

When I spoke to Nancy Agee, she commented on how women are typically better at mastering soft skills:

> I do think women are more naturally nurturing. In fact, I want to write a book one day on what I call *Steel Magnolia Leadership*. You know the movie, right?

> Women have strong values and a core that's unbendable. But at the same time, we women are great at adapting, and nurturing, and caring, and developing others. Women are really good at that.

> I think, in some ways, that sets us up thinking we must go at things more softly or more gently.

I replied, "But it's one thing to go after things gently, versus undermining your own credibility."

> Yes, exactly.

> One thing I have learned is the benefit of having a quintessential open-door policy. Any employee can come into my office at any time. They can e-mail, they can phone me, they can text me, and I expect it. I appreciate it. I think it takes courage for people to communicate openly with higher-ups.

Having an open-door policy creates an honest, caring, trusting environment.

So, when it happens, whether it's for little things or big things, I celebrate that. I tell them, "I know it took courage for you to do this."

I cannot always fix what people want me to fix. You can't always get to the outcome they desire, like, "I want more money. They aren't paying me enough," or something like that.

But having an open-door policy creates an honest, caring, trusting environment.

Linda Rutherford
Executive Vice President, Chief Communications Officer
Southwest Airlines

When I asked Linda Rutherford about the value of building trusting relationships, she shared this.

You must develop trusting relationships to be a trusted adviser. That is the number-one responsibility I have in this role: to be a trusted adviser.

They're asking me for my honest feedback. That's a trusted relationship. I want to honor that.

I'll have people come to me now and ask the question, "Did I come off too strong in that meeting?"

It doesn't have anything to do with our business strategy, but they're asking me for my honest feedback. That's a trusted relationship. I want to honor that. I am glad they are asking me, and they know that I am going to tell them. They know that I will share what I think.

I asked Linda to reflect on her early experiences at the senior leadership table. "Were the executives at that table people you already knew, or did you have to develop relationships from scratch with most of them when you joined the senior leadership team?"

Half the people were the same ones I had known, and they are still there today. Some I knew better than others.

Again, senior leadership roles change over time. You're never done with that. People and relationships are messy, so you just have to kind of figure it out.

Wendy Johnson
Former President and CEO
Dale Carnegie franchise, Atlanta, GA

Wendy Johnson gives much of the credit for what she learned about soft skills and achieving WOW results to her mother.

I learned a great deal about selling from my mom:
- Know what your product value is—it may be something quite different from its physical description.

- Understand what your value-add is—this is really where you make your sale.
- Figure out what's motivating the person you're selling to—it's not just a physical product that you're selling.

Earlier in my career, when I was selling intangible products, I sold a check fraud detection system in South Africa. The product itself was amazing, and we sold it all over the world. The average cost for the product to a financial institution was well over a million dollars, which was a great deal of money back then.

South African banks needed a fraud detection product desperately. But selling the product for its return-on-investment benefit was only one part of the overall solution sale in South Africa.

The competitor companies would go to South Africa—which is literally at the end of the earth, half a world away—and they would attempt to sell a product in just one visit, maybe two. Typically, they would not return. Their customer service, installation, and ongoing support offerings were limited because of the geographic location.

To win this deal, I knew I had to sell *consistency*—client support, follow through, and commitment to excellence. I typically traveled there at least five times before I got a signed contract.

I was not just selling software. I was selling committed service and training, reliability and trust, as well as a return on investment for the product. It wasn't just a piece of software

that was important in South Africa. It was commitment to
service, as well.

I first learned about understanding the client and selling to
their most important need from watching my mom work as a
travel agent. Although she was not a career salesperson, all
those concepts of building trust and understanding and
serving the client came from her.

I believe that my success in my
career was a direct result of
my ability to develop trusting
relationships internally and
externally. Success in business
is all about building these
relationships—both up and down. In a sales situation, people
buy from people they trust. Some women build relationships
only down. You've also got to build relationships *up*, as well.

> **Success in business is all about building these relationships—both up and down.**

Building relationships in your own organization is essential.
Nurturing the people who support you internally allows you to
serve your prospect or client more effectively and
consistently. Developing a mentor or coach relationship
internally or externally will also give you the ability to ask for
advice and guidance during times of uncertainty.

Lieutenant General Kathleen M. Gainey
U.S. Army, Retired

I shared with Lt. Gen. Gainey, "It can be challenging for someone in college to decide what career path to pursue. Some have said to me, 'Why would I even aspire to be in senior leadership? I don't even know what executives do.' For women considering a career in the military, what are some things they may not know about what it's really like at the top of the military career ladder?"

Why aspire to move up the ladder? For me it was to be in a position where I could make things better for people who worked with me and for me. Whatever changes we made would then also help others.

You can get a lot of work done if you don't want to take credit.

One of the things one must realize is that, as an executive, you spend a lot of your time working with people, developing people, and working on people issues—whether it's labor issues or personnel issues. That doesn't stop just because you're at the senior level.

There is an old saying, "You can get a lot of work done if you don't want to take credit."

If you can motivate and get people working together, you can achieve an incredible number of things. When you try and make it somebody else's idea, like saying, "Oh, that's a great idea! You said..." such and such, they may not have said it quite that way, but you can help shape a solution by giving them credit. Then they will run with the ball.

I replied, "That reminds me of a challenge many women complain about: You're in a meeting with a bunch of guys. You finally muster the courage to share your ideas and then a guy across the table will speak over you and propose that same idea. You feel like your comment just floated by unnoticed, while he gets the attaboy response, 'John, what a brilliant idea!'

"Was that ever an issue for you?"

Sure, that was an issue many times.

But, again, if you are not trying to take credit for it, you can help them make it an even better solution. Just say, "I think that's a perfect idea and I think that we could add this capability and make it even better."

Even though it might have been your idea, you are not degrading their idea. You are just saying, "And here's an additional way we can make that successful." You are just being part of that solution.

> **Being a team player goes a long way to solidifying even stronger relationships.**

Sometimes you will find that all the other guys were thinking to themselves, *Well,* she *said that.* They will not ever say it in the meeting, but later they may reveal to you, "You said that same thing."

Then you can simply say, "Yeah, but that doesn't matter."

Let them see that you are not trying to take credit. You are just trying to be part of the team. Being a team player goes a long way to solidifying even stronger relationships.

"Do you think by doing that, it made a difference in how you got ahead?"

I think so because people wanted to work with me. They knew that I was not going to try to be in the spotlight. I did not care about being in the spotlight and I was willing to work to make it a better program, even if I wasn't going to get the credit.

REFLECTIONS:

As Jodi Berg explained, Moments of Truth are important moments in the customer life cycle when it's *especially* important to create the WOW! These moments can include the many big, little, and subliminal interactions your organization has with people who follow your business, view your ads, evaluate or buy your products and services, request after-purchase support, or issue a return or cancellation.

Every. Single. Interaction. Matters.

Moments of Truth even include interactions with potential job candidates and the community at large. Things seemingly out of your control, such as news items and customers' social media posts, nevertheless influence whether people will desire to do business with you and/or work for you. At every single touchpoint, wherever people encounter your brand, they form or confirm opinions about your business.

Every. Single. Interaction. Matters.

Whether your brand WOWs or disappoints depends on the actions and attitudes of every single one of your employees, from the CEO and the board of directors down. Your cultural reputation is based on how satisfied people are with the decisions and actions of anyone representing your organization. Any little slip-up by any one individual can undermine a WOW reputation that may have taken years to establish. Organizational culture matters.

Regardless of your role, the responsibility for establishing and enhancing your organization's WOW reputation and culture lies with you. So be sure to let your own personal WOW shine, wherever you are on the leadership ladder and wherever you may be in the community. You represent the brand. You represent the culture. YOU.

With this in mind, commit to developing and honing your soft skills. Whether you went to business school or not (and if you did, whether soft skills were covered there or not!), it's never too late to work on becoming a more empathetic, approachable, and engaging leader. Here are a few things you may want to focus on:

- Strive to be a pleasure to be around—even when you're stressed, preoccupied, or having a bad day. Be the kind of leader everyone wants to report to.
- Realize that unhappy employees are not likely to ever WOW potential or current customers. They also undermine your culture. So, as a leader, take time to regularly check in with and get to know your direct reports. Develop relationships

with everyone else in the organization too, to the extent you can. Know what's important to each person. Understand each team member's goals and desires and help them get where they want to go—even if it's not on your team.

- Ensure that every one of your team members feels appreciated and finds meaning in their work. Give them credit for their ideas. Encourage them to be creative in terms of delighting customers and job candidates. Keep in mind that when people love what they do and are recognized for going above and beyond, they will naturally strive to do even more. The WOW will build and build.

- When your people trust that you have their best interests at heart, they will have your back and they won't be afraid to ask for your candid feedback. If your own manager doesn't make the effort or take the time to do such things, serve as a role model for them, too. Coach them on how they could create the WOW. You might be amazed by the outcome.

- Be sure to put yourself in your customers' shoes and treat *them* the way you would want to be treated. Would you be delighted with every interaction at every customer touchpoint?

Infuse WOW into your culture by living, breathing, and acting WOW every single day. Be deliberate about it—and you will reap the rewards!

In short, be the kind of WOW ambassador for your brand that everyone should emulate. Infuse WOW into your culture by living, breathing, and acting WOW every single day. Be deliberate about it—and you will reap the rewards!

INTROSPECTIONS:

1 Is your organization's culture focused primarily on people or numbers?

2 Have you ever studied so-called "soft skills"? Do you currently strive to develop and hone this skill set?
   a. Have you ever had an empathetic leader whose style you might use as a model?
   b. How well do you know each team member as an individual: what is important to them, what motivates them, and what their goals are for the future?

3 Think about the best organizational culture you ever interacted with, either as a customer or as an employee or volunteer. How would you describe that environment?
   a. How did team members treat each other?
   b. What kinds of magic did the team create together?
   c. What are some of the key takeaways from that experience that you might replicate or even improve upon within your current culture?

4 What can you do *now*, wherever you are in your company's hierarchy, to serve as an inspirational example and move your company's culture toward WOW?

5 Have you and your team ever mapped out the customer life cycle for your company's products and services? Can you identify every touchpoint and Moment of Truth?

6 As a customer or job candidate at your organization, would you be WOWed at every touchpoint in the process?

   a. What are one or two things your organization might do differently that would WOW people—and position your cultural reputation head and shoulders above your competition?

TEN

Leading Through Challenging Times

Especially in turbulent times, it's up to every leader to be highly visible; proactively listen to fears, criticism, and ideas; and communicate as transparently as possible with everyone. When challenging times drive the need to modify an organization's business practices, technologies, and/or methodologies, it's especially important for leaders to clearly articulate the reasons for change initiatives.

-DEB BOELKES

N o matter what business or industry you are in, every organization faces tumultuous times at some point. Most organizations that have been in operation for decades have had to overcome chaos, disasters, financial hardships, scandals, and sometimes even loss of life. The true measure of a leader often boils down to how adeptly they handle the great trials, tribulations, and tragedies of life, and how effectively they inspire their teams to pull together to overcome completely unexpected adversities.

Arrow Electronics: Leading Through Catastrophe to Create a Culture of Belonging

When I first joined Arrow Electronics, Inc.—as the result of a corporate acquisition—the integration process included an orientation program for all newly assimilated management personnel. I will never forget how the chairman of the board came in to personally tell us the story of "The Great Fire" that had devasted the company less than 20 years before. It was the kind of tragedy that (thankfully) most organizations never have to experience. Some of those that do fail to survive. In Arrow's case, it was a catastrophe that impacted operations and the corporate culture for many years thereafter.

The Great Fire happened in a hotel where the corporate leadership team was conducting a multi-day planning meeting. One evening during the event, a flash fire swept through the hotel conference center, claiming the lives of 13 members of Arrow's senior leadership team. The CEO, an executive vice president, and 11 other senior leaders perished. To this day, that hotel fire still ranks as one of the worst corporate disasters in American business history.

Our chairman went on to share how the catastrophe served as a tipping point, which, understandably, ushered in two years of doubt and uncertainty. During this period, the company struggled to overcome the loss of so many talented executives and to simultaneously deal with a severe recession. It was up to the lone surviving senior executive to hold the grieving company together while he and the board searched for a new chief executive with the right vision, values, and leadership style to shepherd the company out of the crisis.

No one could have anticipated that those who remained would have the fortitude to turn that tragedy into a catalyst for the type of inspiration and drive that ultimately made Arrow one of the world's largest technology distributors. As it turned out, one of the first moves was to promote the executive assistant of one of the lost executives. She was one of the few people who possessed deep awareness of the business issues that had been the focus of the leadership team before the fire. It was a big move for her, but she stepped up to the challenge and played a vital role for many years. She was instrumental in educating other incoming leaders, and she kept the organization running as smoothly as possible. Thrust into a role she had never expected at a tender young age, she went on to become a loving and encouraging corporate matriarch until her retirement over 30 years later.

> No one could have anticipated that those who remained would have the fortitude to turn that tragedy into a catalyst for the type of inspiration and drive that ultimately made Arrow one of the world's largest technology distributors.

The next move was to recruit a new president who possessed a heightened sensitivity for the value of life and relationships, as well as financial astuteness. A former partner of McKinsey & Company, Stephen P. Kaufman joined Arrow as president of the company's electronics distribution business. Four years later, he succeeded the lone original executive as CEO. Eight years after that, Kaufman went on to become the chairman who was now standing in front of us. Mr. Kaufman was the consummate heartfelt corporate patriarch.

By the time he finished narrating this historic tale of tragedy, there wasn't a dry eye in the room. The undeniable takeaways from that session were an understanding of how the current corporate culture came to be, as well as how important, appreciated, and cherished every employee—both old and new—was and would be to this chairman. As a perfect capstone to the story, the chairman's wife brought in a wonderful homemade family-style Italian lunch for all in attendance. These orientation luncheons—homemade and lovingly served by Mrs. Kaufman—were a tradition that endured for as long as Mr. Kaufman was chairman.

Engaging Employees' Hearts and Minds: Lessons from Chairman Kaufman

By the end of the session, not only did I have a far greater appreciation for the new corporate culture, I knew I was right where I belonged. I was impressed that after enduring tremendous loss, the organization had become a family that grew even stronger together. I knew that this transformation was thanks in large part to the dedicated, heartfelt leadership that started at the very top and permeated down through the entire organization—at least until Mr. Kaufman eventually retired. In short, Arrow was a company with values similar to my own—one where I could feel proud to utilize my strong suits.

This transformation was thanks in large part to the dedicated, heartfelt leadership that started at the very top and permeated down through the entire organization.

What a fine lesson that was about leading through extremely challenging times and beyond! Over time, the organizational culture at Arrow helped me refine and elevate the level of empathy and heartfelt leadership my teams and I delivered when working with organizations in crisis mode.

As I pointed out in the previous chapter, WOW Culture Begins with You, you can't win customers' hearts and minds without first winning your employees' hearts and minds. Mr. Kaufman did that better than any leader I have ever known. He engaged employees' hearts and minds from the moment they first walked in the door. He immediately got people on the same page and marching in the same direction through inspirational storytelling and by instilling a strong sense of belonging. Thankfully, Arrow never experienced another crisis of the same magnitude as The Great Fire. But Mr. Kaufman's leadership infused all of our team members—at all levels—with the dedication and pride they needed to carry on through many other challenges and obstacles.

Perhaps most importantly, Mr. Kaufman taught me that you can't win your employees' hearts and minds without exhibiting heartfelt leadership. He exemplified the philosophy that a leader must engage everyone with an appreciation of where they are and who they are. As we have discussed at multiple points in this book, great leaders get to know each of their people on an individual basis: what their lives are like, what their goals are, what motivates them, what their strengths are, and so much more. Being able to tap into your employees' frame of reference is never more important than in the midst of challenging times.

A Consultant's-Eye View of Leading Through Tough Times

Fortunately, tragedies like The Great Fire at Arrow are few and far between. But there are plenty of challenges that organizations and their customers face every day. Well before I joined Arrow, I led corporate consulting and services organizations. Our primary focus was helping global enterprises overcome seemingly insurmountable challenges and redesign broken processes. I learned something about leadership from every engagement—not only about what to do, but about what *not* to do. Here, I'd like to share some of the most important things I picked up about leading during challenging times.

> **Being able to tap into your employees' frame of reference is never more important than in the midst of challenging times.**

Actively assess the employee and customer experience at every level. Why? Because you can't lead your organization through obstacles if you don't know what they are in the first place. As I observed on many occasions, senior leaders are not always aware that certain challenges exist below them in the organizational hierarchy, on the front lines, or in between organizational silos. That's one of the reasons executive teams hire consultants—to ferret out what's hindering operations, how morale could be improved, and how clients' and customers' needs and expectations could be better served.

Have you ever watched the reality TV series *Undercover Boss*, a show that follows high-level executives as they slip anonymously into the rank-and-file of their own organizations? If so, you know that unless an executive started in an entry-level job with their company, they often have little awareness of what really happens each day on the front lines—even if they have been a leader in the organization for years. Similarly, these executives may not accurately understand employees' challenges or customers' experiences.

Commit to identifying—and authentically addressing—your customers' pain points. Often, companies experience challenging times because their customers aren't fully satisfied—or are actively unhappy. Think about it. Have you ever followed the end-to-end journey that your customers go through when dealing with your organization—from the brand awareness process to the purchase and product/service delivery experience to the billing and follow-up customer support processes? How confident are you that every customer has a WOW experience every step of the way?

One way to assess what your customer experience is like is to conduct an annual customer satisfaction survey that covers every touchpoint. Of course, one challenge with customer satisfaction surveys—especially in business-to-business environments—is getting meaningful feedback from every person within your customer's organization who interacts with your own employees. Another challenge is that you may not obtain actionable feedback.

From the customer's standpoint, one of the worst things you can do is ask people to spend their valuable time responding to a long series of questions and then fail to address the problems they identify. Worse yet is to address their issues in ways that make a

> **It's better to not implement a satisfaction survey than it is to set customer expectations and then fail to properly address their noted issues.**

problem worse or create new ones. It's better to not implement a satisfaction survey than it is to set customer expectations and then fail to properly address their noted issues.

Be willing to explore new, innovative solutions. (There's a reason why your old processes aren't getting results!) For much of my corporate career, I led consulting and professional services organizations focused on the design, optimization, and management of call center services for Fortune 500 clients. Occasionally, we had a global client who wanted us to develop what we called bleeding-edge technology solutions so they could deliver beyond state-of-the-art WOW-factor customer interaction experiences. For these engagements, we worked closely with our customers' business process teams and technology gurus to create solutions that had never before been implemented anywhere in the world. While these were high-risk engagements that were not without challenges, it was always interesting. And in the end, we always wowed everyone involved—especially our client's customers (which, after all, was the whole point of the project).

Often, however, we were called in to redesign broken processes— usually after our client had tried to figure out and fix things on their own, but had utterly failed. By the time we were brought in, things were a complete mess—the kind of mess where the organization's biggest customers had complained one too many times to its chairman of the board, threatening to take them to court and terminate multi-million-dollar relationships.

Upon arrival, we usually found the client's management team on pins and needles. They knew their jobs were on the line if we didn't manage to meet a very tight deadline to make things right. Thankfully, these high-stakes projects were just another day at the office for me and my team, but for everyone on the client's team, it felt as though they were teetering on the brink of disaster.

When we agreed to perform these kinds of engagements, we rarely had the luxury of cobbling together some simple off-the shelf solution to automate an existing manual process. Instead, we first had to diagnose the problem. This usually involved following hard-to-find threads through complex Rube Goldberg-like processes. Over the course of the organization's life, systems and processes had been revised over and over, through years of acquisitions and mergers. It was a challenge to untangle these layers as we sought to understand every touchpoint along the customer life cycle experience.

My team and I often commented that our job was like putting together a million-piece jigsaw puzzle where the jigs and the jags no longer quite lined up. We could see where balls were being dropped—often during handoffs between people, systems, and departments. We had to cut out extraneous, outdated, and sometimes even harmful processes, and find creative, more efficient ways to close the gaps that resulted from these unintentional silos. Oh, and did I mention we were almost always working under a tight deadline?

Make sure you and all other leaders are on the same page regarding priorities, strategies, processes, and values. As I mentioned, it was usually in handoffs between silos where we found customers falling through cracks. When we traced the customer experiences from start to finish, all the way up the chain, it was easy to see where the silos started. Once we identified all the places where the balls dropped, we would then present the current process map and the proposed redesign to the customer's senior executive committee.

I would usually take the opportunity to casually say to these executives, "Look to your left and your right. *You* are where the silos originate. Based on our findings, your people are simply adhering to organizational objectives you each define. Our first suggestion is for each of you in this room to get on the same page, as a team, at the top. Then we can redesign and streamline the processes in a way that allows your frontline teams to properly serve your customers in a WOW-factor way."

This often came as quite a shock to those in the C-suite, but they got the message.

Senior leadership teams must work cohesively at the top—not like a bunch of cowboys and cowgirls trying to earn blue ribbons in attempts to outdo each other at the rodeo.

As one astute executive once confided, "What you've shown us is basic stuff. The concepts are simple. The problem is that most of our leaders don't consistently execute the basics day-in and day-out. Or they do it only until the going gets tough. Then they fall back into making short-term profit decisions. Or they go off on their own and do something where everyone's behavior no longer aligns.

Senior leadership teams must work cohesively at the top—not like a bunch of cowboys and cowgirls trying to earn blue ribbons in attempts to outdo each other at the rodeo.

"Or they treat employees in ways that aren't consistent with the values we have espoused, or the values that we want—like having our employees treat our customers well. Obviously, somewhere along the way, it's all breaking down."

Such candid insight is not often conveyed to vendors by senior leaders unless those leaders are utterly frustrated with the behavior of the other executive committee members.

Listen to employees at every level. They often know the most about challenges—and can offer the best solutions. Over my years leading business process consulting practices, I came to discover that the higher people go on the leadership ladder, the less likely they are to take advice from those below them. Instead, when faced with a seemingly unsolvable business challenge, executives are far more comfortable paying high-priced consultants to perform evaluations and make recommendations based on their "expert" analysis.

Perhaps that is due to the way consultants typically present their cases for change—unemotionally and seemingly without bias. Consultants use carefully worded, non-technical language to convey findings based on detailed comparisons of the as-is situation to industry best practices. They explain how current processes undermine the organization's overarching business objectives via professionally prepared graphs, flow charts, diagrams, and timelines. Consultants are skilled at leading the way out of the morass struggling organizations find themselves in and setting a new standard for the industry best practice. A popular anonymous quote often attributed to Winston Churchill says, "Diplomacy is the art of telling people to go to hell in such a way that they ask for directions." Outside consultants are typically in a better position to do that than employees are.

However, at the end of the day, most consultants essentially present what they have learned through interviews and documentation provided by the executives' own staffs. Let that sink in. In most cases, the organization's own employees already possess the information needed to diagnose the problem—and often, they are instrumental in figuring out a solution.

In most cases, the organization's own employees already possess the information needed to diagnose the problem—and often, they are instrumental in figuring out a solution.

As I always told my teams over the years, *everything happens for a reason*. Challenging times may try us seemingly to our breaking points, but remember: It's through navigating chaos and surmounting obstacles that we each learn and grow. Let's take a look at how that played out for some of our executives.

Melissa Reiff
Former Chairwoman and CEO
The Container Store

While Melissa was still the CEO, I asked her to talk about some of the more significant challenges she had to deal with.

When a company has a lot of tenure, it can be very challenging to get people to change. And regardless of tenure, it can still be challenging for many. We can all get very comfortable and *safe* in doing things the same way over and over.

It can be scary to some people. I am compassionate and respectful about that. However, I have told our organization repeatedly, "If we keep doing the same things, we're going to keep getting the same results!"

We must always execute necessary and positive change.

We must always execute necessary and positive change.

Retail is tough. Even though for 30 years we were clicking along, wildly successful in almost every metric, the recession happened. We were impacted like every company, but we successfully endured.

Then we went public in 2013, and, once again, retail got very challenging. We had to be strong, adapt, adjust, and *change*—and that is exactly what we did.

I followed up by asking, "What were some of the surprises or cultural blind spots you had to deal with when you became CEO?"

It is quite different leading a public company versus a private company. In transitioning to a public company, there were a lot of surprises for me.

Now, I was ready for the differences because I did my research as well as possible. But I had never been a CEO before. I had certainly never been the CEO of a public company. I'd never even worked for a public company before. Probably 15 of the 19 members of our leadership team had never worked for a public company before.

We all had some blind spots. I certainly did—for example, when it came to understanding what the analysts wanted and needed after our earnings call to best do their modeling correctly. Working constructively and productively during this process with the board is a must.

I have found that total transparency—the good, the bad, and the ugly—has worked well.

I have found that total transparency—the good, the bad, and the ugly—has worked well. I respect the board, and I believe they respect our leadership team and how we have learned together about operating as a public company.

"You were kind of thrown into that, weren't you?"

Oh, no doubt!

When Kip Tindell made the final decision to take the company public—which I supported, and others did as well—whoa! The IPO experience was certainly a memorable one for us all. Being a public company has so much responsibility—not just to the employees, the customers, the vendors, and the communities, but to *all* stakeholders.

We're in a little bit of a different situation, perhaps, compared to other public companies. Leonard Green & Partners, L.P., a private equity firm, bought our company in 2007. They are a majority holder. They have a strong voice, obviously. And we feel a huge sense of responsibility to perform for them, but still, we have other shareholders and stakeholders that we care about, too.

I have such a tremendous sense of responsibility to all stakeholders—every single one of them—particularly our employees. When we went public in 2013, many of our great employees purchased stock in our company at the IPO opening price. I desperately wanted them to benefit from their investment. But there is only so much you can control.

How the stock market responds is not one of them. I feel very supported by our board, though, with the initiatives we are executing and the direction we are heading.

In terms of other surprises when I became CEO? Thankfully, I was well briefed, because I worked side-by-side, very closely,

with my predecessor, Kip, for many, many years. He was a
great mentor who taught me a lot.

Nancy Howell Agee
President and CEO
Carilion Clinic

While interviewing Nancy, I commented, "I've interviewed
numerous C-level executives and rarely have I found one who said,
'You know, everything has been fairly easy for me.' What have been
some of the bigger career challenges that you've had to deal with?"

Well, two big challenges come to mind. One: Managing
through the pandemic has not been easy for us.

The good news is, I guess everyone was in the same boat. We
all understood each other's pain. But living through the
pandemic has been quite tough.

"During especially challenging times, how do you communicate
with the organization?"

In just the first five months after the start of the COVID-19
pandemic, the executive team and I did over 100 videos. The
utility of video communication works. People like that. We
also e-mailed twice a day, in a very organized way, what we
were doing, the way things really were—being very
transparent.

A lot of people worked from home during the pandemic. But our clinical staff were here, on-site. I felt that if my staff was going to have their lives disrupted, or their lives were on the line, so to speak, and they were going to be on-site, then I was going to be here and I expected the same of my executive team. We made rounds nearly every day.

Our organization is spread over about a four-hour drive, from side to side, geographically. We were somewhere making rounds, listening to people, encouraging them, every day.

For example, just last night I was here until 1:30 a.m. making rounds, and we had a little ice cream social. This was at our major hospital, which is a 725-bed hospital. It is a huge place, but we were trying to be available during all shifts. I think demonstrating availability and communication, being transparent, being clearheaded and calm, and letting people know, "Here's the issue. Here is the goal. We can do it," is important.

> **If my staff was going to have their lives disrupted [during the pandemic]...and they were going to be on-site, then I was going to be here and I expected the same of my executive team.**

I often describe my role as chief cheerleader.

Back when I first became the CEO, we had just gone through a several-year transition—which I was the primary leader of—changing our healthcare delivery system from a collection of hospitals to an integrated clinic model. We literally hired over 650 physicians in two years. We built a lot of buildings. We did a whole lot of things really quickly.

That was right when the Great Recession occurred. We lost a lot of money and had a negative operating margin. The community didn't really understand what we were doing. There was a huge backlash from physicians.

We had to deal with everything from a *Wall Street Journal* investigative article to every agency that regulates us being brought in to say what a bad thing we were doing. It was a very hard time. There were a lot of lessons to be learned through that.

There were many parallels between that and the pandemic we've just been through. Both were financially difficult times.

When I became the CEO, we had recorded a negative operating margin for the three years prior. The first thing the board said to me was, "Would you consider being the CEO?"

The second thing was, "And can you understand that we cannot tolerate a negative operating margin?"

We had to turn the financial ship around. In some ways, it's the same thing now. In just two months, we lost an awful lot of money. Even though we're back to more usual volumes, and although the way we function looks different, we've had to make some very tough financial decisions.

There have been plenty of challenges:
- We had to furlough 1,000 people.
- We had to cut back employee hours.
- We cut pay.
- We began working remotely.
- We accelerated telemedicine.

And we did all this virtually overnight, but it's helped to see us through a really tough time.

The previous time that we had such a financial concern, it was much more structural and, in many ways, within our control. This time, care for our employees, our patients, and our community override the financial circumstances.

Care for our employees, our patients, and our community override the financial circumstances.

Linda Rutherford
Executive Vice President, Chief Communications Officer
Southwest Airlines

Linda and I talked about how things have changed at Southwest over the years. We discussed the Boeing 737 MAX issue that took place in 2019 and 2020. During this time, all 737 MAX aircraft were grounded after two crashes killed over 300 people. It was not Southwest's fault, but it still had to be dealt with. Shortly after that, the COVID-19 pandemic came along. Of course, during that crisis, very few travelers were flying for months on end. Then the federal government mandated COVID-19 vaccines for all federal contractors, which included Southwest Airlines.

I asked, "How do you communicate with your constituents during such challenging times? Has the company brand evolved because of such issues?"

Sure, yeah. We continue to learn a lot.

Culturally, as an organization, we are big about physical touch and in-person meetings. Obviously, that was not possible when the COVID-19 pandemic hit. So culturally, as an organization, we had to pivot to, "How can we do things 'The Southwest Way' but on digital platforms?"

It was everything from creating clever backgrounds when you get into a meeting, to setting the right mood. We had several departments doing different team-building programs like Digital Olympics, where they were having little contests among their teams every day—to have fun and allow our people to let off a little bit of steam, yet still have that teamwork—even though we were not literally sitting next to one another physically. Finding new ways to keep the culture alive has been one of the big things.

Thankfully, we are a very communicative company. We are fortunate that our CEO is an intuitive communicator.

We knew that we would have to step up our communication. The leadership team has been fully on board with that. Our CEO was doing twice-weekly videos for both customers and employees, in addition to a Monday newsline. In addition, our chief operating officer was doing a regular blog post.

We probably communicate more now than we ever have in our history. But you must do that in a time of crisis.

We probably communicate more now than we ever have in our history. But you must do that in a time of crisis, especially one that we had never experienced before like this. We still do not know the end of the story. It has been enduring without an end in sight.

We have learned some things along the way, but we are very dependent on our digital solutions. Thankfully, video is performing very well, from a communications standpoint. It is easy to access. You can get it on your phone. You can get it on your laptop. You do not just read the words. You get to see people, not just hear them. You can see somebody's face and how they are delivering the message. I think it has been very helpful for our employees to be able to connect with the CEO. They see him every week when they are watching these videos.

We have pivoted to more communication—more digital solutions—and rethinking how we can keep our corporate culture fresh, fun, and lively, even in a time that is somber and concerning.

I asked, "Have you ever experienced challenging times when it seemed like there was someone at the senior leadership table who was just out to get you? If so, how did you deal with that?"

One of the worst things you could do to me is question my integrity.

I recall one time, in particular: I was furious because, while working with a group of leaders on a challenge we'd been given, I felt like a peer had questioned my motives and my integrity.

My boss talked to the CEO about it. The CEO was like, "This is a non-issue. This other person obviously misunderstood what was going on. I'm good with what Linda is doing."

My boss came back to me and said, "The CEO's great with it. He now knows what's going on. You're clear."

I then got a *half* apology from the person who created the dust-up. But from that moment on, I knew I needed to be guarded with that person since they might not understand my motives, or give me the benefit of the doubt, or be invested in my development.

That was one situation where I just decided, "I'm going to have an arm's-length relationship there. I'm going to focus on doing no harm and I'm just going to bide my time."

> **You must pick your battles... when you see people's true colors, eventually someone else will, too.**

That was a valuable lesson that I learned from my boss: You must pick your battles. You can't get up every day and fight everything. It is exhausting, and you can become exhausting to other people. You really must decide what battles you are going to pick.

"People can definitely struggle with that."

Especially me, right? I want to fix things. Sometimes I'm moving too fast. When I see a wrong, I want to right the wrong. Or I want other people to right the wrong. Sometimes you just must realize *these things are going to take a little bit of time.*

Throughout my life, I have learned that when you see people's true colors, eventually someone else will, too. Some things you just have to let happen.

Kerry Healey
Inaugural President
Milken Center for Advancing the American Dream

I asked Kerry about the challenges she encountered running for public office. "When you finally ran for office and won, were you running for lieutenant governor of Massachusetts?"

Yes. That was my first office.

"That's gutsy!"

Yeah! I remember my hair falling out. When I got the election results that I had actually won my primary—which was actually more vicious, in many ways, than the general election—I remember feeling my hair release from my scalp and holding a handful of hair in my hand.

"Were you pregnant?"

No. I was just terrified! It was a physiological response.

I was really scared of public speaking and being on television. The first time I had a televised debate, when I ran for state representative in Beverly, I was shaking so hard that the people who were doing the filming thought I might faint on camera.

The studio was freezing cold, and I am very sensitive to cold. My teeth were chattering, like I was at the North Pole. I could not think. I would pull it together when the camera was on me and answer the questions, but after that I realized I really needed help to figure out how I was going to handle the media requirements of being in public office.

I put a lot of effort into becoming more comfortable on camera and understanding how to deal with adrenaline. I started with very practical solutions. For example, the next time I was on television, I wore long underwear under my clothes.

"Then you were probably hot under the lights!"

Yes, and I would be hotter than everyone else, but it helped my nerves. I thought, *Okay. Studios are cold. I get nervous when I get cold. I need to wear long underwear when I go.*

"How do you handle all the criticism that goes with being in the public eye?"

I try to be reflective when people give me criticism or feedback, or when I am being criticized in public.

I try to be reflective when people give me criticism or feedback, or when I am being criticized in public.

I try to take that criticism and really step into the shoes of that person. I try to understand what it is that they disagree with and what they're objecting to. I try to stay open to the possibility that I might be completely wrong and that I need to change.

Wendy Johnson
Former President and CEO
Dale Carnegie franchise, Atlanta, GA

Wendy answered this way when I asked her, "What took you to Atlanta?"

Well, it certainly was not a straight path getting to Atlanta. I have had a checkerboard career. Many of the directional changes I have made along the way were because of personal circumstances, like getting married, or getting divorced, or having a baby.

Each life circumstance you experience forces you to create different visions and goals for yourself. These kinds of life events do not tend to affect men's careers as much. But for women, these events generally create disruption in the trajectory of their careers. It is harder for women to have a smooth ride throughout an entire career because of life events. It is, however, in my nature to adapt quickly to necessary changes. This ability to quickly adapt to change positively impacted my career and contributed to my strong suit of being an early adopter.

I have been in the South since the mid-1980s, so I made that move a long time ago. It was hard for me, because California, where I am from originally, was one of the most beautiful, cool places you could ever know. I didn't want to leave California, but I got married and my husband accepted a job opportunity that took us to Atlanta.

My husband's profession trumped mine, which often happens with couples. So, we moved to Atlanta. Atlanta is a wonderful city, and, overall, the South is a very loving, warm, welcoming place—although it did take some time before I found my social and professional niche in my new home.

So, a change in job for my husband impacted the career that I had built in San Francisco. I started my sales career over again in Atlanta, which impacted my executive stature and my income. I continued to work in many different sales and management positions in the financial, medical, financial consulting, and software industries. During this time, I had my daughter, and many of my decisions regarding my career centered around my childcare requirements.

My marriage failed after only 13 years, and I had to make the decision of whether to move back to California or stay in the South. That was a big decision for me because I love the West and my family was there. I chose not to go back because my daughter was in a wonderful school environment, and I did not want to unnecessarily interrupt her education. But also, I did not want to disrupt my local social and professional relationships and contacts that I had developed in those 13 years.

Career decisions for women are often made around the family. My daughter was at the center of all my career moves. Eight years later, while I was on a sales trip to Johannesburg, South Africa, for a financial software and consulting firm, our country was attacked by terrorists. Yes, that was 9/11.

> **Career decisions for women are often made around the family.**

Here I was, trapped outside the U.S., in another country. My daughter was 16 at the time. Her father was on a business trip, so she was staying with her stepmother. I was in a panic, thinking, *This is just awful. What am I doing here? I have a daughter. These are the last few years I have with her while she is living at home. But here I am, stuck in South Africa. I* was completely unable to protect her at this horrendous time in our country's history.

With air travel completely shut down around the world at that point, it took me a while to get back to the United States. I came back with a whole new vision for my life going forward. It was a cathartic and defining moment for me. I decided that I needed to find a profession that limits traveling so I may be able to be there for my family.

> **I opened my dilemma to the universe. I have found that when you do that, something always happens.**

I opened my dilemma to the universe. I have found that when you do that, something always happens. You are more open to listening to ideas, and asking questions of people leads you to options.

Well, sure enough, I ran into a man at my health club who had just bought the Dale Carnegie franchise in Atlanta. He was looking for a partner, somebody who could manage the business development side of it. So, I spent a few months studying the business opportunity. This opportunity utilized all of the skills that I had developed in my career over the years and presented me the opportunity to develop a whole new set of skills, learning a new industry and running a business.

I then asked Wendy to share how she became the head of the franchise.

I bought a small share initially—less than 20 percent.

But it became quite a wild ride. As time went on, we continually faced financial issues due to my business partner's inability to manage the financial side of the business. Meanwhile, I continued to put more and more of my own money into the company. With each infusion of cash, I eventually grew my portion of ownership to over 50 percent.

About eight years into the partnership, my partner and I parted ways—this sometimes happens with partnerships. One or the other does not meet the other's expectations. With a lack of trust, the relationship fails. It was awful.

Once I owned the majority share of the business, I began to take control of the finances. He pretty much just ran off. Once we had legal separation documents drawn up, he was gone.

"That took a lot of guts on your part. But what choice did you have?"

Well, you know what? I used my whole retirement account and everything else that I had to save the business.

I had no line of credit at the time. I just emptied my entire 401(k) retirement savings into the company. I am proud to say that after a year or so, I got back on my feet, paid off all my debt, and recreated a strong and successful business. It was a wild ride with a great deal of risk.

Lieutenant General Kathleen M. Gainey
U.S. Army, Retired

I commented to General Gainey, "In the corporate world, the marketing department is told to go off and do *this*, but the engineering department is told to do *that*. Before long, they can be working at odds with each other."

I then asked, "Do you have such challenges in the military?"

We most certainly do.

It's all about department heads protecting their money, their people, and their authority. People don't like to share any of those. So, overcoming that is all about trying to work together to develop a shared plan.

- What's the common goal?
- What is it we need to do *together* to achieve that goal?

- How can we get people from each organization to work toward that shared objective?

It's all about department heads protecting their money, their people, and their authority... overcoming that is all about trying to work together to develop a shared plan.

All of that must start at the C-suite—setting the tone, breaking down the barriers, and figuring out, *What are the little projects that we could work on together, to start building relationships and trust?*

So, you start slow and small, and do it in a scalable way. You select a problem that is very important to both parties yet small enough that it can be completed in a six-month period. You ask, "What would be important to you and what could we do together to help make that happen? Let's come up with that solution."

Then, you get those intermediate managers to develop a solution and have them brief the leaders at the C-suite—every 60 days or so. However, as soon as the C-suite leaders start seeing things going astray, they can and must lift the roadblocks that were created or perceived.

Once that project is completed, the leadership and workforce who worked on that project will begin to believe that you are serious about making things better for their organization, not just yours. That is when trust starts to blossom.

REFLECTIONS:

Every leader's primary mission is to get everyone on board and keep them on board, headed in the same direction. It can be challenging to get people to change directions and deviate from "the way we've always done things." To some, change can be downright scary. Others may be open to change, but have reservations or differing opinions on how best to achieve it.

That's why it's important for leaders to develop 360 degrees of authentic relationships within their organization. When you regularly connect with your own leaders, peers, and employees, you increase your chances of accurately understanding any challenges, issues, or roadblocks your organization might be facing. You also develop the strong, empathetic, and trusting relationships you'll need to work together through challenging situations.

Especially in turbulent times, it's up to every leader to be highly visible; proactively listen to fears, criticism, and ideas; and communicate as transparently as possible with everyone. When challenging times drive the need to modify an organization's business practices, technologies, and/or methodologies, it's especially important for leaders to clearly articulate the reasons for change initiatives.

Before a change initiative is put into action, executive leaders and the entire leadership team must clearly lay out what's in it for each stakeholder—from the board of directors and employees to clients, customers, guests, vendors, industry analysts, investors, the media, and the public at large. Articulating what employees have to gain and earning their earnest support is perhaps the most important task. Without the entire team's buy-in and commitment to making the project succeed, even the most well-intended efforts may be undermined by uncooperative staff.

Articulating what employees have to gain and earning their earnest support is perhaps the most important task. Without the entire team's buy-in and commitment to making the project succeed, even the most well-intended efforts may be undermined by uncooperative staff.

Always keep in mind that stakeholders have personal lives, too. Whatever challenges are driving the need for change at work may also be driving changes at home. Storms hitting from multiple directions can dramatically impact a team member's mental health and ability to handle onslaughts coming at them from several directions.

When times get crazy (and even in good times!), break big change initiatives down into small, incremental projects, if possible. The task ahead will seem more manageable, and everyone involved can celebrate little successes along the way. This will help build momentum for the effective implementation of greater things to come.

INTROSPECTIONS:

1   Think back on your career. What are some challenging times you, your colleagues, and/or your organization have been through?

   a. How did you respond to these challenges? What was leadership's response? Was the response helpful, or did it complicate the situation?

2   When something goes wrong at work, or when your organization encounters a challenge, do you tackle the problem on your own or loop others in?
   a. How transparent are you when sharing bad news and obstacles with your team?
   b. If a team member comes to you with a concern or solution, do you listen seriously to their feedback?

3   Do you tend to feel overwhelmed during challenging times? If so, your ability to take appropriate action can be stymied. When this happens, ask a friend or close work associate to listen to your fears, and perhaps ask them to share their fears with you. Knowing you are not alone can sometimes help. Working together to identify a better path forward can help even more.

4   Do you have ideas on how processes could be improved in your work environment? Focus on changes that could increase internal efficiency and also provide a better experience for your customers, clients, guests, and/or business partners.
   a. If so, have you mapped out the current process? Have you identified obstacles and gaps? Can you clearly map out and explain your better approach?

5   Think of the wisest person you ever met—at work, at home, at school, or in your community. Think about how they listened to you. How responsive were they to your questions, fears, and/or ideas? Is there something they did

to make you feel understood and appreciated that you might emulate to help your team members adapt in challenging times?

ELEVEN

Learn from Your Mistakes

I think all of us have done things and then later thought,
Why did I do that? That was not the right way, or a great
way to approach that thing.

*Typically, it happened when I let emotions get in front of
facts. Afterward, I would go back to apologize for the
situation and explain, "Here's what I'm willing to do to
build your trust back in me. I admit, I did the following,
and here's what I'm going to do about it."*
-LT. GEN. KATHLEEN M. GAINEY
U.S. Army, Retired

Some people—myself included—are truly fascinated by the failures that otherwise successful people have experienced. I believe these incidents have a lot to teach us—just as they imparted valuable lessons to the high achievers who experienced them. One reason I am writing this book is because it's vitally important to understand that you can survive mistakes—and be even better for it. As you've no doubt gleaned by now, all of the executive women I interviewed have made their fair share of missteps. Nobody gets everything right the first time! One of my favorite sayings is, "Experience is what you get when you don't get what you want." Ideally, we not only learn from our mistakes, we also grow wiser and use our experience to improve the way we handle things in the future.

> It's vitally important to understand that you can survive mistakes—and be even better for it...Ideally, we not only learn from our mistakes, we also grow wiser and use our experience to improve the way we handle things in the future.

While a mistake or failure might set you back or take you down for the time being, don't let your mistakes keep you down forever. Just get back up onto that saddle and keep riding. What matters going forward is what you do with your newfound knowledge.

The Mistakes That Made Walt Disney...Well, Walt Disney

Are you aware that Walt Disney was fired from one of his first jobs as a cartoonist at the *Kansas City Star* newspaper? His editor told him that he "lacked imagination and had no good ideas." Have you ever thought that Walt Disney lacked creativity? Clearly, Walt learned something from that experience.

When Walt subsequently acquired Laugh-O-gram Films—an animation studio in Kansas City—the company failed, and Walt went bankrupt. Yet, Walt Disney went on to become one of the most successful and creative entrepreneurs of his time. He obviously learned something from that bankruptcy experience, too.

Walt later reflected, "It is good to have a failure while you're young because it teaches you so much. For one thing, it makes you aware that such a thing can happen to anybody, and once you've lived through the worst, you're never quite as vulnerable afterward."

Walt also commented, "You may not realize it when it happens, but a kick in the teeth may be the best thing in the world for you."

A "Major" Mistake in My College Years

Looking back over my own career—and the many mistakes I have made along the way—I would say that one of the biggest errors I ever made happened very early on. In fact, it occurred when I was a freshman in college.

As I mentioned in Chapter 2: Be Open to Outcomes, I began my college education at the University of California, Los Angeles (UCLA). I immediately declared a double major: math and computer science. I chose this double major for two simple reasons.

1. I took advanced placement (AP) math in high school and scored very well on the AP exams, which give me course credit for the equivalent of two quarters of freshman calculus.

2. My father encouraged me to get into computers because he believed they were "the way of the future." He told me that a degree in computer science would position me well for an up-and-coming career path.

Before I go on, recall Jodi Berg's passion for helping people find their superpowers, or things people are really good at doing *and* they really love doing. I wish I had known someone like Jodi back when I was a teenager—someone who could have helped me find my superpowers before I decided on a major and a school.

> I wish I had known someone like Jodi [Berg] back when I was a teenager—someone who could have helped me find my superpowers before I decided on a major and a school.

Since I *didn't* have a Jodi in my life, I made the mistake of not fully getting to know myself, my strengths, my interests, and my educational options before I went to college. I also failed to explore, or even try to learn about, the many potential computer-related career paths that existed at the time. As I now know, certain tech fields might have really piqued my interest. Dialogues with adults working in such positions might have led me to select a different major.

At the time, my rationale for choosing math and computer science was that I was really good at math. But I failed to understand that the only thing I *loved* about math was that I was better at it than all the boys, in terms of test scores and grades. As for computer science, I honestly had no idea what the discipline entailed, and I certainly had no clue about what kinds of jobs one might find in that career field. Like many young people at that stage of life, I was running completely blind.

What I learned from my first computer programming class at UCLA in the early 1970s was that programming entailed sitting at a grungy display terminal in a dank and stale time-share computer lab, typing computer logic instructions onto hundreds of keypunch cards. To me, it was hours of boredom punctuated by periods of frustration when I dropped my box of meticulously typed and sequenced keypunch cards, along with my stack of textbooks, while toiling up or down the computer lab stairs.

When that happened, I not only had to pick up everything, I then had to recompile the deck back into the correct order so my program would run properly. The first time it happened was a nightmare. The second time was the end of the road for me. That was when I made the decision to quit computer science.

Not only did I end up changing majors, I also left UCLA and completely reimagined my career path. After obtaining an associate of arts degree instead of a bachelor of science, I spent five years as a fashion designer. Later, I went back to school to finish my bachelor's degree in business and subsequently obtained an MBA, each with an emphasis in management information systems. In other words, I went full circle—back to computers!—but with a different focus. I found it fascinating to learn about how computers could be applied to running a business.

I went full circle—back to computers!—but with a different focus.

As you've already heard me say, I believe *everything happens for a reason*. My career worked out wonderfully well, and I loved almost every minute.

What If? An Imaginary Do-Over for Young Deb

If I could wave my magic wand, sit down with 18-year-old Deb, and chat with her as a caring mentor, I would advise her to do a little more investigation before walking away in frustration from her coursework at UCLA. I would suggest that she engage in some informational interviews with knowledgeable adults in the computer science field before making any rash decisions.

I know, I know…18-year-old Deb would have replied indignantly, "But I don't even know anyone who works with computers! I don't have a clue where or how to start looking! I don't even know what an informational interview is!" Like many young adults, 18-year-old Deb just wanted to get on with life and not waste any more time.

Nevertheless, 18-year-old me definitely needed some guidance. I should have sought expert advice because I needed a fuller understanding of the many computer-related career options available at the time. I needed a solid objective to work toward— something more specific than simply "getting some kind of job in an up-and-coming industry."

I'll bet that if I had attempted to speak to some of my professors or the dean of the computer science department, they probably could have given me some insights. They might even have connected me to professionals working in some of the major corporations in the area.

It's easy for me to see now what a lost opportunity that was. Within a short drive of UCLA was Jet Propulsion Laboratory (JPL), Rocketdyne, Hughes Aircraft Company, and a whole host of other aerospace and defense contractors. Even computer giant IBM had local sales offices. I could go on, but you get the idea. There were lots of options out there, but I was clueless.

If I had done more homework and sought the advice of adults in the know, who knows how it all might have worked out or where I might have ended up? My life might have been altogether different had it not been for my "major" mistake.

The same could be said for Walt Disney. Nevertheless, he ended up doing alright for himself. I daresay I did, too. It's just too bad that I didn't play all the cards in my hand—and draw a few more from the deck—before I folded and left the game.

> **If I had done more homework and sought the advice of adults in the know, who knows how it all might have worked out or where I might have ended up? My life might have been altogether different had it not been for my "major" mistake.**

The Silver Lining: Discovering and Developing My "Superpowers"

Looking back over the course my life *did* take, I can see that I learned a great deal from that experience. I learned to ask lots of questions, both of myself and of others. I learned that I don't know everything, even now. I learned to ask experts for guidance and seek input from people who have different perspectives.

You may have noticed: I now seek insights from experts all the time. I love to ask deep questions of virtually everyone I meet. I have done so for years now—and I *love* doing it. I guess you could call this one of my superpowers. It's how this book and my three previous books came to be, and it's why I'll probably write more books in the future. So, what I learned from that big mistake early on led to the development of one of my strongest suits—like what happened to Walt Disney.

Everything happens for a reason. Simply learn from your mistakes and move on. Something better is likely waiting in the wings.

Melissa Reiff
Former Chairwoman and CEO
The Container Store

I asked Melissa, "Has there ever been a time in your career when you shot yourself in the foot, and if so, how did you recover from it?"

What a great question. I'm sure there is.

I think there were times when I may have said something that came out wrong. People are human. I am always the first to go, "Oh, my gosh, that's not how I meant it!"

I like to think I'm a great communicator, but sometimes you just say things that people misunderstand or misinterpret. That's why I'm always really, really sensitive and say, "Are you sure you understand what I'm saying? Please, I'm not trying to be condescending. Tell me if I'm not communicating clearly."

I always kind of do that check. I am sure that I have inadvertently hurt somebody's feelings, or I have said something the wrong way, or something like that, which hopefully I was able to amend.

Sometimes you just say things that people misunderstand or misinterpret. That's why I'm always really, really sensitive and say, "...Tell me if I'm not communicating clearly."

Linda Rutherford
Executive Vice President, Chief Communications Officer
Southwest Airlines

When I asked Linda, "Have you ever had a 'shoot yourself in the foot' situation?" she replied, laughing.

All the time! Remember, I'm often wrong but seldom in doubt. All the time.

To that, I asked, "How do you recover when that happens?"

I don't dwell on the failure. That's how you recover. You say, "Okay, that didn't work. I now know to do this differently."

Again, over and over again.

I started out wanting to right every wrong. I then realized I was wearing people out. I had to choose my battles. I probably shot myself in the foot several times with trying to do that. Sometimes you just have to decide, what is the most important thing to worry about or tackle this week? Then those other things just have to wait a little while.

I started out wanting to right every wrong. I then realized I was wearing people out. I had to choose my battles. I probably shot myself in the foot several times with trying to do that.

I pushed an idea kind of forcefully on the company several years ago—which I still believe in the grand scheme of things was a plus for the company—but it still kind of got put into the "this didn't work" disaster category. Here is the story:

Several years ago, two of my team members got an opportunity with *Sports Illustrated*. We were trying to figure out how to break into the New York market. Back then, we could not afford to buy media there. It was super-expensive. So, marketing came to us and said, "We'd love any ideas you can think of to come up with publicity stunts to get Southwest's name out there as we're going into the market."

Then along comes *Sports Illustrated*. They were like, "We'd love to have a partnership with Southwest. We think you're fun and funky. We want to come up with a super-clever way of introducing this year's swimsuit issue."

So they brainstormed and brainstormed. They came up with the idea to wrap an airplane with a cover model. Basically, from the cockpit window all the way down to the tail would be a reclining model who is on the cover of the *Sports Illustrated* swimsuit edition. We all thought it was so damn clever. My boss, Ginger, agreed, "Let's try to go sell it."

Gary Kelly was the CEO at the time. We walked into his office and said, "Look. Here it is."

He gave us the green light!

So, we worked out the whole plan. We took a plane and put it in a hangar. We got it all wrapped. We unveiled it at this giant event in New York with huge publicity. The cover model, Bar Refaeli, went on the *Late Show with David Letterman* and talked about being on a Southwest Airlines plane. We then flew all the models from that *Sports Illustrated* issue out to Las Vegas. They had this big swim party. It was a ton of wonderful, clever publicity.

The plan was that the wrap was going to be on the plane for 45 days, basically through whenever the issue would be on the newsstands. But then, on day eight, we started to get a flood of complaints from flight attendants who told us it was extremely sexist. They did not want to fly on that plane. If that was the plane that ended up at their gate, they were not getting on it to serve our customers.

We were like, "Huh?"

I shot myself in the foot because one of the things I *never* thought about was the employee reaction. I knew the public would think it was clever—and they did—but our own employees, particularly female flight attendants, took issue.

The plane ended up being wrapped for a total of 18 days. That was basically as fast as we could get it out of the

I shot myself in the foot because one of the things I *never* thought about was the employee reaction.

system and into a hangar to get the wrap pulled off. We just very quietly ended that promotion.

I think Gary Kelly would tell you, still to this day, it's the biggest stupid mistake I ever made. He blames himself, too. He's like, "I let you do it. I said it was clever, too. So, we will own that one together."

It was clever. It was marked as a great publicity stunt. But it didn't last as long as I thought it should have. That is probably one of my biggest career gaffes: not considering the thoughts of all the stakeholders.

I still wonder if I had truly thought through all the risks of all the stakeholders, could we have had a communication to our employees that might have headed off some of that criticism? Could we have been ready with some comments, or even a video from Gary, with our head of in-flight, maybe, talking about why we were doing it?

You think of all the different ways we could have maybe mitigated that risk. We just didn't do any of the work because I totally missed getting that stakeholder read.

Kerry Healey
Inaugural President
Milken Center for Advancing the American Dream

While speaking with Kerry Healey, PhD, I asked, "Has there ever been a time in your career when you thought, *Oh, darn. I really shot myself in the foot on that one. I shouldn't have done that!?*"

I probably shouldn't have run for governor. At the time, it made sense because I was the only person from my party who was positioned to do it. At that moment, I had the name recognition, the organization in place, the fundraising capacity, and my governor was stepping down.

I think that my opportunity to run for the top office came a bit more quickly than I would have liked. I would have liked to have had another four years to mature—which is ironic because in another four years I would have been 50, so I would have been very mature. However, I'd been in public life for only four years at that point, so I think that another four years would have been good preparation.

Running for governor seemed like the best thing to do at the time, but it definitely set me back in terms of my political career. I was happy to go on and work on national campaigns. That was an interesting phase in my career.

The way I was able to set myself back on course was, really, just to start over. I started a TV production company. I founded a non-profit focused on rule of law in Afghanistan. I worked on national campaigns—which was something I hadn't done before. I began over again.

I interjected, "You did a little reinvention?"

> Yes. It forced me to reinvent myself. The years following my gubernatorial defeat were great growth years for me. I don't regret starting over. I wouldn't be half as satisfied with my life, as I am now, if I hadn't lost my election. But at the time, it definitely felt like a detour.

The years following my gubernatorial defeat were great growth years for me. I don't regret starting over. I wouldn't be half as satisfied with my life, as I am now, if I hadn't lost my election. But at the time, it definitely felt like a detour.

"That's a great example. You reimagined yourself and started over again. You picked yourself up when you fell and kept going. And it paid off."

I then asked Kerry about the factors that drove her decision to either keep running or stop running for public office. She surprised me with her answer.

> I do not really think I have made that decision yet.

> I have now been out of office for over 15 years. That is a long time. It ended because the people of Massachusetts decided that it should end. So, I ran for governor and lost in 2006. Then, after that, I joined Mitt Romney's campaigns for president in 2008 and 2012, among other things.

> But I did not run myself during those years because I was assisting with those other campaigns. Then at the end of the 2012 campaign, I ended up going to Babson College as president. So, I did not really disengage from politics for another five years after I left office.

I think now the questions are these:

- Would I ever reengage with it?
- Will there ever be a moment when it seems like the right thing to do?

I constantly look at the opportunities. I try to see if there is some way for me to constructively engage. If I feel that, at some point, there is a way for me to be impactful by running for office, then I would consider it.

Wendy Johnson
Former President and CEO
Dale Carnegie franchise, Atlanta, GA

While interviewing Wendy, I commented, "Given how effective you are in terms of dealing with people, selling yourself, and building relationships, I find it interesting that you didn't do any of the Dale Carnegie training yourself."

I believe I would have been a good trainer. But, you know, one reason I never became a trainer was that I was worried that once you become a trainer, if you are good at it, you have little energy left to be creative in the rest of your business. Being a trainer is hard work, and I was trying to run the business.

But the real reason was that you must have a college degree to be a Dale Carnegie trainer, and I did not have one.

Incredulous, I replied, "You mean even though you were running your own franchise, you still had to abide by those kinds of rules?"

Yes, because there is an agency in Washington, DC, called ACCET (Accrediting Council for Continuing Education & Training). Dale Carnegie can give college credit to its participants for their training. However, one of the criteria for certification with ACCET is that all instructors must have a college degree.

"So, you can be the CEO of the organization, but you can't do the training without a degree?"

It is interesting. Not having a degree affects you.

Going through life without a degree means you may have to work for a different-tier company. Without a degree, you look for job opportunities with companies that want seasoned, successful people who have intellectual capital skills and can "hit the dirt running" without a lot of training. You look for companies that do not care about your degree because they do not offer structured career paths or certified training.

> **Going through life without a degree means you may have to work for a different-tier company...You look for job opportunities with companies that want seasoned, successful people who have intellectual capital skills and can "hit the dirt running" without a lot of training.**

If I had it to do over again, I would have finished that final year of course work to get that bachelor's degree. It might have presented different opportunities.

Lieutenant General Kathleen M. Gainey
U.S. Army, Retired

I asked Lt. General Gainey, "Has there ever been a time in your career when you shot yourself in the foot?"

Sure! I think all of us have done things and then later thought, *Why did I do that? That was not the right way, or a great way to approach that thing.*

Typically, it happened when I let emotions get in front of facts. Afterward, I would go back to apologize for the situation and explain, "Here's what I'm willing to do to build your trust back in me. I admit, I did the following, and here's what I'm going to do about it."

"That's not easy to do," I commented.

No. I've swallowed a lot of pride.

"Can you describe a time when you had to go back and say, "Hey, I'm sorry."

Sure. One time was a very public event: It was the very first time I was in USTRANSCOM, where somebody sent an e-mail that I took the wrong way. I immediately shot back something very ugly. It was like, "Stop."

One of the big key lessons learned for me was this:

> **Before you respond to an email, sometimes you just need to... write your response in a Word document...Print it. Come back in an hour, or a day, and reread it. Then think, *How could I rephrase that?*

Before you respond to an email, sometimes you just need to not use the *reply all* feature. Just write your response in a Word document—one that's not even attached to an email.

Print it. Come back in an hour, or a day, and reread it. Then think, *How could I rephrase that?*

"Good point about emails."

We all get tired. We all do stupid things.

Another time I listened to an industry partner come in and say, "Your people are all messed up! You said you value *this,* but *this* is what your team did!"

I took his word for it. I called up the person who did *that* and I said, "That's not how we behave. That's inappropriate, and here's what I want to have done."

He walked out of the office and started doing what I laid out. Fortunately, his boss learned of this.

She looked at the situation, gathered the facts—that I had not—and came to my office to speak to me. She said, "Ma'am, I'd just like to make sure you get the whole story. Here is what they said. Here's what my guy did. Here's *why* my guy did that." She provided me the full context that I failed to ask her subordinate for.

Then she continued, "Now, he's taking your guidance, and doing exactly as you asked, but I think you should know that the industry partner had not done their job. They violated these regulations. They had not done *this*."

I replied, "Woah. I obviously didn't take the time to get the whole story."

"So, do you have any change in guidance for me?"

"Yes. Let's go back and fix this."

Then I sat down and wrote an apology to her subordinate. I walked down to see that individual and apologized to him—in front of his peers.

Then I also left him my apology note, saying, "Wanting everybody else to know it was totally inappropriate for me to jump down two levels and not take the time to fully understand the situation."

I had failed to take the time to wait, talk to his boss, and find out what the truth was. I was working off of emotion, not off of facts. I did not even take the time to ask for the facts.

"That takes a big person to do what you did, in terms of the recovery and the apology. You not only issued a written apology and verbally apologized to the person, but you also did both in front of other people. That was a class act."

Well, it was just a total embarrassment. But I was willing to humble myself in front of others and admit, "The behavior you saw me demonstrate was inappropriate and here's my apology. I want all of you to see that I was wrong. This guy was right and he was doing the right thing. I was lambasting him for it, not realizing it."

> **I was willing to humble myself in front of others and admit, "The behavior you saw me demonstrate was inappropriate and here's my apology. I want all of you to see that I was wrong."**

I think one of the things about the C-suite is, you can run yourself down. I was tired. I was irritable. I let my emotions and my tiredness impact good, sound decision-making.

That's another thing for those aspiring to the C-suite: Be careful because you will run yourself down and not realize it. You've got to have somebody who can tell you, "We're going to unplug here for a day because you're just not making good decisions," or, "You need to go get a couple of days of eight hours of sleep."

When I retired, for the first year, I was sleeping 10 or 12 hours a day. I was just totally spent—exhausted.

You don't realize that because you're running on adrenaline. But you're often making bad decisions. You're rushing to a solution instead of waiting and gathering enough facts. You're just trying to play whack-a-mole, instead of saying, "Which issue do I want to address and why? Is that really a priority?"

"Had you observed somebody else take that kind of recovery action before? Did you have role models in doing so?"

Yes, I did. I had several great examples to follow.

My dad was pretty good about going back to people and apologizing when he jumped at them. I would hear him talk about those situations and how he handled them.

You don't realize that [you're exhausted] because you're running on adrenaline. But you're often making bad decisions. You're rushing to a solution instead of waiting and gathering enough facts.

That made an impression on me; however, I realized it too late. I did not follow his or others' examples as early as I should have because I did not think I was in that bad of shape.

REFLECTIONS:

One of the most important things we can do to build trust in the workplace (or anywhere) is to do what we say we are going to do. Yet, some of our ideas turn out to be better than others. Sometimes, what initially seemed like a great idea turns out not to be as great as we expected.

When you make a mistake, or when you don't get the results that you (and perhaps others) had hoped for, ask yourself what you might choose to do differently if given the chance for a do-over. Don't beat yourself up. Accept the fact that no one is perfect—and remember that all mistakes give you the opportunity to learn a lesson so you can do better next time.

If you can correct the situation, then do so as quickly as is reasonably possible. I say "reasonably possible" because making rash assumptions could cause you to have a knee-jerk reaction that

> **When you make a mistake, or when you don't get the results that you (and perhaps others) had hoped for, ask yourself what you might choose to do differently if given the chance for a do-over.**

makes a bad situation worse. Here are some basic steps to take in a few common situations:

If you were the only one harmed by your mistake: Assess the situation, learn from the experience, and move on. I admit that this advice falls into the "easier said than done" category. We truly are our own worst critics—and I have found that to be especially true with high achievers.

The worst thing you can do is let feelings of guilt over a misstep consume you. Guilt over a miscalculation that impacted only you is a sign that your ego is getting in the way. Letting guilt fester gets you stuck in an unhealthy mindset of unhappiness and self-loathing. In the extreme, guilt can lead to depression. Don't go there.

Feelings of remorse, on the other hand, are about intention and come *from your heart*. Remorse *can* be a valuable first step toward learning. So, if you make a mistake that impacts only you, be your own best empathetic friend. Remind yourself that everyone errs now and then, no matter how smart or experienced or well-intentioned they are.

The ability to rationally assess the cause of an unexpected negative outcome is a healthy sign of maturity. What you learn from the experience can lead to personal, professional, and spiritual growth.

Over time, these personal lessons learned can take you to heights of which you may have never dared to dream.

If someone takes offense to something you have said or done:
Do your best to remain calm, especially if the other person confronts you in anger. Rather than getting into a debate or responding in kind, simply say, "I'm sorry" and politely ask, "What would you recommend I do differently?"

Then listen. Listening with the intent to understand is one of the most important things you can do. It's the one thing almost everyone wants from us at any time, and it's *especially* crucial if someone believes they have been wronged. Once the other person has suggested what you could have done differently, acknowledge their feedback and thank them for their input. If the person ultimately feels that they have been heard, that their problem has been acknowledged, and that their desires going forward have been taken seriously, your relationship has the potential to become stronger than ever before.

> **Listening with the intent to understand is one of the most important things you can do. It's the one thing almost everyone wants from us at any time, and it's *especially* crucial if someone believes they have been wronged.**

This is also a golden opportunity for you to learn a valuable lesson: about how your actions affect others, about leadership, about communication, about your organization's priorities and values, etc. If your own emotions are heightened, wait to consider the feedback more fully at a later time. Having some distance will enable you to evaluate the situation calmly and rationally.

If an action you have taken harms people in some way: Own up to what you did—or failed to do. Put yourself in their shoes and be honest with yourself about the consequences of your decision. Admit to yourself that you did something wrong. Then apologize as soon as possible. Don't let things fester.

- Briefly describe what you did by saying something like, "I was wrong to have (done whatever) and I am sorry."
- Briefly describe how you might have felt if the shoe were on the other foot.
- Briefly say what you will do differently going forward to ensure it won't happen again.

Admitting when you are wrong and explaining how you will handle things differently in the future allows those who were wronged to accept your apology and forgive you.

Whatever you do, don't get defensive by including "but" or "if" in your apology; for instance, "I'm sorry if I hurt you, but..." This will only serve to undermine your sincerity.

If the wrong was made in public: A written apology will leave a lasting impression that you mean what you say. In your communication, you may also want to share any lessons you have learned and explain what you plan to do differently in the future.

Apologizing can be difficult and humbling, but it shows sincerity and repairs trust. Keep in mind that "experience is what you get when you don't get what you want." It's amazing what a learning experience can teach you in the long run—and how "a kick in the teeth" can set you on the path to future success.

INTROSPECTIONS:

1. Think of a time when what you thought was a great idea turned out not to be so great—and the results were not what you expected. What did you learn from that experience?

   a. Did things turn out all right in the long run? If so, what actions and decisions led to the acceptable outcome?

2. Think of a time when you said something that came out wrong, or was taken out of context, or was interpreted in a way that you didn't intend. How did you handle the situation? How could you have rephrased what you said to have achieved a better result?

3. Think of a time when a major decision you made or an action you took harmed someone (or multiple people). Did you apologize?

   a. What did you do to correct the situation?

   b. If you could have a do-over, what would you do differently?

4 What was the biggest mistake you ever made, career-wise? How did you recover?

   a. Knowing what you know now, what would you do differently? Or are you glad things worked out the way they did?

5 Consider your strong suits and "superpowers." Did past mistakes help you identify or hone any of them?

TWELVE

Hindsight Is 20/20

I think I would have been more intentional about this leadership journey earlier in my career. I was more satisfied with staying in positions. I was not willing to move— probably because of my family. I think I should have been a little more open-minded about relocating.

I also should have been a bit more intentional about professional growth.

-NANCY HOWELL AGEE
President and CEO, Carilion Clinic

When I look back over my life and career, I can clearly identify times when I should have paid more attention to the little red flags that went up in the back of my mind. I now know that I had good instincts (or women's intuition, or gut feelings) even before I became an adult.

If I were magically granted the opportunity to live my life over again and do just one thing differently, I would choose to call a time-out on myself whenever those little red flags popped up. I would encourage myself to analyze why the flags were there, and what they might be telling me about the situation I was in. I honestly think those were times when a guardian angel was trying to get my attention: "Hey, Deb, think about this!"

> If I were magically granted the opportunity to live my life over again and do just one thing differently, I would choose to call a time-out on myself whenever those little red flags popped up. I would encourage myself to analyze why the flags were there, and what they might be telling me about the situation I was in.

Sometimes I heeded those subtle warnings and instinctively removed myself from the situation. But more than a few times, I wasn't brave enough, or mature enough, or pragmatic enough to stand up for myself and say *NO*. Those times when I failed to stand up for myself are the ones I regretted later. As the title of this chapter says, hindsight is 20/20.

My Initial Business Plan: Creating Custom Couture Masterpieces

As I have shared previously, after working for five years as a fashion designer, I went back to college to finish my undergraduate degree and then get my MBA. I chose to go back to school because I was sick and tired of working for bosses who were role models of what *not* to do as a leader. I knew that staying in organizations where the owners carried on like spoiled, belligerent children would soon become intolerable. I truly believed I could do a far better job as a leader—if only I had more in-depth knowledge of how to manage all aspects of a business.

In hindsight, I now realize I had more business acumen than I gave myself credit for. While working at my father's agricultural pump business every summer growing up, I had learned to complete many foundational tasks like bookkeeping, and I also had a good understanding of the "soft skills" needed to engage employees and customers. I probably could have attained success as a leader with this skill set alone, but I have never regretted that I got an MBA.

One regret, however, was not honoring my *intention* for getting that MBA—and that's the story I would like to share with you here.

After earning my MBA, my intent was to run my own fashion design business, focused on creating custom garments for wealthy women who wanted to have a distinctly gorgeous look of their own. My ability to listen to the needs and desires of such affluent women, combined with my ability to transcribe their ideas into designs that fit and flattered them, was something I excelled in. In other words, creating custom classic couture masterpieces that women loved and felt good in was a strong suit of mine.

> After earning my MBA, my intent was to run my own fashion design business... Creating custom classic couture masterpieces that women loved and felt good in was a strong suit of mine.

I discovered this *superpower*—as Jodi Berg would call it—quite serendipitously after my first husband, a U.S. Naval officer at the time, left on deployment. Upon his departure, I quit my swimwear design position in Southern California and moved east for the duration of my husband's absence. As I discussed in my first two books, *The WOW Factor Workplace* and *Heartfelt Leadership*, during my high school years, a wonderful family took me in after my mother's death and became my "adopted" parents. While I was working on my associate of arts degree in fashion design, they relocated to New Canaan, Connecticut—which is not far from New York City. They generously offered me a place to stay rent-free while I took undergraduate business classes at the University of Connecticut.

To pay for my tuition and books, my "family of the heart" convinced me to work part-time creating custom designs for the wives of corporate executives who lived in the area. I loved doing so, and my clients loved my creations. They came back every time they needed a unique ensemble for a special occasion. In fact, I had to turn down some of their business to ensure I had time for my studies!

One day while I was creating a truly gorgeous wedding gown for the daughter of one of my clients, my adoptive dad said, "You need to make this your full-time business when you're done with school. These women love what you do, and they seem happy to pay you whatever you ask. We can turn our barn into your design studio and help you get started. This business of yours is a real winner."

I was thrilled. I had never dreamed of having such a fabulous business. Now I not only had a proven business model with a healthy and growing client base, I also had a place to call *my studio.* I was more excited than ever to finish my business degree so I could run a sure-to-be-successful business of my own. It was a dream come true.

"You Will Follow Me": A Red Flag Ignored

Unfortunately...

When my husband came back from deployment, he wasn't so keen on the idea of my establishing a couture design business in my folks' barn. In fact, he informed me, "When I'm done with my next assignment, we're going to live in California, not Connecticut."

I replied, "But the client base for my custom designs is in the New York area. The fabric houses are in New York City. My clients love going to the city with me to personally select their fabrics. They love having me help them select just the right accessories at the stores on Fifth Avenue. The whole thing is a special experience for them. L.A. just isn't the same. It's much too casual. For my custom classic couture business to be successful—at least the way I have proven it can be—it must be in the New York area, where I've already established a reputation and a great client base."

He responded, "I'm not following you. You will follow me."

What a gut punch that was.

I struggled to accept that conversation, but the discussion was over. My husband was not about to change his mind. As I thought about it later, I considered my wedding vows: to love, honor, and obey (*obey* is a traditional marriage vow that is commonly omitted these days). I had made that commitment. I would simply have to find a way to succeed back in California, whatever that meant.

As you already know, I ended up completely changing course. I spent nearly 30 years going up the ladder in the world of technology. I never looked back at the fashion design business after that fateful conversation. It hurt, but I accepted the situation for what it was and moved on.

If I could have foreseen the future and realized how the cards would ultimately play out over the next decade, I might have elected to fold my hand, right then and there. The marriage was not destined to succeed for a variety of reasons. Marriage is a two-way street—a loving partnership of mutually respectful give-and-take—not a relationship in which one person dictates and the other obeys. But I was committed to honoring my vows, at least at the time.

> If I could have foreseen the future and realized how the cards would ultimately play out over the next decade, I might have elected to fold my hand, right then and there.

In hindsight—from a career standpoint, at least—I now believe I should have been true to myself. I should have played to my strong suit rather than try to force-fit myself into glass slippers meant for Cinderella.

Of course, who knows how my life might have played out if I had said goodbye to my first marriage at that point? I certainly would not have my two wonderful sons—now fathers themselves—whom I love so dearly. I wouldn't have the wonderful daughters-in-laws I cherish, nor would I have four adorable granddaughters of whom I am so proud. Seeing them succeed as they grow up is one of my life's greatest privileges.

Moreover, I cannot begin to imagine what my life would be like without the man who subsequently became my wonderful partner, best friend, and soulmate—whom I've now been married to for over three decades.

So, even though hindsight may be 20/20, I'm quite certain everything happens for a reason. When you play to your strong suits and learn from your mistakes, life usually has a way of working out for the best. Perhaps it is a good thing that we cannot go back and have do-overs.

When you play to your strong suits and learn from your mistakes, life usually has a way of working out for the best. Perhaps it is a good thing that we cannot go back and have do-overs.

To Prevent Regret, Live Your Life With Intent

I recently had a reflective conversation with a retired executive friend about a certain key question I like to ask my leadership development clients: *Are you happy with your life and do you love what you are doing?*

I explained the reason why I ask this question: It causes people to do some soul searching. I've found that a common initial response is for executives to express contentment with all the *privileges* and the *money* and the *trappings*…the things that *other people* think are representative of a successful life.

But then I'll ask my clients again: *Are you* really *happy with your life and do you* really *love what you are doing?* Then I wait for a more thoughtful and reflective response. If they can honestly answer *yes* to that question, then indeed, they have reason to be satisfied with their success.

But I often find that underneath the confident façade they project to the world, many of my clients are not truly happy. Some will finally confide that they feel stuck with nowhere to turn. They are afraid to make a career move or a lifestyle change because the money is too good to walk away from. They like the comfort of knowing that others are impressed with their status and wealth.

> I often find that underneath the confident façade they project to the world, many of my clients are not truly happy. Some will finally confide that they feel stuck with nowhere to turn.

Eventually they say something like, "How could I possibly leave this job (or this relationship)? If I did, it would seriously impact my kids (or my kid's schooling, or my parents, or whomever). I cannot just walk away from this life I've worked so hard to attain."

I then asked my retired executive friend, "Did that ever happen to you?"

She replied to me this way:

I call all that *the bumper cars of life*. It's when you've got all these responsibilities, and you've accumulated all the trappings, but then suddenly things happen that you never anticipated.

Our ultimate success in life is based on what you talk about so often, Deb. It's about keeping a positive attitude and taking charge of what you can control.

I've learned over time that it's important to set an intention for my actions. Whenever I discovered that I was not really doing what I had wanted to be doing with my life, that's when I knew I had to take a time-out. I would make a concerted effort to get away and quietly explore deep within myself—to get in touch with my real, authentic self. I would ask myself that tough question: *What do I really want to do?*

Once you identify what that looks like, you can assess what it might take to get there. It helps to consider alternative approaches. Most of all, you can't let yourself settle into that victim mindset of *I'm just stuck here. I've got to keep doing this because of...x, y, or z.* You must get yourself out of that kind of victimhood thinking.

You can't let yourself settle into that victim mindset of *I'm just stuck here. I've got to keep doing this because of...x, y, or z.* You must get yourself out of that kind of victimhood thinking.

Instead, ask yourself, *What can I take charge of?* Then architect a path for yourself and make it happen. It's up to you to do that. No one else can do it for you. Others might advise you, but only you know what's right for you, in your heart.

I used to advise my own mentees that sometimes, if they thought they couldn't change their circumstances at work, or if they were working for a bad leader—and there are a lot of those—they could either whine about it or they could ask themselves, *Where else can I get some inspiration?*

There are a ton of places to do that. In the end, each of us is responsible for our own self-development. It's not the responsibility of your boss. It's not human resources' responsibility. *You* are in charge. It's totally up to *you* to discover the truth about what will truly make *you* happy.

It's not easy to do, especially if you have kids at home and you have a busy life. But you must carve out some quiet time to reflect and get in touch with what is in your heart. Then you must put an action plan in place for whatever it is you want to accomplish.

It may not be possible to make whatever it is happen overnight. But it won't happen at all if you don't put in the effort and put an intentional plan in place.

Great advice.

> **Each of us is responsible for our own self-development. It's not the responsibility of your boss. It's not human resources' responsibility. *You* are in charge. It's totally up to *you* to discover the truth about what will truly make *you* happy.**

While hindsight might be 20/20, an even more powerful truth is that life is all about learning and growing. The seeds of opportunity are often found in situations where we don't get what we want and end up somewhere we really didn't intend to be.

Life is a never-ending set of rounds until someday the game is over. In the meantime, it's about evaluating the cards we are dealt, discarding the cards we don't want or that don't make sense to keep, and then drawing new cards from the deck to see where that takes us. You don't always get a winning hand. But with some calculation and luck, and with the courage to take a risk, you might ultimately come out a winner.

Remember, experience is what you get when you don't get what you want. So, when things aren't working out the way you would like, take time to reflect, learn from your experience, put a new plan in place, and move forward. Ask yourself: *Am I really happy with my life, and do I really love what I'm doing? OR—might I look back on this period of my life and regret the choices I have made?* Then, move forward with intent and confidence while playing to your strong suits.

Melissa Reiff
Former Chairwoman and CEO
The Container Store

I asked Melissa, "If you had it to do over again, would you do anything differently?"

You know, whatever the lawyer thing is in me, I always felt that calling. But I am so grateful and happy with my career and I hope that I have made a difference.

I kind of wish I had gone back for more education. But then, the reality was I did not want to go back just to do that because I was perfectly happy. So no, I do not regret that.

There are certainly things as a mother that I would have done differently—of course.

Maybe I would not have been quite so intense about everything. As they say, *Don't sweat the small stuff.* I would also try to better prioritize those things that are truly important.

But I am *beyond* proud of my two children—Jacob and Piper—the people they have become and the families and careers they have. They are my everything, along with my husband, Ron.

Oh, there is one thing I would have done differently: I definitely would have taken more business classes at SMU. I would have taken more finance and accounting courses because I have had to learn all that "on the job." I had to be responsible for the P&L, the balance sheet, and all—along with our great CFAO at the time, Jodi Taylor, of course. But it has also been great fun and I have loved it.

You know, my background was marketing, training, creative, advertising, PR, sales management, etc. Then I came to really love and respect supply chain, tech and finance, and even accounting. I love distribution. I love analytics. I love data. I love CRM—customer relationship management. I love it all now because I get to do it all. That has just been a blast.

But I think if I could have had a better foundation for all that accounting, finance, and specifically business acumen, it would have certainly helped. It would not have hurt, that's for sure.

I would have taken more finance and accounting courses because I have had to learn all that "on the job."

Jodi Berg
Retired President and CEO
Vita-Mix Corporation

When I asked Jodi, "What would you want to share with people about important lessons learned?" she responded:

One of those important lessons learned, something that I value, is this: When we are passionate about something—you can call it *instinct*, you can call it *your radar*, you can call it *intuition*, you can call it whatever you want to call it—but when you're passionate about something, then you will be in tune with things that are happening in that space. You have an awareness.

If you question that at all, just consider what happens when you are buying a different car. The moment you start looking at a new car, it suddenly seems like that model car is everywhere.

It is not that these cars just dropped out of the sky. It is that you now have a different lens with which you look at the world. Your lens is now allowing you to selectively pick up on the car that you are interested in.

So, if you are passionate about something, you can see things or pick up on things that are in that space—things that you might have otherwise ignored.

Another important lesson that I learned along the way was this: Sometimes it is not necessarily better to learn and do something the same way everyone else has done it. What is important is to focus on what you are ultimately trying to achieve. Then you can figure out how *you* can do it, based on *your* passions and what makes sense to *you*.

You are more apt to be successful overcoming obstacles if you intuitively know what works for you. My mom always called it the *Quarter Turn Theory*. She came up with her *Quarter Turn Theory* because she believed if you focus on something, but if you are not intentional and careful, you will take a quarter turn and you will end up going in a different direction.

If you focus on something, but if you are not intentional and careful, you will take a quarter turn and you will end up going in a different direction.

But it works the other way, as well. If you feel like you must do something in a certain way, just one little quarter turn can change the entire trajectory of who you are as a person and the impact that you can have while you are on this planet. In my case, it was a catastrophic illness that almost killed me. Hopefully, other people will not have to go through that kind of a mind shift!

If I could figure out how to help people do that, in a way that people could grasp—a formula or something so they don't have to go through a near-death experience—imagine the impact that people could have.

Exponentially more important, imagine the personal fulfillment and joy that individuals could have. You do not have to go very far—perhaps just go into a bookstore or read any sort of magazine—to realize that people everywhere struggle to find internal fulfillment and joy. I have two young adult daughters. Even with me sharing this message and living it, they still struggle with this.

Once you see it, it is not complicated. But you must have that moment where you go, *aha...AHA! Okay...I see it!*

Then you can do something differently.

"Yes, if we can just find a way to have an aha experience without having the kind of scary experience, like the one that caused you to realize, 'Oh my gosh, there's only so much time on this planet and I'm going to live my purpose now!'

"When all of a sudden it comes to you, when you just start focusing on what really is meaningful to you, what really matters to you—forget about trying to get ahead, forget about trying to earn this big title, or whatever it is—and do what is really meaningful to you, it's amazing how you will create that WOW experience, not only for yourself, but for everyone around you."

That is when you end up becoming successful, because you are not inhibited by the obstacles that come your way. You just overcome them.

Like I said, in my case, the opportunities just kept laying themselves out in front of me when I was not even looking for them or asking for them. I was just working and loving it.

That is when the leaders above you say, "Oh, wait a minute. This person who is so successful making things happen should be doing this and that for us."

I'm just a sample size of one, but when all those opportunities were presenting themselves—like when I was first asked to head up the household division, then when I had this vision for what Vitamix could become—I was asked to be the president and CEO.

All the while, I was a mom with two young daughters. I was so busy. I was trying to be a great mom *and* I was trying to lead this company to achieve this vision. Sometimes we can convince ourselves that we are doing the right things for our kids.

I had an executive coach at work. I wish that I could have had an executive coach for my life, someone who would have looked at me at home. They might have told me, "I know you think you're doing what's best for your kids, but through their lens, you're not."

In hindsight, I now realize that I did not take the time to see life through their lens. I saw life through a mom lens, a mom who wanted to gift and bless and grow, with the ultimate purpose of helping my daughters become strong, confident contributors to the world, in a way that gives them joy. That was my purpose as a mom. Every decision I was making was an attempt to make that happen.

But I did not see that they just needed more of my time. I would do that differently.

"What else might you have done differently?"

Sometimes I wish I had married a different person. But if I had married anyone else, I would not have the two wonderful daughters I have today. They are amazing!

I do wish I had divorced a lot sooner. Yet, although I know it would have been better for me, I don't know if that would have been better for my daughters.

Every other option also would have come with regrets—just different ones.

Every other option also would have come with regrets—just different ones.

Nancy Howell Agee
President and CEO
Carilion Clinic

Nancy Agee had this to say when I asked her, "If there was anything that you could wave your magic wand and do over again, is there anything in particular you would have done differently?"

I think I would have been more intentional about this leadership journey earlier in my career. I was more satisfied with staying in positions. I was not willing to move—probably because of my family. I think I should have been a little more open-minded about relocating.

I also should have been a bit more intentional about professional growth.

There have been a couple times in my life when I have reported to someone I felt was not a good leader. I tolerated it and worked around it, instead of confronting it. I have always said I would never do that again. Thankfully, I have not had to. But there were two times when I thought, *This is not a good situation. He is not a good leader.* The good news is I waited it out. He is gone, and I am not *(smiles)*.

But in hindsight, these are the kinds of things that are not about *you*. It is about how an unethical leader is affecting the organization. I learned some lessons going through that. I think it is good to take the risk of confronting it by saying, "I'm not happy about this situation."

But you risk losing your own job and your own credibility. In my case, I should have gone above this person and taken that risk. The good news is that at some point, some of us did, and it changed the organization.

It is tough to do. I get that. It is tough to do. It's tough to risk complaining about a boss. I have a little brass turtle I keep on my desk to remind me that a turtle never gets anywhere without sticking her neck out.

> **I have a little brass turtle I keep on my desk to remind me that a turtle never gets anywhere without sticking her neck out.**

"Is there anything else you might have done differently?"

Honestly, I think I would worry less.

Linda Rutherford
Executive Vice President, Chief Communications Officer
Southwest Airlines

Linda Rutherford had this to say when I asked her, "If you had it to do over again, what would you do differently?"

I would probably tell my younger self to be braver than I was.

I also think I would have had a reckoning—a lot sooner—about *Don't sweat the small stuff. This will all be okay.*

For several years, I was trying to be great at everything and not let a ball drop. I now think the pressure that put on me was unreasonable in terms of what I was doing to myself. If I could, I would look back and say to myself, "You should have cut that out about three years sooner than you did," to give myself some grace.

I also wish I could have realized that kids are resilient. They are forgiving. The most important thing they need is you. They need you—the unstressed you. I think that would have been something I would have told myself to do.

"Do you think you put yourself under more stress at home as a mother, or at work as a careerwoman?"

It was most certainly as a mother.

I was just talking to a colleague of mine about the ages of our kids. She said, "Now is a really good time to kind of dig into the business. Your kids are grown, and now you'll feel less guilty."

I was like, "You just voiced exactly what I was thinking."

There is just that pressure that we put on ourselves to be everything—the super-mom, the super-executive, the super-friend, the super-spouse. That cape gets torn after a while. You just can't do everything constantly.

So, yeah, I think there is just that pressure that we put on ourselves to be everything—the super-mom, the super-executive, the super-friend, the super-spouse. That cape gets torn after a while. You just can't do everything constantly.

Now that I'm on the other side of all that, I see that if I was afraid of being brave, there was no reason to be. I now know I would be welcomed into the tribe and I would be appreciated for being brave.

"In hindsight, was there a point in your career when you now wish that somebody had said that to you then?"

I do think my boss of 23 years, Ginger Hardage, did say it at some point. That was a turning point for me.

Kerry Healey
Inaugural President
Milken Center for Advancing the American Dream

With such a vast array of leadership career experiences—from serving as a public policy maker to running higher educational institutions and more—I asked Kerry, "If you had it to do over again, what would be one of the bigger things that you might do differently?"

I would try to figure out how to better integrate my personal life and being present for my family during periods of intense professional engagement.

I was married for 30 years, and my children grew up during the time that I was engaged in politics. If I had the opportunity to do it over again, I would have paid more attention to the experience my family was having during some of those more immersive work years. My job impacted their lives as well.

I then asked Kerry to share some of her best advice to help women advance.

I think women should test their fearlessness more. They should push themselves into situations that make them uncomfortable, so they will learn to build skills that allow them to succeed in places that are unfamiliar to them.

One lesson that I learned—and another piece of advice I have for anybody who wants to go into politics—is this: You cannot have any unconsidered opinions. You must make lists of everything that people expect you to have an opinion on. You must know *why* you believe whatever it is you believe. You must be open to criticism, like, "That's not a good argument," or, "Your belief system is wrong for these reasons." If you cannot defend a belief, then you should not hold it.

> **You cannot have any unconsidered opinions...You must know *why* you believe whatever it is you believe...If you cannot defend a belief, then you should not hold it.**

This notion of not having unexamined beliefs is extremely important in politics. I think that being able to defend your beliefs gives you confidence over time. Some people may feel ambushed if someone criticizes them for a particular action or belief, especially if that belief or action is something that was done without reflection.

My general advice would be to acquire as many skills as you can in several related fields. Ultimately, bringing more skills to the table from a broader base is going to make you a better leader. So, in a nutshell, be a generalist, never stop gathering skills, and learn how to deal with the media.

Wendy Johnson
Former President and CEO
Dale Carnegie franchise, Atlanta, GA

I asked Wendy, "If you had to do it all over again, is there anything you would have done differently?"

I would say that there are a couple of things I would have changed.

I still think about the many times I picked up my daughter from school or daycare while I was on a conference call. Here's this little girl who can't wait to tell me about her day, and I'm whispering to her, "Shhhh! Shhhh! Quiet. Quiet!" She couldn't talk to me because I was too busy talking on a conference call.

I wish I had enforced better starts and stops on myself. I should have clearly delineated when I was a mother and when I was the businesswoman. I just dragged her along sometimes—when I think she

I wish I had enforced better starts and stops on myself. I should have clearly delineated when I was a mother and when I was the businesswoman.

wanted me to be present. I feel that sometimes she did not have the attention she needed and deserved.

I think that the current work-life balance movement is very good for working parents because it's honoring that you are a parent, and there are things you need to do. You need to be present for your children. If you have a stay-at-home husband, that is fine. He can go to all those events when you don't get to.

I think it is nice that businesses honor family responsibilities more today than they did when I was raising my daughter. I felt I had to keep my family under wraps. I would have loved to have been proud of being a mom, and more open about my experience as a mom. Instead, I think I was so worried about being judged negatively that I just didn't talk about my family.

I didn't dare talk about my child or bring pictures out at work. I did not even have pictures of my child on my desk. I just didn't because I was burned so many times by what I felt were off-putting comments like, "Who is taking care of your child?" and all that, mainly because I was traveling. I think if I had not been traveling so much, maybe I could have gotten away with talking more about my family.

Honestly, I felt looked down upon—at least by some of the other women in the office. It was funny that it was not just men. It was also women whom I felt chastised me. Men simply didn't want any excuses. They just wanted to be able to tap you to do something whenever they needed you to do whatever it was that needed to be done.

Back then, when a woman told her male boss she was pregnant, it was usually a discussion the male boss hoped would never happen. If the woman was a hotshot executive, and she told her executive boss she was pregnant, what would that mean? It is supposed to be a happy moment for her, but instead it was always a difficult conversation for everyone.

Unfortunately, sometimes people get married without even discussing whether they even want to have a child—and what that would look like, and what each of their expectations are. I would most definitely do that differently. Part of the failure of my marriage was poor communication. He never really articulated that he wanted me to stay home. It was just something I sensed from the way he reacted and behaved at times. But we never really talked about it.

If he had actually *told* me he wanted me to stay home, I honestly don't know what I would have done. I think it was obvious that I was happier working. It was obvious to me that the Wendy who worked before the baby, the Wendy who stayed home with the baby, and the Wendy who went back to work after having a baby were each totally different. I needed to have my business life.

I do believe there is something to be learned from this work-life balance movement. As Americans, when we go to Europe, we find lunch for Europeans can last two or three hours. You will have a glass of wine or a beer. We don't do that in America. We just work, work, work. That's all we do.

I do feel like this new focus on having more work-life balance is going to be a good thing for executive women. I hope we are serious about making sure that people can fully live a

I think it was obvious that I was happier working. It was obvious to me that the Wendy who worked before the baby, the Wendy who stayed home with the baby, and the Wendy who went back to work after having a baby were each totally different. I needed to have my business life.

family life *and* be a successful careerperson.

In fact, one of the newer generations—the millennials—have changed it to life-work balance. Life comes first, prioritized ahead of work. What does that say? It says, *My life matters, and my children matter.* I think this is a very good thing.

Lieutenant General Kathleen M. Gainey
U.S. Army, Retired

When I asked retired Lt. General Kathy Gainey, "If you had it to do over again, is there anything you would have done differently?" she had this to say:

Oh, there are lots of little things I would have done differently—situations, decisions, approaches, lots of little things. After I did something and it did not turn out quite right, I'd think, *What could I have done differently?*

My husband, Ed, was always great about being my sounding board. We would share things and he'd say, "Well, what are you going to do differently? What were the other options you could have taken?"

One of the things he taught me was this: Every time you are trying to develop a solution, look at three different ways to do it. Do not look for just one solution; look at three different ways.

Then, after you select the criteria that you are going to use to make the best possible decision, evaluate all three courses of action against those criteria. Each of the courses are going to have good and bad aspects.

Maybe what you find, once you have had a chance to look at the various pros and cons, is that you should develop a hybrid of those options. But if you look for only one solution, and that is the only solution you pursue, it is going to have pitfalls.

He taught me how to broaden my analysis skills.

I asked, "Is there anything else you would do differently if you had it to do over again?"

One thing I would do is find time to sleep more. I would have made better decisions if I had learned how to get eight hours of sleep each night.

I lived for years on six, and five, and four hours of sleep. As a result, I do not think I made as good of decisions as I could have. Nor was my temperament always as pleasant as it could have been had I received more sleep.

What was I accomplishing, line-by-line, in those hours that I stayed up and answered emails?

What was I accomplishing, line-by-line, in those hours that I stayed up and answered emails?

Was I really comprehending what I read?

Were my answers well-thought-out and coherent?

"What would you have done to get more sleep?"

Not answer as many emails, but instead prioritize them and focus on the truly important ones. Also, I should have asked my staff to prioritize the paperwork I did take home to read.

But there is a fine line. You are trying to learn. You are trying to grow. You are trying to answer questions.

Over time, I just came to realize how important good, sound sleep is, when it comes to making good decisions. Unfortunately for those I worked with, that was very late in my career.

REFLECTIONS:

Given what they know now, here are some of the most common things our women on top suggested they would have done differently—and that you might take into consideration as you move forward:

Enforce better work-life balance:
- Regularly ask yourself: *Am I really happy with my life and do I really love what I am doing?* The more honest you are with

yourself, the more balanced, fulfilled, and—yes, successful!—you will be.

- Be more present (or in the moment) in your personal life and for your children. What your loved ones need and want most from you is often your time and presence.
- Prioritize what's really important—don't worry about the small stuff. Learn to delegate nonessential tasks to others.
- Give yourself some grace—there is no need to be perfect at everything or to do everything.
- Get plenty of sleep.

Be intentional about your professional development:
- Take business courses, financial management classes, or whatever professional development opportunities make the most sense for your career trajectory. The broader your skill set, the more effective you will be as a leader.
- Know what your goals and passions are. Take charge of actions and decisions that are under your control and move forward with purpose.
- Don't stay in one position too long if there is no room for growth.
- Be openminded about relocating, and about considering new positions and career fields.
- Be able to articulate why you believe what you believe. Be open to changing your opinion when new information presents itself.
- Learn to deal with the media.

Be braver:

- Do things your own way.
- Listen to your intuition.
- Look for multiple solutions to every problem. This gives you more options and greater confidence and enables you to pivot with agility when circumstances change.
- Confront unethical behavior—report a problem manager to higher-ups.
- Know your life partner's expectations and vice versa. End a marriage that isn't working.
- Be more open at work regarding the fact that you are a mom—and that your children are an important part of your life.

Many of my executive friends and clients would concur with these bits of advice. This to-do list just might be one of the most important pages you will find in this book, in terms of succinctly guiding you on your journey. Tag it, highlight it, recommend it to others, and refer to it often.

INTROSPECTIONS:

These "Introspections" are a bit different from those in previous chapters in that they should be answered and acted upon (more or less) in order. Think of them as a blueprint for living a more purposeful life—one that you'll be able to look back on with pride and fewer regrets.

1   Are you truly happy with your life?

2   Do you really love what you are doing?

3   Do you feel stuck where you are, either at work or at home (or both)?

4   What's keeping you stuck there?

5   If you could wave a magic wand, what would you really want to be doing?

6   If you could change just one big thing, what would that one big thing be?

7   Assess what it might take to make that happen.

8   Consider alternative approaches.

9   Determine how you can take charge of what you can control.

10   Now, set an intention for action.

THIRTEEN

Special Section: Juggling Career and Motherhood

We hear a lot about work-life balance. I think that sometimes, as women, we put intense pressure on ourselves to make sure that balance comes down to the day and the hour. When you put yourself under that kind of pressure, then there can be days—or weeks or months—where it just feels like you're losing at everything.

That was sort of a stress spiral for me until I figured out for myself that it was more of a yin and yang. It was not going to be perfect every day, or every week, or every month. But I would do the most important thing that day, or the most important thing that week. Sometimes your kids win. Sometimes your spouse wins. Sometimes work wins. It's more like achieving work-life harmony.

-LINDA RUTHERFORD
Executive Vice President, Chief Communications Officer
Southwest Airlines

I regularly book public speaking engagements and lead discussion groups for women in leadership programs. One of my most-requested topics is *How to Achieve Work-Life Balance.* Virtually everyone wants guidance on how to manage it all.

Let's face it: "Having it all" is not easy—but it can be done. The key is to find what works best for our own personal situations at any given stage of our ever-evolving lives. Of course, just when we think we've found the perfect answer, life has a way of changing on us. But that's what life is all about. It's a journey of learning and preparation for handling even bigger challenges in the future. So, cherish those gray hairs. You earn each one.

I managed to raise two ambitious sons—now grown up with beautiful families of their own—while leading my own successful career. But I must admit, it was not without a great deal of loving support. And even then, there were plenty of roadblocks and bumps to navigate around, mountains to climb, and quicksand pits to crawl out of along the way. My hat is off to military wives and all single moms who raise successful kids while managing their own careers without a life partner or other support structure to rely on for assistance. Single moms are superheroes in my opinion.

Single moms are superheroes in my opinion.

There Is No Blueprint for Having It All—But We *Can* Learn from Each Other

As I interviewed our now-familiar C-level executive women, it was interesting to discover the various magic tricks each of these women employed to juggle home life and kids' schooling along with extracurricular activities, involvement in community affairs, and, of course, their own high-powered careers. Their stories are a testament to there being no one best, sure-fire approach to having it all.

Why wouldn't we want to learn from each other, and then adjust those lessons to fit our own individual situations? We don't have to reinvent the wheel. Women have been raising amazing kids while enduring challenging times for millennia—and they didn't even have Zoom, cell phones, cars, or even electricity for most of that time.

A friend who was a senior executive at The Walt Disney Company shared a simple life lesson that really struck a chord with me. Her story might be meaningful to you, too, regardless of where you are on the career ladder:

I grew up in a family of five kids. It was competitive! In the summers, I worked for my dad, selling shoes. I loved the challenge of working on commission and engaging with customers. I found the retail world fun and money-making. was eventually offered the opportunity to go to the Federated Department Stores corporate training program in New York City. I remained with Federated corporate for 10 years as I gained expanding experience developing their private label.

From there, I was recruited by Disney. Disney has long been admired for being hyper-focused on the cast/employees, and, perhaps more importantly, on the guest experience. They have an *exceeds expectations* culture. Mediocrity is not part of their playbook.

I started as a director at Disney. Over 20 years, I moved up the ladder to a senior executive position and traveled frequently to Disney parks and resorts throughout the world.

While the Walt Disney Company experience was life-changing for me, perhaps one of the most impactful "life lessons" I ever learned—one that impacts me in many ways to this day—was one my husband helped me learn while I was at Disney. It's a lesson I became very passionate about.

One night I arrived home an hour late for a planned dinner date with my husband. He was so disappointed about my late arrival, yet he just patiently and lovingly asked me if I would ever be an hour late for a Disney meeting. With that one simple question, he made me realize the importance of dedicating adequate time to family—and living in the moment. What a wake-up call that was. It was also a tremendous gift.

> **[My husband] patiently and lovingly asked me if I would ever be an hour late for a [work] meeting...What a wake-up call that was.**

I think most women (and even men) struggle with this. Executive roles require such a commitment—they are full of responsibility and accountability. But running a family requires a commitment, too. In my mind, it comes down to how you prioritize your time.

I believe we all have *one life* to live, not two (a work life and a personal life). Our work life and our personal life are all lived within the same time span. Prioritizing that time is the key—and the hardest thing to do.

Our *one life* is so important. People just need some tools to help them succeed in all the different aspects of it. Thanks to my husband's question, I quickly realized what I had done—as if it were no big deal—but believe me, I never did it again.

That experience made me a better leader, and it became part of my leadership style, which others could emulate. Many of the cast members on my team followed my lead. Some told me that their *one life* was better as a result, which led to stronger performance at work.

I learned firsthand that it takes better planning, and especially knowing when to say *no*. It also takes great organizational skills. If you maintain a calendar with solid back-to-back meetings, you will most likely be late to everything. Being late is a bad habit to get into. If you are overcommitted, the quality of your work can't possibly be exceptional.

A big thank-you to my dear friend for this insight. Now, take a breath and read on for my own *one life* story.

> **If you are overcommitted, the quality of your work can't possibly be exceptional.**

My Childhood: The Catalyst for Self-Reliance and a Purposeful Life

If you read my first book, *The WOW Factor Workplace*, you may recall that my mother was an alcoholic. I came to realize that at some point she had lost her sense of purpose in life. Long before she died at the end of my senior year in high school, I took over responsibility for running the household.

Always the overachiever, I learned to juggle my schooling and extracurricular activities with grocery shopping, cooking, and other household chores. Someone had to do it! My dad was busy running his own company. If I wanted some semblance of a normal life—whatever that meant—I needed to take over doing whatever I thought moms were supposed to do.

A very kind neighbor who observed much of this once told me, "What you are going through only serves to make you stronger. Someday you will look back on this as a blessing because you'll be able handle anything." I never forgot her insightful words.

I did not want to end up like my mother or be dependent on anyone else for fulfilling my purpose in life.

My life goal back then was to someday have a career and earn my own living. Most importantly, I did not want to end up like my mother or be dependent on anyone else for fulfilling my purpose in life. The thought of that happening terrified me.

First Comes Love, Then Comes Marriage...But How Does the Baby Carriage Fit into a Career?

I met my first husband at a fraternity party when I was a college freshman. We had known each other only briefly when he proclaimed, "No wife of mine is going to work for a living. She'll be a stay-at-home mom, just like June Cleaver on *Leave It to Beaver.*"

My immediate response was, "I hope whoever she is enjoys that." Since we were just friends, I simply shrugged it off. But I still remember that conversation like it was yesterday.

Fast forward four years, and we were married. I was 21. My new husband never once mentioned that June Cleaver idea again, so I figured it was no longer relevant—especially since I had been working as a fashion designer for more than two years by the time we got married. Still, his comment remained a little red flag in the back of my mind.

Fast forward seven more years. By then we had both earned MBAs, and we had each moved on to new careers—mine in the Fortune 100 technology world. Although we never discussed it, along the way, I made a deliberate decision to delay having children until I was well established in my new career. I wanted to feel totally capable of handling my professional life along with whatever challenges I would inevitably encounter while trying to be a role model mother.

Meanwhile, even though I was just 28, family and friends were asking us, "Why don't you have children yet?" Some admonished me, "You can't wait forever, you know. The clock is ticking."

One day my husband gave me an ultimatum: "What's the point of being married if we aren't going to have kids?"

I was stunned by that. Was that the only reason he had married me? What about the vows *for better, for worse, for richer, for poorer, in sickness and in health, to love and to cherish?* What a wake-up call. I now felt backed into a corner.

Trying to make sense of it all—and stay true to my vows—I concluded that my delaying motherhood was not fair to my husband. I rationalized that I certainly wouldn't be the first woman on the planet to not feel ready for motherhood. Besides, I had never failed before. I could do this.

Finding My Way as a Working Mom

I kept working right up until the evening I went into labor. Our beautiful son was born the next morning at 5:40 a.m. While still in the recovery room, I called into my weekly staff meeting. My boss was aghast. He kindly but emphatically notified me that I was now officially on maternity leave.

I truly enjoyed being at home with my newborn. While he never said it to me, I'm sure my husband expected that I would decide *not* to go back to work. Yet, when my six-week maternity leave was up, I was ready to return to my professional role. I missed it. As much as I loved my son, and as much as I relished the pride and joy inherent in motherhood, I also loved my job and the personal fulfilment that my career gave me.

I was passionate about my career goals, *and* I was just as passionate about the goals I had set for myself as a mother. I intended to teach my son to make his own sound decisions so he would someday become a responsible, upstanding, independent, self-supporting citizen who loved and respected women as equal partners in life. I wanted to serve as my son's role model for living a wonderful life—which included having a fulfilling career and a loving, supportive marriage.

The hardest thing for me about going back to work was finding someone I trusted enough to care for my infant son in the loving way that I instinctively did as a mom. I was blessed to find a stay-at-home mom in our neighborhood who agreed to care for him throughout his first year. A former schoolteacher, this mom had quit teaching when her first child was born. Now that both her son and daughter were in elementary school, she missed having a baby at home to dote on and care for during the day. She was thrilled to care for my baby, and her children enjoyed coming home after school to play with him following his afternoon nap. It was a win-win for all of us.

As much as I loved my son, and as much as I relished the pride and joy inherent in motherhood, I also loved my job and the personal fulfilment that my career gave me.

I must admit, the first day that I went back to work was extremely difficult from an emotional standpoint. I had never experienced such a feeling of loss as I did that day. But being the overachiever that I am, I just doubled down. I basked even more in the joy of being the best mom possible in the early mornings, at night, and on weekends. Meanwhile, I relished being back at work, too.

Once my son was walking at about twelve months of age, we switched him to an in-home daycare for toddlers where he was one of six little ones—again, in our neighborhood. There he learned about socialization, acceptable behavior, and manners. The woman who ran the daycare had two assistants, so it was a very attentive and learning-focused environment—perfect for that phase while he was still in diapers.

Over the next few years, my husband periodically made comments about how nice a *Leave It to Beaver* lifestyle would be, and better yet, how fantastic it would be if we had *three* children. At that point, I drew a line. Having three children was not in my plan. Two was enough for me, and I told my husband we would just have to agree to disagree on that one.

Son number two was born almost three years after number one. This time when I went back to work I hired a live-in nanny—which made my life much easier. With a nanny, I was better able to manage my now-increasing travel schedule without panicking about delayed flights and getting stuck in L.A. rush-hour traffic at the end of the day. This arrangement seemed perfect to me at that time.

The Most Difficult Decision of My Life
Unfortunately, my husband wasn't so happy with the situation. Upon my return to work, I quickly realized he fully expected me to give up my career and stay home with baby number two. (He certainly had no intention to become a stay-at-home parent!) In his mind, raising kids and doing household chores were the wife's responsibility—all day, every day—not just at night and on weekends.

No matter how perfect I tried to be as a "Supermom," I clearly wasn't living up to my husband's expectations—because they weren't compatible with the future I wanted for myself. I knew I would never transition to the *Leave It to Beaver* lifestyle he hoped for.

After a great deal of angst, I finally suggested we part ways. We both deserved to live the lives we each wanted. More importantly, it wasn't good for our children to live in a home with two unhappy parents in conflict.

> No matter how perfect I tried to be as a "Supermom," I clearly wasn't living up to my husband's expectations—because they weren't compatible with the future I wanted for myself.

I suggested to my husband that there were plenty of women out there who would find great personal fulfillment in a life that revolved around home and family—and he deserved to find one of them. In exchange, I hoped he would respect the fact that I would never be June Cleaver. Whether correctly or not, I associated my own mother's decline into alcoholism with the loss of purpose I believe she felt after stepping away from her career. I did not want to go down the same path, for my own sake and for that of my children.

Leaving that marriage was the most difficult decision of my life because I took my vows seriously. I had intended to make a lifelong commitment. I agonized and prayed for guidance for months before coming to a final decision. But in the end, I believed my most important obligation was to be the best possible role model parent.

I knew all too well from my own childhood that having parents who were unhappy with themselves and in their marriage was not a good foundation. My sons deserved happy, well-adjusted parents who loved and respected each other—even if they did not live under the same roof. I knew in my heart that I would be a far better role model, and that their dad would be a far better role model too, once we each had the ability to pursue the lives we truly wanted.

A New Life and a New Love—But Not Without a Few Wrinkles!

So, when IBM offered me a promotion along with a paid relocation to Phoenix, I accepted. The promotion enabled me to provide the boys with the standard of living we were accustomed to, on my salary alone. Meanwhile, I racked up tons of frequent flyer points as my sons traveled between our home in Arizona and southern California where their dad still lived.

Another year later, I remarried, and life was wonderful. The flying-back-and-forth arrangement was acceptable until my oldest started school. But it soon became clear that the boys needed to be in one place during the school year, and our idyllic existence came to a screeching halt.

Unfortunately, when the boys' father and I went back to court to renegotiate the custody arrangement, the California family court was emphatic that California had jurisdiction over the children. The boys must attend school in California. Therefore, they would live with their dad during the school year and with me in the summer. That ruling was devastating for me.

How could I now have both my career *and* my children in my one life? How could I serve as a role model mom if I was not with my boys—at least half of the time? How effectively could I guide them toward becoming responsible, upstanding, independent, self-supporting citizens who loved and respected women as equal partners in life?

There was only one answer. I had to return to California. My new husband was an angel and agreed to do whatever would work best for our family. By the way, he has been my most ardent supporter, my best friend, and my soulmate since day one—and he still is, more than 30 years later.

I tried desperately to transfer back to southern California within IBM, but the timing was terrible. The U.S. economy had taken a serious downturn, and IBM was downsizing. At that moment, there were no appropriate IBM positions in southern California that interested me. But then God opened a window. I was recruited to join a southern California-based technology firm—thanks to an IBM friend who knew my dilemma.

How could I now have both my career *and* my children in my one life?

Upon our arrival back in California, the boys requested to spend every other week with each parent: one week on, one week off. That is precisely what we did. It was the next best thing to perfect, under the circumstances. I arranged for their after-school care and made appropriate arrangements for their summer activities.

Everyone had equal time together throughout the rest of their growing-up years.

Playing to My Strong Suits at Work *and* at Home Helped Me Achieve My Greatest Goals

While I wouldn't recommend what I went through if you can help it, I will say that having the boys spend every other week with each parent worked well for my career. By then my role entailed a great deal of travel. For a few of those years, my job was even based in New York. Thankfully, at my level, I had the flexibility to work from home, or at the local branch office, during the weeks the boys were with me.

I am grateful that the time I spent in New York did not present a problem for my boys. They simply knew I was home and attended all their school and extracurricular events every week that they were with me. I never missed a game, or a school open house, or a band performance, or a wrestling match, or a track meet during my designated week. We had season tickets for the children's philharmonic orchestra. Their stepfather and I took them traveling in the summers—from Canada to Malta to Australia. We even hosted formal prom-night dinner parties in our home for their many friends. It was glorious.

On the evening of our oldest son's high school graduation, he requested that my husband and I take him out to the best restaurant in town—just the three of us. There, he thanked us for being amazing role model parents. (As my son's stepfather, my husband found this recognition to be especially meaningful.)

My son thanked us for teaching him manners, accountability, leadership skills, and how to navigate the world. He said his friends looked to him for advice, all because of what he had learned from us. Talk about a powerful thank-you. Goal achieved.

At the end of the day, we must all accept that life is a gamble. You make the best decisions you can with the information you have at the time. Thanks to the 100 percent support and undying love of my soulmate-husband, juggling motherhood *and* my career was not only sustainable, but fulfilling and enjoyable. And I couldn't be prouder of our amazing sons, their loving wives, and each of our four adorable granddaughters.

> **[My son] said his friends looked to him for advice, all because of what he had learned from us. Talk about a powerful thank-you. Goal achieved.**

While I wouldn't necessarily recommend the path I took, my advice is this: At every step along the way, make the most of the cards you are dealt, and always play to your strong suits.

Melissa Reiff
Former Chairwoman and CEO
The Container Store

I asked Melissa Reiff, "Did you always intend to be both a mother and a career woman?"

Yes. I can remember, from a very young age, wanting both a successful career and wanting to experience the beauty and wonderment of being a mother.

I had my first baby—a son—when I was 24 years old. At that point in my career, I was working for a Lamar Hunt company, World Championship Tennis, a company I also worked for during college at Southern Methodist University. My position at that time was to assist in preparing for our tennis tournaments—some outside of the U.S. These tournaments included all the big names in tennis at the time, such as Jimmy Connors, John McEnroe, Guillermo Vilas, etc. I remember being in Puerto Rico working at a tournament when I first guessed I was pregnant.

As I recall, I took only about three weeks for maternity leave.

I next inquired, "At that time, were there any rules or regulations within your industry or workplace regarding working while pregnant or after having a child?"

No. At least none that I can remember.

"What was the biggest challenge you faced when you first returned to work following the birth of your children?"

Nursing. My husband would bring our son to me at work so I could nurse him. I also worked very hard to keep breast milk frozen in the freezer.

"Who watched after your children while you were working?"

Eventually, I left World Championship Tennis and began working with a company called La Papillion, Inc. We were a manufacturer representative company, and I was able to work out of my home. My husband had his own business, so he also worked out of our home. We were able to watch our son together.

When I got pregnant with our daughter, our work became more demanding, so we hired a nanny to help us.

"Overall, what were some of the biggest challenges of balancing your career with motherhood?"

At the time, I was one of *very* few mothers who had a career. It was challenging trying to get to know the other mothers, and I was not always available to attend every activity or event at school, etc.

I also had to manage any guilty feelings that I had—which was sometimes hard. But I was lucky in that I had a very supportive husband who was a terrific and involved dad.

"Looking back, what was something you did while raising your children that you are now very glad you did?"

I believe we set a good example in terms of work ethic, commitment, compassion, and kindness.

In terms of raising my daughter, I am proud that I set a good example for her—as women can *have it all*. It's not easy, but it can be done, especially if you have a secure, confident, and supportive partner or husband. That is a necessity. And I'm very lucky I had that—married 44 years now and still going strong!

> **It was challenging trying to get to know the other mothers...I also had to manage any guilty feelings that I had—which was sometimes hard.**

Jodi Berg
Retired President and CEO
Vita-Mix Corporation

When I asked Jodi Berg, PhD, if she always intended to be both a mother and a career woman, she responded this way:

There are pros and cons to having children at any stage in one's career. My intent was to find fulfillment. But I always knew that I wanted to have children.

That said, I do feel there are *a lot* of women out there who need to know that juggling a career and motherhood is not always a Cinderella story.

When I was young, my dream would have been to work until I had children, and then stay home and raise them. But I also knew I did not want to be reliant on anyone else to ensure I was fulfilled. I also didn't want to get married just to have children. So, I needed to prepare myself for a career that brought me fulfillment.

In my early 30s, I married someone whom I thought was going to be able to care for a family financially so I could stay home. Unfortunately, my husband worked on and off—not enough to contribute financially in a significant way—so I did not have a choice but to work and pay for childcare.

> **There are *a lot* of women out there who need to know that juggling a career and motherhood is not always a Cinderella story.**

As my career advanced, I found fulfillment in what I did. But I always wished I'd had the option to stay home with my girls.

I was 34 when my first daughter was born, and I was 36 for my second. I was allowed to take three months of maternity leave and still work when I could. So, I always worked from home during my maternity leaves.

I now regret that I did this. Looking back, I wish that I had walked away from work for at least those first three months, each time.

While both of my daughters were young, I was a director of an international division, which required me to travel overseas for weeks at a time. So, they had to spend their younger years in daycare.

I wanted to be with them as much as possible, so I brought them with me to trade shows in the U.S. I also had them join in when I was hosting our international distributors for dinner in my home.

Once they were in middle school, my husband gave up on working for someone else and became an entrepreneur. While he started companies out of the house, he was home for the girls.

I then asked Jodi, "What was one of the biggest challenges you faced when you first returned to work following the birth of your children?"

Exhaustion was my biggest challenge.

I was working all day, then picking up my daughter(s), feeding everyone dinner, then bathing the babies, etc. Then I was nursing at 4:00 a.m. It was like holding down two full-time jobs.

> **Exhaustion was my biggest challenge...It was like holding down two full-time jobs.**

I had given up caffeine when I was pregnant the first time. After struggling through months of withdrawal, I never went back to drinking caffeinated beverages. While working full-time and taking care of my daughters, including nighttime feedings, I was still the only one fully awake in afternoon meetings at work.

Giving up caffeine was the best decision I ever made.

"Who watched after your children while you were working?"

When they were infants, I had them in an in-home daycare. As toddlers and up through elementary school, I had them in a daycare center. During elementary school and the beginning of middle school, I had them in in-home after-school care. When they were in middle school and high school, my husband was home for them.

"Looking back over the years now, what were the biggest challenges of balancing your career with motherhood?"

I was never the mom I truly wanted to be. I did not realize this until my girls were older. There were SO many moments that I was not a part of. There were things that happened that I did not know about because I was not overhearing them talk while driving them around or getting to know their friends.

If only I had married someone who understood the need to share relevant information, this challenge may have been overcome. As it was, I waited until they were in high school to file for divorce, thinking they would not need after-school care. But because my ex chose to demonize me in their minds, they did not want anything to do with me for a few years.

The person you marry and raise your kids with makes all the difference.

The person you marry and raise your kids with makes all the difference.

"What were some of the best things you did while raising your children?"

- I *always* took the time to explain why a rule existed.
- I made sure I was consistent in my expectations and rules.
- I *always* answered every question they asked with honesty.
- I told them I loved them every chance I got.

- I told them to make themselves proud whenever they left the house or got out of the car.
- I was a role model of joy, peace, and confidence, and I displayed a deep passion for living with purpose.

My daughters are now in their early 20s, and they are beginning to realize what happened. They are both living with me now, and we are beginning the discovery and healing process for them. This is helpful as I can better understand the emotional roller coaster they were on.

Nancy Howell Agee
President and CEO
Carilion Clinic

When I asked Nancy Agee, "Did you always intend to be both a mother and a careerwoman?" she had this to say:

Not really. I married a little later in life, so I had not decided about having children.

Once I was married, I very much wanted a child, but then I found I had infertility issues.

At that point in my career, I was a director for an enterprise-wide department and was taking on additional responsibilities as I moved toward becoming a VP. I was also going through an infertility work-up, which is no fun—the medications make you a hormonal basket case.

Certainly, an earlier start would have been easier and would have given me a longer runway. I convinced myself that the stress of pursuing a career was impacting my ability to conceive. It was a rather low point for me. But I finally did have a son.

I took off 12 weeks for maternity leave—half of which was paid time as I had accumulated a fair amount of personal time off (PTO). In truth, I worked from home after about the third week, so I stayed engaged with work throughout most of my leave.

I then asked Nancy, "What was one of the challenges you faced when you first returned to work following the birth of your son?"

One challenge? There were many!

Perhaps the biggest challenge was that breast feeding wasn't as common back then. It was hard to find a private location, and I had to adjust my pumping schedule to my work schedule.

"Who watched after your son while you were working?"

I used a local church daycare. It was a tough decision, but it ended up being a great nurturing environment.

"What were one or two of the biggest challenges of balancing your career with motherhood?"

There was never enough time in the day. Balancing all the activities of a child, from picking him up after school, to an unexpected sick day, to attending soccer games, to getting dinner, all set against a background of career and work responsibilities were ongoing and evolving challenges.

I never felt I was in the right place. While at work, I wanted to be with my son. While with my son, I thought about work.

On top of all that, I never felt I was in the right place. While at work, I wanted to be with my son. While with my son, I thought about work.

"What was one of the things you are most glad you did?"

Oh, that's so easy. Zach was in an amazing Montessori program. Then he was in a great private school. He thrived. While I might have wished to have been with him, it's clear he had a great start and wonderful experiences.

Now he is an amazing young professional who is married to a wonderful person, and he is a terrific father. I couldn't be prouder of him. So, it all worked out well!

It's interesting now that Zach has a son of his own, he and his wife have made the decision to put their son in a similar Montessori environment.

Linda Rutherford
Executive Vice President, Chief Communications Officer
Southwest Airlines

I asked Linda Rutherford, "Did you always intend to be both a mother and a career woman?"

I will tell you *yes*. I enjoy working, and I enjoy the joy of working, and getting to do what I like to do. I knew when I got married that we would have at least one child. We kind of brokered a deal. I wanted to go through the experience to decide whether I would want to do it again. And so, yes, I knew I would be a working mom.

I had an excellent role model. My mother was a single mother and very early in life. She was very proud of the work that she did to ensure that she could provide for my sister and me. She also found joy in the work that she did. I think she was a great example for me to learn from.

I followed up with, "At what point during your career did you have children?"

I was about 10 years into my career. At that point, I was a middle manager.

The plan I had set for myself was just to dive into my work, and work hard to put what I called *deposits in the goodwill bank.* I wanted people to know my work ethic. I wanted them to see the kind of work that I do and see the contributions that I was able to make so that when I needed to ask for some grace—either because I was on maternity leave, or coming

back from maternity leave, or managing work and kids'
schedules—that I would
have the benefit of the
doubt. That way, I could do
whatever it took to make
sure that my job was done,
and it was done well.

> I wanted people to know my work ethic...so that when I needed to ask for some grace...I would have the benefit of the doubt.

"How many children do you have?

I have two—27 months apart. I now have a soon-to-be-25-year-old and a 22-year-old.

"When you had your first child, did the airline industry have regulations about having children for women who were not flight attendants?"

Nothing that I had to worry about. Obviously, not being a flight attendant, I didn't have to worry about it, although my doctor's advice was, "Don't travel after month seven."

My role as a public relations specialist was to focus on media relations. My part of the network was the western United States—everything from El Paso to the West Coast in our route network—which entailed a lot of travel. I had to manage that a little bit while I was nearing giving birth and then when I was off for a while on maternity leave. Never before did I have to stop traveling or manage my work in different ways.

"How long did you have for maternity leave?"

With my oldest—Matthew—I was off for 12 weeks. That was just an adjustment—going from being a couple to being a family. I think that was very necessary time for us to take.

Then, shortly after my daughter, Allison, was born, during my maternity leave, Southwest Airlines had an operational emergency. My leader at the time said, "I can't even believe I'm calling to ask you this, but we could use your help."

I wanted to be needed in that regard, so I was like, "Yeah, great!"

Consequently, I took a little less time off with Allison than I did with Matt. I just went back to work earlier than planned and sort of accelerated the plans we had in terms of care for the kids. It was a much easier transition going back to work having two children than when the first one arrived.

"What did you do in terms of childcare with your first one?"

There are all different kinds of ways that you could do that. I didn't want to go instantly into a traditional daycare environment if I could help it. I searched for someone who kept a small group of infants in their home. I was able to find someone who was about a mile from our house—a lovely woman who kept four infants. It was the best home-away-from-home situation.

My husband and I are great partners. We shared getting everything ready in the morning, the drop-offs, and the pick-ups. That was an ideal situation.

I moved my son into a more traditional daycare environment before my daughter was born. A lot of that was for socialization—being able to play with kids his age, sort of expose him to all the childhood diseases to get his immune system up and begin to deal with different types of adults.

Then, when Allison came along, I was a little bit more comfortable. I put them back into a home environment where they could be together.

I chose a different home environment—one with a woman who had an assistant and took care of two levels of kids. So, I was able to kind of put my then-baby and -toddler into that environment together—which I was happy about.

Then, after that, it just became a patchwork of solutions. Quite frankly, we used church daycares, we used traditional daycares, and we had some at-home care until they were ready for school.

My husband and I are great partners. We shared getting everything ready in the morning, the drop-offs, and the pick-ups. That was an ideal situation.

I am a big believer in the Montessori program. As soon as they were both age eligible, I got them into Montessori. They had before- and after-school care as part of that, all in the same facility. Everything we did before this was aimed at getting them ready to go into the Montessori environment.

We moved both into Montessori at the same time. They took the kids starting at about age three. So, she was three and he was about to turn six.

"At least you had a little bit less juggling than if you were trying to take one to one place and one to another place."

Yeah, but there were a few times we did that when they were not together. That was not ideal—to have two drop-offs and two pick-ups.

"What would you say were the biggest challenges that you faced following the birth of your children?"

I think you must become a logistics expert. When you are on maternity leave, you are figuring out what the care is going to look like when you go back to work. When you go back to work, it is about managing the home time and the work time so you can still take care of everything that needs to be taken care of—like doctor appointments and play dates and all of that.

Then there is summer. Summer is fun—when they get to be school age. For summertime, it was all about figuring out how to string together all the camp experiences that they could have to occupy their time and give them something to look forward to while they were out of school.

[Following the birth of children], you must become a logistics expert.

Honestly, I loved the excuse to be able to travel during spring break and all those holidays off from school. When the kids were on spring break we literally went, "Well, they're on spring break. We have to be off, too!"

My husband and I are both very big believers in public education. So, when they aged out of the Montessori program and the kids were enrolled in public school—going into first and second grade and so on—we were fortunate that the public school program had campus-specific after-school programs.

When they would arrive there in the morning, they could eat breakfast there if they wanted to. Then they would go to school.

There would be an after-school program where they could get homework help. They could also play games and expend some energy in the gym or out on the playground, or whatever. That worked well for us. Again, once they were both in elementary school, they were able to be together. That worked out well.

You know the feeling of *I'm not fully focused on work. I'm not fully focused on my family. I'm not fully focused on my children. I'm not really focused on my friends.*

"What were some of the biggest challenges in terms of juggling motherhood and your career?"

We hear a lot about work-life balance. I think that sometimes, as women, we put intense pressure on ourselves to make sure that balance comes down to the day and the hour. When you put yourself under that kind of pressure, then there can be days—or weeks or months—where it just feels like you're losing at everything.

You know the feeling of *I'm not fully focused on work. I'm not fully focused on my family. I'm not fully focused on my children. I'm not really focused on my friends.*

That was sort of a stress spiral for me until I figured out for myself that it was more of a yin and yang. It was not going to be perfect every day, or every week, or every month. But I would do the most important thing that day, or the most important thing that week. Sometimes your kids win. Sometimes your spouse wins. Sometimes work wins. It's more like achieving work-life harmony.

"I certainly know that feeling guilty thing—you worry that you may not be making the right choices for your child when they are first born, then again when you are going back to work. How did you deal with the guilt feelings that you inevitably have as a mother?"

It's kind of funny. This is a phrase that I use to describe it to other people: I feel as though you have a couple of choices. You can decide that your children are the center of the world and everything you do revolves around them; or you can decide that there's a world and there's a place for everybody in it—so you sort of assimilate children into your life. I did the latter.

I think that worked for our family. I think that worked for our marriage. I think that showed them some examples about the benefits of hard work. I think it helped them shape their thoughts about being career-minded and what they wanted to go out into the world and do, in terms of making a difference.

There is always guilt. Right? There is that one time you were traveling, and you did not make the soccer game. But you cannot be everywhere. It was probably good that their aunt was there instead of you, and that is fine. She needed to be able to see the kids do that, just like I would have.

Those feelings of guilt are just there because you want to be perfect. Again, the sooner you realize that there is not necessarily perfection, but there is trying to do your best. Then you live your life.

What you're looking for is more of a harmony. I don't think you can call it balance, but harmony.

What you're looking for is more of a harmony. I don't think you can call it balance, but harmony. You ask yourself, *Have I done the best I could with the time that I had available for the people who needed it?*

"You mentioned having trouble being present. You want to be here, but you are not fully here, and you are not fully there. You are not fully the mom. You are not fully at work. How do you deal with that? What is your advice, aside from *just let it go?*"

My daughter could call here in the middle of the day, having a stressful moment and needing to talk to her mother. I need to realize that is what she is doing. She is 22 years old, self-sufficient, out on her own, with her own busy schedule. But if she is calling, there must be a reason.

At the end of the day, my best job will be a mother. That will be the best job. That goes to the top of the list. If there is a competition for my time, it is going to be the kids who get that attention and that focus first. If I am 10 minutes late to a meeting, we will figure it out. I will get caught up or we'll reschedule the meeting. We will figure it out.

"Logistically, how do you fit in time for yourself?"

I'm probably not as good at that as I should be. I mean, there are things that I really enjoy doing. I enjoy spending time with friends. I enjoy traveling and I make sure that I make time for that. I think that I have a healthy dose of being able to do things with my spouse, as a couple. Then there are things that I like to do on my own, with others, and I have the freedom to do that—which I enjoy, as well. I don't feel like there was a stress to do that any certain way. We just sort of figured it out as we went along.

"Did you ever feel left out or excluded at work if you needed to leave early to go to a special event with your kids, or did you just fit all that in, too?"

You know, you always get nervous about those meetings when it's 5:30, and then it's 5:45, and then it's 6:00. That happens on occasion. But that might be more about me telling myself that we would just have to eat dinner later than I thought we would.

If I needed to be at a game at 6:00, then I was at the game at least by 6:10. It was important to me to be where I said I was going to be. Although my kids cajole me to this day that I'm never on time!

"How did you and your husband work this out? It sounds like you have a pretty good partnership. Do you feel that was fairly balanced between you?"

First, we have a great partnership.

We are both very organized. We were both committed, during the weekend, to sit down and say, "Okay, what's in the week ahead? What do I need to be prepared for? Let's talk about meal planning. Let's talk about where we need to take the kids—somebody has to go to gymnastics; somebody else has Little League practice."

It is kind of figuring out the movements of the family and keeping all of that organized, along with our respective travel schedules, as it related to work.

We both had a commitment to communication, a commitment to the fact that we each needed to do what is important. There really was not a competition. It never got competitive.

Overall, what my husband, Mike, would say is that he enjoys working but he does not live to work. So, we always had a great partnership. If I were sitting in that meeting later than I expected, and it was going to be like 6:45, then he would be like, "Alright. I'll pick up Allison from dance. No problem."

> **[My husband and I] both had a commitment to communication, a commitment to the fact that we each needed to do what is important.**

He always made sure he had some built-in flexibility if something were to happen to my schedule. He is always very giving in that regard.

"So, he had a little more flexible schedule?"

Yes, he always has. It was just the nature of his work and who he works for. He's always had that flexibility.

"What are the kinds of things that you did while you were raising your children that you can now look back and think to yourself, *I'm so glad I did that, either with or for my children*."

First, you never get time back. Even if there were 101 things to do, I'm glad that we made sure that we took time for the kids so we didn't miss out on the special moments, because you can't ever get those moments back.

We are a big traveling family. So, the memories that we were able to make through the

You never get time back.

years—of the different trips, the vacations, the outings that we took—I think that my kids look back fondly on all of that, and they've grown.

"Were there other little moments along the way, like in elementary school or junior high?"

Oh, yeah. For example, when the kids would do their art projects and they would fill in those ad-lib things that the teacher would have the kids fill in, like "My mom does _____" or "My dad does _____."

One day we were cleaning out their rooms because we were having some renovation work done to the house. We dragged all that stuff out and started reading them. My husband and I both said, "These are really well-adjusted, resilient kids. Yay!"

We just want them to be contributing members of society, willing to work hard, make the world a better place, and not be a jerk. It's pretty simple.

I'm a big scrapbooker and I take every one of those pages as an opportunity. When I walk into the room and I see them flipping through that scrapbook—from a trip we took 10 years ago—and smiling, then I know that the time and the effort were worth it.

My husband had to travel for his work, and I had to travel for my work. Yet, we somehow made it work so that we were never both gone at the same time. We did not necessarily have to depend on friends or family for those types of logistics.

When we were both at home, we made a big point about having dinner together as a family—whatever that looked like. I am not saying that dinner was fancy, but it was time for us to spend together, kind of decompress, hear how school went, and hear how their friends were doing. If there was anything that was bothering them, we would have a chance to talk about that then, too.

During the COVID-19 pandemic, the kids were at home because their colleges went virtual. My son graduated in May of 2020, in the middle of the pandemic, and was looking for work. We would still sit down together, even with them being adults.

I can now kind of reflect on it and think, *I'm glad we made that investment of time*, because it became a habit. They didn't mind sitting down to have dinner with us, even though they were grown up and they probably had a hundred other things they also wanted to do.

"Now you're at a point where your kids are grown. Are they still at home?"

No. They are gone now. I have a University of Texas graduate who is on her way to graduate school, and I have a college graduate who is adulting in Houston. It all went by so quickly, but we did it.

I can now kind of reflect on it and think, *I'm glad we made that investment of time, because it became a habit.*

Kerry Healey
Inaugural President
Milken Center for Advancing the American Dream

I asked Kerry if it was difficult balancing motherhood with running a political campaign for lieutenant governor. She had this to say:

My kids were seven and ten when I was elected lieutenant governor, so I did have quite a bit of juggling to do at that point in my career. I made a conscious decision to wait until my children were in school before beginning my political career, but now women run for office with infants and while they are pregnant. I wanted to make sure I had extra support in place for my family before stepping into the arena. For example, in addition to babysitters, my mother-in-law lived with us for many years. She was a former teacher and principal, and I trusted her to make many decisions for my children's education and upbringing while I was in office. I remain deeply grateful to her for her support at that time.

> **Some of the things I did would probably be universal, like depending on friends and family for backup during demanding professional moments.**

I am financially more fortunate than many women who struggle to balance work and a career, but some of the things I did would probably be universal, like depending on friends and family for backup during demanding professional moments.

Wendy Johnson
Former President and CEO
Dale Carnegie franchise, Atlanta, GA

I asked Wendy Johnson, "Did you always intend to be both a mother and a career woman?"

Absolutely not. I thought I would just get married and have babies. I never dreamed otherwise. I knew that I would have to work at something to make money, but I always assumed my main job would be as a mother and a wife. An executive career was not encouraged or presented as an option.

When I joined the airlines, I flew to Miami for the training. The first evening, we met as a group with our instructor. After the meet and greet, the instructor asked each one of us, "Why are you becoming a Pan American stewardess?"

My answer was, "To make myself a better wife and mother."

That honestly is what I said: "To make myself a better wife and mother," and I obviously believed that, or I wouldn't have said it.

Six years of flying for Pan Am internationally completely changed the landscape for me. I left the country every time I went to work. As a result, my vision for myself began to change from the exposure to cultures all over the world and the responsibilities that I had in the job. What came from that experience was that I discovered I wanted a career. I wasn't even interested in motherhood. I wanted to get married, but motherhood wasn't in the forefront. At that point, I figured it would happen someday, but I wanted to be an executive woman. Our experiences and our responsibilities change our direction and form new paths.

I followed that up by asking, "At what point did you meet your husband?"

> **My vision for myself began to change...I discovered I wanted a career...I wanted to get married, but motherhood wasn't in the forefront.**

Well, I have been married twice. I met my first husband on an airplane when I was a flight attendant. He was on his way back from Australia.

He had just sailed the Transpacific Yacht Race coupled with a business trip to Australia. I met him on a flight back from Hawaii to San Francisco.

I believe he was a bit surprised. He might have thought I was giving him a little bit of a bait and switch when I decided to become a career woman. I still feel kind of guilty about that. But that's what happens when you grow. He wasn't against it, and he was proud of me, but he made fun of it a little bit.

For instance, when I went to work for Transamerica Corporation—the Budget Rent a Car division—he and his family called it "Bu-jay" Rent a Car because Budget Rent a Car was low end, at least to people in their world. "Bu-jay" was sort of a tongue-in-cheek joke, but it was a put-down, and I resented it.

"At what point in your career did your daughter come along?"

Later, after I married my second husband. I had my daughter at 37 years old, after two miscarriages. So, when she came along, I was very grateful that I got to be a mother.

I had put motherhood on hold until the age of 37, when women begin to get to that stage of life where they may have infertility issues. Today there are so many women in their late 30s or early 40s in fertility clinics. Some women harvest their eggs, just so they can ride it out and not interrupt their career path.

At the time I finally became pregnant with my daughter, I was working for a cash management firm that handled payroll tax for large companies.

During my pregnancy, I was afraid to tell anybody I was pregnant because I had witnessed over the years an immediate change in management's view of women once they became pregnant. Whether it was conscious or unconscious, it seemed they began thinking that *she'll probably not come back*, and they proactively started to backfill the position.

In those days, despite laws requiring companies to keep your position open, they would immediately, albeit unofficially, start planning your exit. You could feel it. You had to start transferring your responsibilities to other people. You would start to feel like you were losing your job.

> **Whether it was conscious or unconscious, it seemed they began thinking that *she'll probably not come back*, and they proactively started to backfill the position.**

In those days, many women thought you *should* stay home. There was a perception, amongst both men and women, that if you chose to come back, what kind of mother were you. They would ask, "Don't you miss your baby? Who is watching your baby while you are at work?"

So, you kept quiet about all of it. You just didn't commit. Keeping quiet was the best thing to do when you were pregnant.

I finally got to the point where I thought, *If I'm going to have children, I need to do it now.*

It came as quite a shock when I realized that when you go to the obstetrician at age 37, they check a box that says *geriatric*—and yes, they have a little box like that on the form! If you are over 35, it is considered a geriatric pregnancy. Then you know you have waited too long.

I didn't start telling people until I began wearing maternity clothes. Today, it's the style to let your pregnant stomach show—and everybody gets to look at your growing belly. But back then, you kept it very private. So, as soon as I knew that people would recognize it was a maternity top or dress, then I knew I had to say something. How wonderful it is that women today can openly enjoy this special time in their lives at work.

> **How wonderful it is that women today can openly enjoy this special time in their lives at work.**

"What was your role at the time?"

At that time, I was not in management. I was running a sales territory in the Southeastern U.S. I was traveling a lot while I was pregnant. I kept on going right to the end. I have to say, because it was a very small company, it was probably better than if I had been with a major corporation. They needed me and they were hoping I would come back. You really want them to hope you will come back. It feels good and it makes it easier for you.

Financially, I needed to work right to the end. I was bound and determined to not let my pregnancy affect anything. I was not going to be different from anybody else in the job. No excuses.

I think that's just sort of our generation—no excuses.

There was no question that I would take my six weeks of maternity leave off, and I loved being a mother. But I quickly realized that the highlight of my day at home was going out to the mailbox to get the mail. So, I finally concluded, *I love my baby, but I do believe that I can work and still be a great mom.*

For me, it was a lonely time, because a lot of people were encouraging me to stay home. There was prejudice against working mothers. I felt that, anyway.

Even today, there are people who say that being a mother is the best job a woman will ever have, and it is more meaningful than anything she'll ever do.

I don't know if it's a male thing or a female thing—that a mother should be at home. Unfortunately, there were a lot of women who let me know that they believed I needed to be at home. "What do you do with your baby when you travel?" is just one question I would get from fellow employees.

It made me feel a little defensive. They would certainly not ask a man that question.

It was a challenging time for those of us who were working moms back then because the whole model of how families worked was in transition. We were in the forefront. It was one thing to be a working mother if your household income made it so that you *had* to work. But try to be an executive woman in an upper-middle-class household with a child. Now that was a choice.

Eventually, they passed great laws that helped to protect women, so they would be valued even though they became a mother. Their job performance was what mattered.

"Did your husband support you in whatever your decision was? Or was that an area of contention?"

Yes, he supported me, but he didn't help me.

It was alright with him if I went back to work. He loved the additional money coming in. But he did very little of the childcare work, nor did he do any of the shopping, or cooking, or cleaning. I did almost everything—although he did take the dry cleaning, and he blew off our property with the leaf blower. He would do whatever I asked, but the operative word was *ask*.

I had to fight with him to hire a cleaning lady at different times. I had a live-in nanny for a while just because I really needed some help. I couldn't work and be a mother and wife without help. I just couldn't.

Sometimes, in the middle of the night, the nanny and I would collide in the hallway when the baby would cry. We would both go running in and collide, because I thought, *I'm the mom*, and she would say, "I'm the nanny." Then we would laugh and say, "Okay, which one of us is going to pick up the baby?"

Oh, my husband had a lawn service. Right?

"Your husband wasn't getting up in the middle of the night?"

No, not usually. He gave me only Saturday nights off so I could sleep in on Sunday morning. He took the baby duty on Saturday nights. I think that was probably typical back then.

When I was with Pan Am, if you became pregnant, you lost your job. You would be fired as soon as they found out. So, women were working while they could hide their belly. As their uniform would become tighter, the supervisor would say, "Hmmm. I think she might be pregnant."

Then you would lose your job. It was in the regulations—in the human resources handbook. The handbook said that if you got pregnant, your employment was terminated. Before that, you would be terminated if you got married. Then they changed the rule to just being terminated if you were having a baby.

Of course, all of this would change. At the time, I was a recruiter. I was hiring and interviewing stewards and stewardesses for Pan Am, in a territory in the west. I had been trained by an industrial psychologist on how to conduct interviews for the position.

In the middle of all this, there was a settlement of a class action lawsuit that demanded airlines allow a woman to have a baby and keep their job. My job abruptly changed from recruiting new hires to interviewing the returning mothers. Everyone who wanted their job back was automatically rehired. It was a real breakthrough for women.

"How much maternity leave did you get?"

I was given six weeks off. But they were flexible because you could tack your vacation time on to it, so my leave drifted into almost two months.

Companies may not value you until they think they might lose you.

Companies may not value you until they think they might lose you. I think they really wanted me to come back, so they were more flexible than other companies might have been.

"Were they contacting you while you were at home on your maternity leave?"

No. They were pretty much hands-off. But remember, there were no cell phones and there was no email. It took guts to call someone on their home phone. So, they really left me alone, which was good.

But then, within a few months after having my child, my company had a serious lawsuit against it, and I had to go find other work.

My job had been perfect because I worked from home. So, when I found a job with a company owned by Citicorp— Quadstar—it became necessary to hire a live-in nanny, just to be able to go back to work. I would have to go to an office every day.

Before I hired this woman, managing childcare was very hard for me. I was dropping my child off at all these little daycare places for two hours, just so I could go on a job interview. On top of that, my baby was being exposed to all kind of illnesses. She also had congenital heart disease, so having live-in childcare was important for me.

This woman cared for my daughter even while I was not working—for about 30 or 45 days, in between jobs. Having her was an absolute necessity because I was unable to go on job interviews without childcare.

I employed this nanny for almost two years. She lived with us Monday through Friday and then she went home on weekends. I picked her up at the train station on Sunday night. Then I took her to the train on Friday afternoon. So, for the workweek I was covered. And, we had some privacy.

I do not know how women today have a baby at home and at the same time do their jobs and conduct Zoom calls without childcare. I just do not know how that would be possible.

It was a marvelous experience for me, coming from the West, to live in Atlanta at the time. I had a tremendously wonderful experience having our nanny live with us. She was in her 70s.

> **I do not know how women today have a baby at home and at the same time do their jobs and conduct Zoom calls without childcare.**

At first, she had to train me. I had never had live-in help before. It was different when I grew up. My mom had a cleaning lady once a week, but that was it. We did not have any kind of in-house employee when I grew up, so I didn't know how to handle it.

The nanny did not want me to treat her like a friend, but that was my natural inclination. I thought I would be nice and treat her like a houseguest, but this made her painfully uncomfortable. She helped me to create a perfect work ng relationship. She was with me for about a year and a half. After that time, I went through a divorce, and I became a single working mother—a new and different challenge.

"Then, a year or year and a half later, what did you do?"

I went to work for a company in the medical field—specifically, environmental medicine. I started out in sales and then ended up as VP of sales and part-owner of the company. We were providing medical surveillance for employees of major engineering companies that cleaned up the planet—hazardous waste cleanup. Ninety percent of the time, it was a regular office job that did not require travel. This really made life easier for me.

By that time, I had my daughter in a Montessori school/daycare program—a combination of daycare and school. They had early morning sessions, so I would drop off my daughter in the morning. At that time, my best girlfriend's daughter was in college. She needed a job, so I paid her to pick up my daughter at 2:30 or 3:00. She would bring my daughter home and give her a snack.

I think the biggest challenge for a working mother—without a full-time nanny of some kind—is the fact that when summer comes and during holidays, when schools are not open, school is an incomplete childcare option. So other layers of childcare must come into play. You are always struggling to find temporary or short-term solutions.

You must be very organized and plan months ahead. By February or March, you must already have every day of the summer planned out. If you do not have summer all planned by then, you will really be in trouble. It creates unbearable stress.

"I'd like to ask you about dealing with guilt feelings. Young women today are working, and they are worried, *Am I making the wrong choice by working? What will be the impacts on my child? What will be the long-term implications on them and the family?* Did you ever feel guilty about working while being a mother?"

I totally felt guilty about working and I had a reason to work. I was a single mom. Yet, I do not know if society made me feel guilty or if it was just me making myself feel guilty. But I was always worried that I was stretched so thin. I could let my daughter have only one outside activity. I felt guilty that she could not do after-school lessons AND swimming. There was only so much that I could fit in and juggle. So, I had guilt feelings about that.

I had guilt feelings that she was in daycare instead of a myriad of playdates each day. Now, she was having a great time at daycare and had special friends there. But I still felt guilty because all the other little girls had mommies who picked them up, and they had a playmate, and they could come home and have milk and cookies. My daughter did not have that.

> **I do not know if society made me feel guilty or if it was just me making myself feel guilty. But I was always worried that I was stretched so thin.**

There were very few mothers with kids in her class who asked my daughter to play after school at their house. I don't know why. I could have picked my daughter up at their house at 5:30. The daycare after-school kids were left out. So, I felt guilty that it impacted the social aspects of her life. I felt sad about that, and I felt sad that she was made to feel different from the other kids with stay-at-home moms.

"What would you say was the biggest challenge of balancing your career and motherhood?"

I would say that the biggest challenge with juggling a career with motherhood was lining up childcare. The bigger my positions got, the more impromptu my need to travel became. Whatever childcare I had set up—and was perfect—got changed all the time. The biggest challenge was making sure that I had the right childcare.

The biggest challenge with juggling a career with motherhood was lining up childcare.

I believe that any executive woman who has not solved her childcare issue is going to be full of angst and stress—to the nines— because your children are as important to you as they are to a stay-at-home mother. It's very challenging.

When somebody calls you and asks, "Can you be in South Africa on the fifteenth of this month?" you don't answer, "Let me check and see if I can get childcare."

Those were not words you could use. An answer like that would be death to your career. So, instead, you say yes. Then you get off the phone and you go crazy, right? Now, you must find a way to do it because you have said yes.

So, I would say that lining up childcare was my biggest challenge as I grew in my roles.

"Even with a live-in nanny, you still have challenges with childcare because sometimes they get sick or have a death in their family to deal with."

Right. But I was married at the time I had the nanny. My husband would try to help in that case.

"How did you fit in self-care, friendships, personal relationships with male adults beyond the workplace, and exercise? How did you fit those things into your life?"

Of course, we are completely forgetting about the person, Wendy. There is the career, there is juggling, there's childcare, and there are other challenges, like the challenge of being a career woman and a mother—who is single in her 40s. Then there is the person.

Your personal life landscape is always the last priority on the list. For a single mom, you—as an individual—pretty much do not exist. I had just eight nights a month that were mine alone. That was it. So, it was very limiting. At least it was for me.

> **Your personal life landscape is always the last priority on the list. For a single mom, you—as an individual—pretty much do not exist.**

Now, it was by choice. I could have had 20 nights to myself if I had wanted. I could have just hired a babysitter. But I chose not to do that because I always thought, *I'm a mom and I*

need to give that my all. I'm not here all day for my daughter,
like other moms.

My daughter was around eight years old when I took over as
the full-time parent. She still needed a babysitter. I was a
runner, but I could not take a run without a babysitter. I could
not do anything without a babysitter. It was not like I was in a
subdivision with a lot of teenagers or somebody who could
drop by for 20 minutes while I took a run. I was isolated.

So, I had to fit it all in, in different ways. If I had five minutes, I
used the five minutes. I would empty the dishwasher—you can
empty a dishwasher in five minutes. Done. So that's the kind
of life you live—you make use of every minute. I joined a club
where I could work out at lunch, so I was able to get a
workout in before I came home. Then, as she got older, I could
take a walk in the neighborhood. But when she was younger,
no.

I believe that if I were to do this over, the world today
embraces working mothers more readily, and I think I would
have made more time for a personal life. I wouldn't feel the
guilt.

"Did you feel left out or excluded at work because you had to leave
to go pick up a child? You couldn't say, 'Oh, I'll do the softball
game with the team, or I'll go to the bar to socialize with the gang
after work,' like single people can."

Yes, I would say that certainly the drinks after work were a
rare occasion. I just couldn't do that.

"What about the mental state of being present? Some women really struggle with being present. You move through things, you are checking boxes, you move on to the next thing, and you are exhausted. You are over-scheduled. When you are here, you're thinking about there. When you are doing this, you are thinking about that. Your body is here, but your mind is there. Was that an issue for you?"

> Absolutely. Unfortunately, it was more of an issue when I was being the mom than when I was being the executive. You had to be present at work in a meeting—to take notes and action items, and listen to a client, to know how to write a proposal for them by listening to their needs, and so on.
>
> It was easier to skate at home, like when I was cooking breakfast and my daughter was talking to me, yet I'm not listening. I think Alex felt that I wasn't always present because I was thinking about something at work.

"So, the challenge for you was being present for your child. Do you think that had something to do with the nature of your job—in a more senior-level role, with more responsibilities—that gave you more fulfilment?"

> Yes. At least for me, the day-to-day gratification or reward for being a mother was not always evident. Of course, there are those wonderful, sweet moments where they curl up in your arms and say, "I love you, Mommy"—all those wonderful little moments that you have. But a lot of your life at home is repetitive and challenging. Each stage has its own nuances.

I think it is almost easier to be present for work. I've never had this discussion with other working mothers, but when I got to work, I was not worried about my daughter because she was at school or being taken care of at daycare (unless my daughter was sick). But you know the kind of pressure you can be under at work forces you to be very present when you are there.

Every day is not a Hallmark moment. I just know that I could be the best for my daughter if I was working at something that gave me great pride and provided for us.

It was not as though I did not get gratification from being a mother. Motherhood is just wonderful. I am so grateful that I got to be a mom. I don't feel that I missed anything. Every day is not a Hallmark moment. I just know that I could be the best for my daughter if I was working at something that gave me great pride and provided for us.

As for me, I needed a purpose. I needed feedback. I needed validity. I needed to grow. Growth was important to me.

It is difficult to be a stay-at-home mom and it's very challenging. I respect the women who do it because it's hard to find the value part of it on a day-to-day basis. They are magnificent. This isn't about right and wrong. It is about what is right for you. It is all good.

"Especially when you were raised in an era when moms stayed home."

Right. My mom did work after my father died. So, I was exposed to having a working mom, but I was in high school by that time.

As a working mom myself, I often worked right up until 6:00, the deadline for daycare pickup. I now feel guilty that I did that. I've found that a lot of the younger generation today insist on work-life balance. Some don't work past 5:00, ever, and I don't blame them.

I'll never forget one night when my daughter and I were having dinner and she said, "Mom, when I grow up, I'm going to have four kids and I'm going to be a stay-at-home mom!"

It was like a knife going through me! I said, "You know, I think that's wonderful. It's going to be perfect because I'll be retired by then and I can babysit and help you with your four kids."

Then she grew up. Now, fast forward 20 years and she's a career woman. She's a mini-me! She just loves being an executive woman. I have come to the realization that while her life growing up was not easy and was definitely challenging, being different could have been a good thing.

If she were sitting here with us today, she would say, "No, my mom is awesome. It was okay that she was a career woman. That's what I am today. She was a great role model."

That's what she would say. She wouldn't say anything about, "I didn't get to take more lessons or activities," or, "She didn't pick me up in the carpool lane."

While [my daughter's] life growing up was not easy and was definitely challenging, being different could have been a good thing.

I remember the husband of one of my friends saying to me, "I hope you are banking all that child support money that you're getting, if you're not going to stay home and use it to raise your child."

His wife nearly killed him for saying that. There is this assumption that if you are getting child support, then you should stay home. But it was not enough for us to live on. I could not just stay home and live a decent life that my daughter would be proud of. I still had to work.

"What kinds of things did you do while raising your daughter that, looking back, you are glad you did?"

Well, I brought her in to work a lot. Depending on the situation, sometimes I had to when my childcare failed.

Everyone was very kind about it when she was little. When I was working at the environmental medicine company, she was shy and afraid of everybody. So, she would get a coloring book and go hide under my desk and stay there. Nobody even knew she was there. But she was absorbing everything she heard and observed.

Sometimes, if I had a big presentation to make, I would practice my slideshow at home in the evening. I would have my remote control and I would project my slides on the wall, and I would give my presentation to her. She would sit there with her legs crossed on the floor and listen intently. Then, when I was finished, she would say, "It's my turn!"

Then she would present the slideshow herself. She would make up all kinds of stories about the slides. I really felt like she was in training to become a great presenter—which she is now. I am so glad that I involved her in that way.

She often helped me with my projects. For example, when there was a big project, or a marketing event where we had to staple things and stuff bags, she was always on the production line, being a part of that.

Everybody in the office always knew her. As she got older, she was easier to bring in because she was not in the way, like a little kid. Some of the younger employees would play with her and throw Koosh balls with her. I think I made work touchable and friendly for her. I am certainly glad I did that.

I also took her on a lot of pleasure trips—just the two of us—to other parts of the world. For example, I took her to Hong Kong. One day we got

I think I made work touchable and friendly for her. I am certainly glad I did that.

on a bus to go into Kowloon, and I handed her some local currency. I said to her, "You're in charge of the money today."

I think she was probably 10 years old at the time. She had so much fun making the monetary conversions.

I exposed her to many parts of the world, which gave her a much broader perspective of the world than most kids ever get.

From what I have seen, both in my own career and because of my experience creating a women's leadership development program at Dale Carnegie, having a family and advancing an executive career is a big challenge that women must uniquely face.

I almost sold my women's program to a large telecommunications company. I was so close, but then they reorganized and moved all their people to Dallas. Life is timing, right? They were very vocal about the fact that women have a harder time advancing because it required moving from city to city. They have a family, and they have a husband. Many times, the husband's career is the one the family worries about the most. That is still sort of the tradition.

It seems harder for a man to risk his career and move to another city for his wife. The wife's position must be quite lucrative and on a real upward trajectory for a family to do that. This really hurts a woman's chances of getting ahead, up the organizational ladder to higher-level positions.

Lieutenant General Kathleen M. Gainey
U.S. Army, Retired

I commented to Lt. General Gainey, "I understand you were 38 years old when you married your husband, Ed, who was also a senior military leader. Do you have children?"

No, we do not have any children.

Part of the reason for that was that I was going straight into battalion command. When you are in command in the Army— unlike other services—you cannot get pregnant when you are in command. When you are in command, pregnancy means you are not deployable. If you are not deployable, you cannot be the commander because you cannot deploy with your soldiers.

So, that meant there would be at least two years that I would not be able to have children. I would have then been age 40, starting a family. Being a special ed schoolteacher, I knew that the later you wait, the higher the likelihood of having serious complications.

Ed and I talked about it, and we concluded we could always decide later to have kids, and that we could always adopt.

But I suddenly realized that I no longer had that biological clock ticking inside me that said, "Yes, I want kids." That was a real surprise for me as I had always wanted kids. I love children.

So, we said, "We'll wait." Then we started talking about whether we really did want kids. He said, "If we really want children, I'm happy to. I don't feel like I *need* kids, but I'm happy to have kids."

I suddenly realized that I no longer had that biological clock ticking inside me that said, "Yes, I want kids." That was a real surprise for me as I had always wanted kids.

Then, I started talking to my mom, and she said, "Don't rush into that. Not everybody needs to have a family. You are not going to get pressure from your dad and I that we need a grandchild. Have children only if you want to."

My father-in-law, Mr. Donnelly, was not happy about it. He wanted a grandchild. He wanted us to have kids.

But you know, we have a family. It is made up of all those lieutenants, and captains, and colonels we have mentored and coached our whole lives. They come through this door for lots of visits, they call on the phone, and we mentor and coach them, still to this day.

> **We have a family. It is made up of all those lieutenants, and captains, and colonels we have mentored and coached our whole lives.**

I just went and officially retired one. I just went to the promotion for another one. Others bring their kids and their grandkids down here to see us. So, in a way, they are our family. And we take care of our nieces and nephews and their kids.

There was a benefit of our not having children and that was the freedom to take care of our parents and focus on them in their later years.

I then inquired, "The other women who were with you in the general officer ranks, were they similar to you, with no children?"

About 70 percent of them were married. About 30 percent of them were not. Of the 70 percent who were married, half of those—a third of the total—had children.

Of those who were my close friends, all but one were dual military—meaning their husbands were also military. Now, that is not the norm. There are a lot of women who are married and have civilian husbands. But those at the flag officer rank who had kids, most I knew were dual military.

Of those with children, most of them had full-time nannies, or a mother-in-law, or their own mother who lived with them, to help take care of the kids, at least when they were young.

REFLECTIONS:

It is entirely possible to manage both a successful, high-powered career and motherhood at the same time. One of the most important foundations for successfully living such a lifestyle is to ensure that the important people in your daily life, such as your partner and perhaps your family or friends, are supportive of your choices and goals. Especially if you cohabitate with another person, their objectives, expectations, and dedication to family should blend well with yours.

If you are in a relationship, it's important to have candid conversations with your beloved about your respective expectations and objectives. You should also talk through each of your philosophies about educating and disciplining toddlers, youngsters, and teens *before* you enter a formally committed relationship or marriage.

> It is entirely possible to manage both a successful, high-powered career and motherhood at the same time. One of the most important foundations for successfully living such a lifestyle is to ensure that the important people in your daily life...are supportive of your choices and goals.

These discussions will help to ensure that you both have a solid basis upon which to build a fulfilling and harmonious life. If your respective personal desires and expectations regarding how to best raise a family are not well aligned, it is important to discuss how you will work through these things in the years ahead. Know what you are getting into.

The stories shared here reflect but a small sample of all the possible permutations and alternatives when it comes to juggling career and motherhood. There is no "one right way" to fit both of these roles into your life. (In fact, the "right way" is whatever works best for you!) But I noticed that the women on top who found it relatively easier to "have it all" credited their significant others with being both supportive life partners and loving, involved parents. Even then, most found it beneficial to have the assistance of a live-in nanny (or close family member) when the second child came along, at least until both children were old enough to attend the same daycare or school.

Sharing the load with others who are also invested in your child's future should not be seen as a weakness or failure, but as a prudent decision to enhance everyone's well-being.

Just like building a successful executive career, raising children demands large amounts of time, energy, and emotional investment. Sharing the load with others who are also invested in your child's future should not be seen as a weakness or failure, but as a prudent decision to enhance everyone's well-being.

Of course, childcare is only one hurdle working mothers face as they seek to advance their careers. Some common challenges to be mentally prepared for may include:

- Nursing an infant while working.
- Arranging for daycare and after-school care—a challenge that constantly evolves and lasts for years, until the children are old enough and responsible enough to be on their own after school.
- Managing the logistics of life in general: preparing meals, bathing and dressing little ones, pediatrician appointments, arranging and attending extracurricular activities, being home to care for a sick child, filling in when the caretaker is ill or quits, etc.
- Being present and focused—in the moment—at work, at home, and in your community.
- Meeting your own personal needs for fitness and adult socialization.
- Missing some of those special moments in your children's lives—*and* having to say no to some personal opportunities of your own.
- Feelings of guilt—you cannot always be everywhere.
- Exhaustion.
- Accepting the fact that you are not perfect.

As Linda Rutherford shared, it is wise to strive for harmony instead of perfection. Do not expect things to be perfectly balanced every day—or every week, month, or year! At any given time, try to do your best at the things that are most important to you.

INTROSPECTIONS:

1   If you are not yet a mother:
   a. Have you considered if/when you might want to
      have children?
   b. Would you like to be a stay-at-home mother, or
      would you prefer to have both a career and
      children?
   c. How might you manage the responsibilities of
      child-rearing, and do you expect your spouse/life
      partner to share in that effort?
   d. Would you (and/or your life partner) consider a
      modified career path to better harmonize with your
      family goals?

2   If you are in a new, committed relationship/marriage:
   a. Have you and your beloved candidly and honestly
      discussed your respective desires and expectations
      about having a family and how the two of you will
      handle the responsibilities of a baby and children?
   b. If you have not done so, have that conversation.
   c. If you have discussed this, are you both on the same
      page? If not, what will you do about that?
   d. Do you and/or your beloved plan to modify your
      career path(s) to harmonize with your family plans?

3   If you are an experienced mother:
   a. What lessons have you learned that you wished
      someone had shared with you before you had
      children?

b. What would you have done differently, if anything, based on what you know now?

c. Do you have any mentees or colleagues who might be appreciative of your sharing these lessons?

FOURTEEN

Reflections on Success

I always knew that I had determination, perseverance, and a strong passion to be happy and successful in whatever career I pursued.

I am proud that I have exceeded many of my dreams as well as discovered and accomplished new ones. However, I also know that no matter your age, you must continue to learn and ask questions—be inquisitive.

-MELISSA REIFF
Former Chairwoman and CEO
The Container Store

There is yet another certain question I love to ask successful executives: "Have you been successful in the way you expected?"

The answers can be quite varied, and I'm often surprised by what I hear.

When someone turned the tables and asked me that very same question recently, I was honestly surprised at my own answer. But it was the truth, and it was heartfelt. Essentially, my answer was this:

> **Our priorities change over time. What may have been of utmost importance at one point in your life can take a back seat to other priorities as your journey progresses.**

My original career goal was to become the CEO of my own company. I have achieved that goal, so I guess I can say *yes*—I have been successful in the way I expected. But achieving that success felt different from how I thought it would. Along the way, I was not always in control. I had to play the cards I was dealt. Getting here has been a humbling experience.

I would also add: Our priorities change over time. What may have been of utmost importance at one point in your life can take a back seat to other priorities as your journey progresses.

Purpose and Priorities Beyond My Professional Life

While I ultimately achieved my original career goal, it took longer to get there than I thought it would. Interestingly, the actuality of being a CEO became less important to me as I moved forward through life. My younger self might have been surprised to hear it, but becoming a CEO didn't turn out to be the crowning glory of my personal success.

Now that we've almost reached the end of this story, I'll share a little secret with you. As career-focused as I may seem to some people, my top five life priorities these days are as follows:

1. My faith
2. My husband
3. My children
4. My country
5. My career

As you can see, my career is well down the list—although it's still more important than a great many things I'm asked to lead or be involved in. As I evaluate my success in each of these priorities, I am quite satisfied that I have done the best I could along this journey of mine.

Before diving into a more extended examination of my career success, I'd like to take a brief look at my top four priorities and how I evaluate my success in each. Perhaps some or all of these priorities align with your own. If so, I encourage you to reflect with me!

Priority 1: My faith. While I have not spent much time talking about my spiritual beliefs in this book, suffice it to say that my faith in God is very important to me and has been a guiding force throughout my life. No one is perfect—I'm certainly not—but I am extremely grateful that even when I have stumbled, my God has always lifted me up and blessed me in ways I could have never imagined. My faith has consistently shaped my values and my

> I've been extremely blessed, because for over 30 years, my husband and soulmate has always chosen to see the best in me.

choices, and has motivated me to keep going in difficult times. My faith in God has proven to me that everything *always* works out for the best, even if it may not seem like it at the time. And it has contributed indelibly to my success in all other areas of my life.

Priority 2: My husband. My first marriage ended, yet I learned a great deal from that experience. Marriage is a two-way street that requires mutual respect, trust, support, communication, forgiveness, friendship, fun, and so much more. I believe I got it right this second time. I've been extremely blessed, because for over 30 years, my husband and soulmate has always chosen to see the best in me. This time around has been beyond my expectations.

Priority 3: My children. I'm extraordinarily proud of the fine, upstanding, and responsible adults my sons have become. I am certainly not the only person who influenced their upbringing, yet I believe the difficult choices I made along the way turned out—for the most part—to be good ones. There's a little sign displayed in my kitchen—a gift from my younger son—that reads *If I could have picked my mother, I would have picked you.* Seemingly "little" (but in reality, tremendous) things like this affirm I succeeded in motherhood in the way I had hoped.

Priority 4: My country. I am proud that one of my sons became a U.S. Marine Corps officer and fighter pilot. I was proud to be a military wife. I'm proud that my father, both of my grandfathers, and every generation of great-grandfathers—going all the way back to the American Revolution—served in the U.S. military. I hold a deep respect and appreciation for anyone who steps up to serve their country, knowing they may someday be called upon to make the ultimate sacrifice.

Yet, it's been only in the last decade that serving my country—in my own unique way—became a top five priority of mine. Had it always been such a high priority for me, I suppose I might have served in the military, as Lt. General Gainey did, or in politics, as Dr. Kerry Healey did. Instead, it took me over 50 years to realize that I wanted to serve my country in a more meaningful way than simply belonging to the Daughters of the American Revolution (DAR).

I have always believed it is the responsibility of every citizen to hold their elected representatives accountable for keeping the promises they made to constituents when they ran for office. So, eight years ago I founded—and still to this day lead—a grassroots educational organization dedicated to helping the citizens of my community become more knowledgeable about the important issues of our time. Our ultimate goal is to empower constituents to become more discerning and motivated voters.

> I have always believed it is the responsibility of every citizen to hold their elected representatives accountable for keeping the promises they made to constituents when they ran for office.

We don't tell anyone how to vote, and the organization is not affiliated with any political party. Instead, we invite various elected representatives, candidates for office, and well-known subject matter experts to speak to us each month. Because of these meetings, our members become more fearless and adept at asking relevant and important questions of our elected officials and political candidates. This endeavor has been far more successful and gratifying than I ever expected. Because the world keeps changing, there will always be more to do on this front.

Helping Others Achieve Success: The Unifying Thread in My Career

Regardless of how I prioritized my career at any point in time, my professional success was never about the title I held, or the industry I was in, or the business function I led. Throughout my career—and even as a wife, mother, and leader in my community—I have always measured my success by how well I helped others define and achieve their own personal visions, dreams, and ambitions. As I look back now, I can see that this has been the single most consistent priority for me, year after year, no matter where I was or what I was doing—in my job, at home, or somewhere out in the world.

In my book *Heartfelt Leadership*, I told a story about a time I was forced to lay off my entire department. It was the most difficult thing I had ever had to do up to that point. After much deliberation on how I might go about it, I concluded the best approach would be to follow the Golden Rule: *Do unto others as you would have them do unto you.*

Whether in the best of times or in the worst of times, I consider myself most successful when I enable others to feel good about themselves by helping them along on their journey, and by working side-by-side to accomplish great things. With that in mind, I knew that whatever I said to each person had to be authentic, from the heart, and honest. I would have to act with compassion, candor, and integrity.

> I consider myself most successful when I enable others to feel good about themselves by helping them along on their journey, and by working side-by-side to accomplish great things.

When the fateful day came to pull the trigger on my dreaded assignment, I asked each member of my team, one at a time, to meet with me in my office. As each one came in, I closed the door, sat down next to him or her, and revealed what was going to happen. After their initial stunned reaction, I told each person how much I honored, respected, and admired them. I talked about the strengths they brought to the team.

When I asked, "What is most important to you in life, and what makes you excited about your career?" I listened closely to each response.

We then discussed what they might really love to do going forward. We brainstormed about the types of jobs they would like to have. We reviewed the kinds of companies in our local region or elsewhere that might allow them to best play to their strong suits. I gave each person my wholehearted commitment to help them identify and work toward future opportunities—and I followed through.

Regardless of whether it's the best of times or the worst day ever, doing things like that—*helping people become the best versions of themselves*—is how I measure my success. But surprisingly, I never fully came to this realization until someone asked me whether I had been successful in the way that I expected.

I knew I had been successful when every one of those team members came back at a later point to thank me for helping them find the path to an even better career.

As I said before: It's not the job. It's not the title. It's not the trappings of power. I now know that for me, success is simply the process of holding myself accountable for helping others become the best versions of themselves. In the case outlined above, I knew I had been successful when every one of those team members came back at a later point to thank me for helping them find the path to an even better career.

Feedback like that confirms to me that I've been successful. Any other measure of success feels shallow and unfulfilling. So, reflecting on my current list of top five life priorities, I believe I have been far more successful in many more ways than I ever dreamed I would be.

The Definition of Success Isn't Set in Stone

Everyone on planet Earth has their own unique list of priorities. Our priorities are often different from one another's, and they may change over time. I appreciate that for many people, having a successful career might always be at the top of the list—and there is nothing wrong with that. Personally, I've come to realize that creating and sustaining meaning and fulfillment in life is more important to me than having a successful career.

Of course, that's current Deb talking. Between you and me, my top five life priorities have changed with every passing decade. What was important to me at age 20 didn't include a husband or children. By age 30, those individuals had been added to the list and other things fell off. By 50, caring for aging family members became important, and so on. That's just the way life works.

So don't ever feel that long-term goals you once mapped out for yourself must be forever set in stone. You are not a failure if your trajectory changes—especially if those changes are driven by passion and purpose.

> **Don't ever feel that long-term goals you once mapped out for yourself must be forever set in stone. You are not a failure if your trajectory changes—especially if those changes are driven by passion and purpose.**

Simply consider your life a continuous game of cards, with round after round of play. Some rounds you'll get a winning hand; sometimes you won't. The secret to success is found in knowing what to keep, what to throw away, and when to walk away.

The Art of Finding Success in a Losing Hand

As every card player knows, each hand can be a winner, and each hand can be a loser.

I learned that lesson in spades when I published my first book, *The WOW Factor Workplace*, in December 2019. I was so excited to launch that book, especially after years of interviewing executives and collaborating with my then-writing partner. Most of all, I was passionate about helping aspiring leaders all over the world become the best versions of themselves as best-ever bosses in best places to work.

Convinced this book was sure to be a tremendous success, I planned a very special launch party for 100 friends and business associates at the local Omni resort. I ramped up my social media presence and wrote several magazine and newspaper articles to spread the word. I also purchased cases and cases of paperback versions of the book to sell at all the upcoming book festivals and speaking engagements I was booking.

But (you may have guessed where this story was going!) I had not planned on a global pandemic shutting down the entire world. Within three months of my book launch, COVID-19 had changed life as we knew it. Who would have thought that *two weeks to slow the spread* would turn into months of complete lockdowns in country after country? Who would have imagined that a calendar full of in-person speaking engagements and book festivals would simply be erased, just like that?

The success I had so carefully and diligently worked to set up ultimately became one of the biggest losing hands I ever played. As I mentioned earlier, while every hand can be a winner, that same hand can be a loser. We must accept that we aren't always in control, no matter how perfectly we think our hand has been set up through calculated antes, discards, and draws from the deck.

Sometimes we shouldn't measure our success based on the attainment of a certain goal. Sometimes success is more about maintaining a winning attitude through thick and thin. Sometimes success is simply being gracious in defeat. Sometimes success is about believing in yourself, especially in the worst of times. Sometimes success is just showing up—or getting right back in the game with a positive, can-do attitude—after an embarrassing humiliation. In reality, success can be as simple—and as important—as learning from each round of play, whatever cards you are dealt.

> Sometimes we shouldn't measure our success based on the attainment of a certain goal. Sometimes success is more about maintaining a winning attitude through thick and thin...being gracious in defeat...believing in yourself...[and] just showing up.

As you journey through life, always keep in mind that lasting success is born of faith, a positive attitude, passion, patience, persistence, and humility.

So, never give up on whatever is most important to you. Keep the faith and a positive attitude, no matter what. Be passionate and persistent, yet patient, because timing can be everything. Now may not be your time just yet.

And finally, be humble. As Rick Warren observed in *The Purpose Driven Life*, "Humility is not thinking less of yourself; it is thinking of yourself less."

That is what success as a heartfelt leader is all about.

Melissa Reiff
Former Chairwoman and CEO
The Container Store

When I asked Melissa, "Have you been successful in the way you thought you would be?" she shared this:

I always knew that I had determination, perseverance, and a strong passion to be happy and successful in whatever career I pursued.

I am proud that I have exceeded many of my dreams as well as discovered and accomplished new ones. However, I also know that no matter your age, you must continue to learn and ask questions—be inquisitive.

> **No matter your age, you must continue to learn and ask questions—be inquisitive.**

Bearing in mind that children and family are likely to be a top priority for many women, I then asked, "What words of wisdom do you have for career women considering whether or when to have children?"

There is no *perfect* time to have children, and I believe there are many advantages to having them when you are younger, but there are also advantages to having them when you are a bit older and hopefully wiser. Decisions like whether or when to have children are so personal. For me, I could not imagine NOT having children and missing out on the most beautiful experience of life.

Jodi Berg
Retired President and CEO
Vita-Mix Corporation

When I asked Jodi, "What words of wisdom do you have for career women now considering whether or when to have children?" she said:

I have two things to share.

If you feel you are being emotionally abused, be aware that your children may also be suffering from abuse—even if you are not seeing it. Don't be afraid to seek help as soon as you see a concern.

Don't be afraid to seek help as soon as you see a concern.

We are on this planet only once. Decide what matters to you and do the best you can with the cards you are dealt. Play a hand that you will be proud to have played.

Nancy Howell Agee
President and CEO
Carilion Clinic

When I asked Nancy, "Have you been successful in the way you thought you would be?" she responded this way:

> Oh gosh. I think I have been more successful than I ever could have imagined. I am blessed with so much richness in a job I love, people I work with, and colleagues across the country. I think I am finally at the stage where I'm now beginning to think about legacy.
>
> Yeah, I'm very happy with where I am and what I'm doing.

I followed by asking, "What words of wisdom do you have for career women now considering whether or when to have children?"

Kids are a joy and a blessing... and far more resilient than you think.

> Do it! Kids are a joy and a blessing...and far more resilient than you think.

Linda Rutherford
Executive Vice President, Chief Communications Officer
Southwest Airlines

When I asked Linda, "Have you been successful in the way you thought you would be?" she answered:

More than I ever would have imagined.

I certainly did not have this—where I am right now—set as a goal. To be here and do what I'm doing—to get to work with the people I'm working for, and for this amazing company— has all been such a blessing.

So, yes, I am far more successful than I ever thought I could have been, and I am proud of the things that I have been able to bring to Southwest Airlines.

> **To be here and do what I'm doing—to get to work with the people I'm working for, and for this amazing company—has all been such a blessing.**

That includes several things, like bringing forward opportunities to showcase Southwest in branded entertainment TV shows and movies, starting up a social business function, and putting a focus on the employee experience. It's been exciting to bring those things to life, and then working with team members who are far smarter than I am, who pick up the torch and run with it.

I am very proud of the capabilities I have been able to bring into the organization, that maybe would not be here if I had not been here.

I followed up by asking, "What words of wisdom do you have for young women who are thinking about whether to have kids, or wondering if they should just pack it in and focus solely on the kids or their career?"

You know, everybody is different. You must do what feels right for you. You must do what feels right for your family and for your marriage. No one else can define that for you.

If you're feeling guilty, figure out what the source of that guilt is. It can't be something that outside forces are putting on you because no one can make you feel that way.

If you are doing what you know your family needs you to do, or wants you to do, or encourages you to do, then allow yourself the grace to not be influenced by outside factors. Stay focused on what you know you need to do for yourself, what you need to do for your marriage, and what you need to do for your family.

> **Stay focused on what you know you need to do for yourself, what you need to do for your marriage, and what you need to do for your family.**

The other thing I would say is about this working-mom guilt. I admit, I have felt it. There are always other people who make other choices. Sometimes they judge you harshly because your choices were not their choices. I know that can add stress sometimes. You just must stay true to yourself and true to what you think you can do.

You get only so many trips around the sun. You get only one lifetime, and it needs to be spent the way you want it. You are in charge. You are the one who is in charge of your life. You are the one who is in charge of how you spend your time.

One of the greatest moments is when your child will stop to reflect and say to you, "Wow, yeah, this life was pretty good."

My daughter volunteered at a hospital in Austin while completing her undergraduate degree. She texted me and said, "Hey, Mom—wanted you to know the cleaning lady at the hospital stopped me today and told me that my mom raised me right. Just thought you ought to know that."

I was so blown away. I was showing it to everybody who would stop for ten seconds, saying, "Look at this text! Look at this text!"

That is the payback.

Kerry Healey
Inaugural President
Milken Center for Advancing the American Dream

When I asked Kerry what her long-term objectives had been in the early stages of her career, she had this to say:

Once my husband's career was established, once the children were in school, and so forth, then I really focused on assessing, "What have I learned over the last ten years, being a consultant for the U.S. Department of Justice? What would my agenda be if I went into public office?"

I realized I had built a very broad agenda. There were criminal justice reforms that I considered essential. I was very concerned about child abuse and neglect. I cared about domestic violence and sexual violence. Those were all things that I had the opportunity to study, in depth, over the previous decade.

While the first ten years of my career seemed very introspective and academic, it was during that time that I built the foundation upon which the rest of my public engagement was predicated.

When I then asked her, "Have you been successful in the way that you thought you would be?" Kerry was one of the few women on top who responded this way:

No.

But I am not disappointed in the ways that I have been successful.

Honestly, I am completely surprised. I had no intention of being a college president. I couldn't have imagined the position I'm in today. I never thought I'd be building a new cultural center in the heart of Washington, D.C., dedicated to advancing the American Dream.

So, I think you can't really plan your life. You just don't know what opportunities you'll be given. But you can prepare by learning a broad variety of skills and being open to new challenges.

You can't really plan your life. You just don't know what opportunities you'll be given. But you can prepare by learning a broad variety of skills and being open to new challenges.

To that I responded, "Would you say you have exceeded what you thought you would do?"

> No. It was just different from what I expected to do. But it has been a good life, nonetheless!

Wendy Johnson
Former President and CEO
Dale Carnegie franchise, Atlanta, GA

When I asked Wendy, "Have you been successful in the way that you thought you would be?" she had this to say:

> You know, I have spent some time thinking about this question. It really is a good question for me.
>
> I must admit, my life just happened to me. My professional journey just happened to me. I didn't always chart the course.
>
> The constantly changing business world, coupled with personal requirements, impacted my career direction. The circumstances that were presented to me over the years—searching for industries that provided opportunity for women, downsizing, rightsizing, companies going out of business, acquisitions, IPOs, and, finally, family requirements to reduce travel—all impacted my career path.
>
> I never dreamed I would be a successful small business owner for the last 20 years of my career. I had originally envisioned a long-term career and advancement in one industry and one

company. The beauty of life's circumstances that required me to work in many industries and entirely different jobs over the years, prepared me well to be a successful small business owner.

I next asked Wendy, "What words of wisdom do you have for career women who might be considering whether or when to have a child?"

When I was a young girl, my dad came home from work and sat down in the big leather chair to read the newspaper while my mom cooked the dinner. Then, the family sat down to eat together. I liked that part.

Fast forward to our adulthood. We were different. We women were trailblazers.

> **When I was a young girl, my dad came home from work and sat down in the big leather chair to read the newspaper while my mom cooked the dinner...Fast forward to our adulthood. We were different. We women were trailblazers.**

Recently, I went to Camp CEO with the Girl Scouts. We were all CEO women, mentoring 16-year-old girls for a weekend—or for a couple of days—in the wilderness. At night, we (the CEO women) would get together and talk. Most of the women had never had children. They just blazed right through it.

I think a woman should be up front with her company that she is going to have children. I also think that whole communication about children is important. Legally, they are not able to ask you about it, but there is no law against you talking about it. I think it's good to be more forthright with your company, saying something like, "I can't guarantee you anything, but I love working here. I want to come back."

Be more out there, up front, and open about it—and enjoy it.

I have not spoken with younger women today about whether they feel they can just go out and get pregnant and not worry about it. But I would say that once you do have a child, you must have your childcare absolutely, completely nailed down. Otherwise, you will be so stressed and so maniacal that you will not be a good mother or a good wife or a good employee. It will be a big mess.

Some women think that because they can work from home now and conduct meetings on Zoom, they can get away with less childcare. But that is just not the case. Right now, we are laughing and tolerating children jumping into Mother's lap during a meeting and dogs running around in the background. But that does not further your executive image. We cannot afford to risk this. Childcare is still the best option.

My advice is this: Enjoy motherhood *and* enjoy being an executive. It is okay to do both.

Enjoy every aspect of your life. Maybe then, other people will do so, too.

Especially as a leader, you should set the stage. Thankfully, these days, there is an increased openness and celebration of family in the workplace. Take advantage of that and go for it!

Lieutenant General Kathleen M. Gainey
U.S. Army, Retired

When I asked Lt. General Gainey, "Have you been successful in the way you thought you would be?" here is what she had to say:

> I have been *far more* successful than I ever thought I would be. I never, ever would have dreamed I would have achieved all that I have.
>
> My parents and my brothers all laughed when I called to tell them that I had been picked for general. They were like, "You're kidding!"
>
> I never, never dreamed it. And my husband, Ed, was like, "Holy crap!"

I asked the general, "Was it a surprise to you to be selected for general?

> Totally!

I had been given a great opportunity to show that women can make a difference. Now it was up to me to make that difference.

"What did you say to yourself when you learned you had been selected for general officer?"

> *Do not mess this up!*

I had been given a great opportunity to show that women can make a difference. Now it was up to me to make that difference.

"How many other women were at that level while you were there?"

When I first made brigadier general, I think we had 13 female one-star generals. When I made three-star, I was the third female in the Army to get selected for three-star. We had three-star generals in some of the other services (Air Force and Navy), so there were others too, but overall very few in the beginning.

When I retired, we had *nine* female three-stars at the same time.

"Out of how many, in total?"

Three-stars? Probably 200.

The whole group of women about my age were quickly moving up and advancing.

"You weren't trying to get there?"

Not at all. *Not at all.*

"How do you think it happened?"

When you take care of other people, and motivate them, and get them totally excited about what they're doing, they're going to succeed. When they succeed, you look good.

By taking care of people. By building teams. By making people believe in themselves, and motivating them to do their best. I also always stressed being a team player, as well as a leader.

When you do that, when you take care of other people, and motivate them, and get them totally excited about what they're doing, they're going to succeed. When they succeed, you look good. Your organization looks good because they are doing their job in the best way they can.

REFLECTIONS:

It's not unusual for high-achieving women to be surprised at their own success. While many point out that they have always been passionate, persistent, and determined to succeed in the various positions they have had along the way, most admit that they never dreamed of attaining their ultimate position—or even envisioned themselves in the industry where they ended up! Most didn't chart the course they took. Rather, life just had a way of fortuitously working out—often better than they ever expected.

It's not unusual for high-achieving women to be surprised at their own success.

Most high-achieving women who are also mothers say their children are one of their top life priorities—and that balancing children and career has been one of their biggest ongoing challenges. If you are contemplating whether to become a mother, bear in mind that there is no perfect time to have a child. You must do what feels right for you, your marriage, your stage of life, and your family. It doesn't matter what others may think. Only you can make that determination. It's your life, and you must be true to yourself.

Certainly, there are many advantages to having children when you are younger: You typically have more energy and can expect fewer complications with pregnancy before age 35. On the other hand, the benefits of motherhood later in life include your level of maturity and self-confidence, along with a more well-established professional reputation.

Yet one consistent piece of feedback from all our mothers on top is that having children can be one of the richest, most fulfilling, and joyful blessings of your life. Enjoy motherhood. Enjoy your career. Enjoy all aspects of your one life at every phase of life.

If things don't always work out the way you hoped, the great news is that children are more resilient than you might expect. And so are you. Believe in yourself and help others do the same. It may help to remember that mistakes are learning opportunities, and that value can still be found in a losing hand. Sometimes, keeping a good attitude and persevering even when things don't go your way is the greatest measure of success.

As you continue on your life's journey, keep in mind the words of Jodi Berg: "Decide what matters to you and do the best you can with the cards you are dealt. Play a hand that you will

Placing other priorities—such as your family, your faith, or other passions—above your career does *not* mean that your professional life isn't important to you.

be proud to have played." If you find at any point that your career is not at the top of the list of things that matter to you, don't feel guilty. Placing other priorities—such as your family, your faith, or other passions—above your career does *not* mean that your professional life isn't important to you. To avoid regret, seek fulfillment wherever your purpose and passions lie. And as always: Play to your strong suits!

INTROSPECTIONS:

1   So far in your career, have you been successful in the way you expected?
   a. What serendipitous twists and turns has your career taken that you never anticipated?
   b. How much of your career happened by design?

2   What are your top five life priorities right now?
   a. Are these priorities different than they were five years ago? Ten years ago? Twenty? If so, why?
   b. How do you define "success" in each of these five categories? What actions are you taking to work toward those goals?
   c. What type of feedback lets you know when you have been successful in each of these categories?

3   Have you ever worked carefully and diligently for a certain type of success, only to end up with a losing hand? If so, how did you respond? Were you able to salvage any successes from the situation?

Listen to Your Heart

When you are truly passionate about something...give it all you've got, even if it takes until your final day. At least you will have enjoyed living a life of meaning and purpose, your days will have flown joyfully by, and the people who know you will be amazed at all you accomplished. You might even amaze yourself as you achieve your own kind of success.

-DEB BOELKES

t may sound strange at first blush, but people routinely ask me, "Do you ever sleep?"

The number of things I may accomplish on any given day rarely seem all that exceptional to me, but most people who don't know me well can't believe I accomplish all that I do. As you might recall from Chapter 7: Leverage Those Strong Suits, one of my CliftonStrengths top talent themes is Achiever. In other words, I have an internal drive to accomplish something tangible every single day, and this drive usually gives me the energy to work long hours on multiple projects at once. The fact of the matter is, I simply listen to my heart and do what I enjoy.

Each morning I prioritize actions that will allow me to leverage my strong suits and tackle what I consider most important to get done that day. By the end of the day, even if I get only one task done, I have the satisfaction of knowing it was the most important thing that I wanted to do. And better yet, I will have enjoyed doing it. If I can do two, or five, or ten, or twenty important things in a day, all the better—but who's counting when you're having fun?

Each morning I prioritize actions that will allow me to leverage my strong suits and tackle what I consider most important to get done that day.

When focusing on my passions and personal priorities, I rarely feel burdened. In fact, prioritizing my passions and playing to my strong suits gives me energy. I can't wait to get started each morning, and my days just fly by. When something becomes a drudge, I stop doing it. It's that simple.

Based on the many lessons I've learned throughout my life, and as we conclude our *Strong Suit* journey together, my best advice to you is this: *Listen to your heart.*

Especially when it comes to the big things in life, only you can decide what's right for you. Those situations might include deciding on a new career path, evaluating whether you are ready to be both a mother *and* a career woman, going back to school, or getting married.

Do not hold yourself accountable for achieving things *others* want you to achieve. Do not feel responsible for pursuing someone else's definition of success. The only way you can ever be truly happy—and successful—is to define what success means to *you*, in your own terms, and listen to your heart. Your heart never lies to you.

> **Do not feel responsible for pursuing someone else's definition of success.**

If You Feel a "Calling," Be Sure to Listen!

Looking back, I now see that whenever I was "inexplicably" driven to do something far out of the ordinary—and the idea would not go away—it was a *calling*.

A calling is something you just know in your heart is the right thing to do. You know instinctively that it will make the world a better place. Even if you don't have a plan and you might not get paid to do it, you can't help but jump in and pursue your calling.

Take notice of what captivates you, what excites you, and what engages you. Eventually you will find your calling—if your calling hasn't already found you. Be open to the possibility that over time you might even have several callings. That simply means you can have an even richer life.

> **Even if you don't have a plan and you might not get paid to do it, you can't help but jump in and pursue your calling.**

I still make a habit of listening to my heart, and I still pursue callings. I simply can't *not* do the kinds of things that 1) will play to my strong suits, 2) make the world a better place, and 3) I know I will enjoy. As a result, my days are filled with passion, purpose, and joy.

If you ever feel strongly drawn to pursue an idea that ticks the three boxes I've just described, then you should answer that call. When you are truly passionate about something, you *will* find a way to do it—no matter how difficult or crazy it may seem.

> **When you are truly passionate about something, you *will* find a way to do it—no matter how difficult or crazy it may seem.**

Then give it all you've got, even if it takes until your final day. At least you will have enjoyed living a life of meaning and purpose, your days will have flown joyfully by, and the people who know you will be amazed at all you accomplished. You might even amaze yourself as you achieve your own kind of success.

So, as we come to the end of this journey together, I'd like to send you off with these special wishes:

- May you choose to pursue your callings and live your life without regrets.
- May you choose to be a role model in all that you do, because everyone needs a role model far more than they need a critic.
- May you choose to help others become the best they can be—and inspire them to do the same—so you and everyone along your path can help the world become a better place.
- May you choose to accept God's grace in every mistake. Simply live, learn, and grow as you go.
- May you choose to be a confident, caring, loving, and authentic woman on top in all of your endeavors—whether you are the only person in the room or the one on stage.

If all this sounds a little scary to you, don't worry. For more insights, you can always read or listen to my other books:

- *Women on Top: What's Keeping You From Executive Leadership?*
- *The WOW Factor Workplace: How to Create a Best Place to Work Culture*
- *Heartfelt Leadership: How to Capture the Top Spot and Keep on Soaring*

If you need a little more advice, visit my websites— HeartfeltLeadership.com and BusinessWorldRising.com—where you can read my blogs, watch my videos, listen to my podcasts, sign up for my monthly newsletter, and even contact me directly.

Of course, you can connect with me on LinkedIn, too. Just know I'm here for you, so reach out. I'm inviting you to!

And now, my final wish for you is this: May you achieve every success that you set your mind to. Just listen to your heart, do what you enjoy, believe in yourself, and play to your strong suits.

So, go on now…success is out there waiting. I hear it calling you. I'll be rooting for you.

Sending you big hugs and heartfelt best wishes,

Deb

Success just got easier®

About the Author

Deb Boelkes is the award-winning author of *The WOW Factor Workplace: How to Create a Best Place to Work Culture, Heartfelt Leadership: How to Capture the Top Spot and Keep on Soaring,* and *Women on Top: What's Keeping You From Executive Leadership?*

Having spent 30 years climbing the career ladder within male-dominated Fortune 500 technology firms, Deb knows firsthand the challenges women can face in their efforts to reach the top. That's why in 2009 she founded the leadership development firm Business World Rising (originally called Business Women Rising): to accelerate the advancement of high-potential women and men to the top of "Best Place to Work" organizations.

In *The WOW Factor Workplace,* Deb changed our expectations about achieving joy and fulfillment from our jobs. In *Heartfelt Leadership,* she changed our expectations of those who lead.

Women on Top transformed the way women pursue their careers, and *Strong Suit* provides the candid mentoring every woman needs to become the best leader she can be on her way to the top.

Deb speaks to corporations, industry associations, and universities the world over—both on stage and as a podcast guest expert—on career advancement, leadership development, and creating Best Place to Work organizations. She is regularly quoted and featured on radio and in publications ranging from *CNN Business* and *Thrive Global* to *Authority Magazine, Diversity MBA Magazine, Advancing Women*, and industry-centric periodicals like *Women Leading Travel & Hospitality.*

Deb received her bachelor's degree in business administration and her MBA in management information systems from the University of Rhode Island. She lives on Amelia Island in northeast Florida with her husband, Chris. Together they have three grown sons and four granddaughters.

For more information on Deb Boelkes, go to BusinessWorldRising.com.

How to Work with Deb

Deb Boelkes' greatest value lies in inspiring leaders to embody a new kind of leadership style ... one that fosters an inviting and energizing culture and esprit de corps; one that produces and sustains greater employee and customer loyalty; one that consistently delivers a healthy impact on the bottom line ... heartfelt leadership.

Neither heartfelt leadership nor the creation of an engaging Best Place to Work culture can be learned through standard training techniques. Passions must be stirred and inspired. Hearts must be reached. That's what Deb does best.

Deb gives enlightening keynote speeches. She produces eye-opening symposiums, conducts energizing workshops, and consults with executives and high-potential leaders at all levels.

There has never been a better time to take your leadership and your organization to a whole new level ... to a Best Place to Work level ... through heartfelt leadership. Contact Deb today.

Deb Boelkes

FOUNDER, BUSINESS WORLD RISING, LLC

Deb.Boelkes@BWRising.com

Office: +1 (904) 310-9602

DebBoelkes.com | BusinessWorldRising.com

HeartfeltLeadership.com

LinkedIn.com/in/debboelkes/

Other Books in the Series

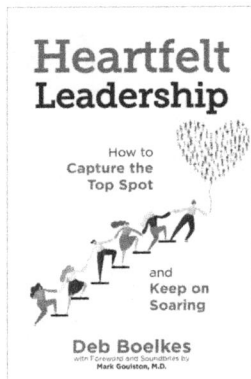

Women on Top
What's Keeping You From Executive Leadership?

Deb Boelkes
Author of The WOW Factor Workplace and Heartfelt Leadership

the WOW Factor Workplace
How to Create a Best Place to Work Culture

Deb Boelkes
with Foreword and Soundbites by Mark Goulston, M.D.

Heartfelt Leadership
How to Capture the Top Spot
and Keep on Soaring

Deb Boelkes
with Foreword and Soundbites by Mark Goulston, M.D.